H

1950

NATION-BUILDING IN KENYA

T_3

Nation-Building in Kenya

The Role of Land Reform

John W. Harbeson

Northwestern University Press

EVANSTON — 1973

John W. Harbeson is associate professor of political science
at the University of Wisconsin–Parkside.

CONTENTS

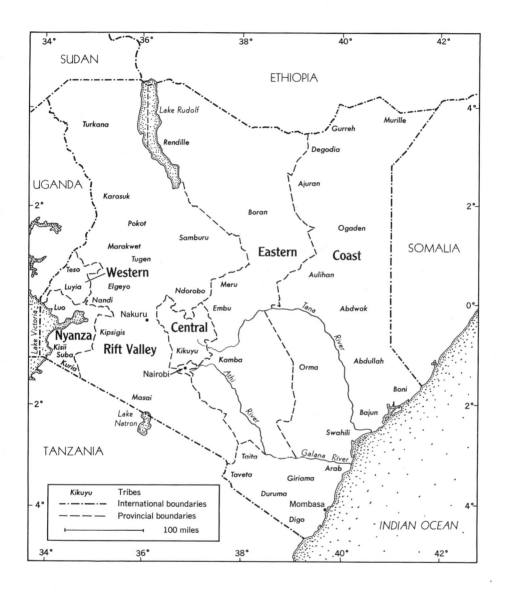

REGIONS OF KENYA AS DEFINED BY THE REGIONAL BOUNDARIES COMMISSION, 1964

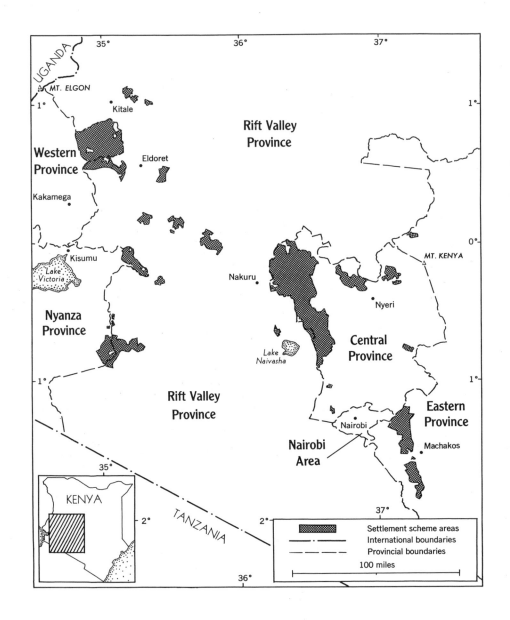

KENYA LAND SETTLEMENT SCHEMES, 1965

ACKNOWLEDGMENTS

I have accumulated a great many debts in doing the research for this study and producing it in final form. Many of these debts do not begin to be repaid by their acknowledgment here. My research would have been impossible without the interest and cooperation of all the individuals I interviewed. But I must express particular thanks to N. S. Carey Jones for opening his files to me and spending a whole day answering my questions, thereby giving my research its first big boost. Victor Burke helped me gain clearance for my research in Kenya and was generous in giving me his time to answer my questions and seeing that I got the assistance I needed in the Department of Settlement. The World Bank and Commonwealth Development Corporation took an interest in my research for which I am very grateful. The African settlers who took the time to explain their point of view made an indispensable contribution to my study, and I hope that its publication may in some indirect way repay them. My colleagues at University College, Nairobi (now the University of Nairobi), provided a good measure of intellectual stimulation as I worked. My students there, some of whom served as interpreters, all taught me a great deal about the country in which I was studying.

Much of the information and many of the interpretations in chapters 2 and 3 have been derived from interviews and private files. Particular thanks are due to Dan Etherington, Sir Wilfred Havelock, the late Peter Wise of the Commonwealth Development Corporation regional office in Nairobi, and T. C. Creyke of the International Bank for Reconstruction and Development for giving me access to very helpful materials on the land-resettlement program. Several interviews, including those with the individuals just named, were particularly helpful; namely, those with Ronald Ngala, Mark Mwithaga, Sir Ferdinand Cavendish-Bentinck, R. J. M. Swynnerton, Professor Eric Clayton, Lord Cuthbert Alport, N. S. Carey

Jones, Humphrey Slade, James Gichuru, Alexander Storrar, G. R. Henderson, Philip Ndegwa, Victor Burke, Malcolm MacDonald, Lord Howick, Lord Perth, Duncan Nyanjom, and Solomon Karanja. I fear to name these individuals because so many interviews with other people were so helpful. My friend and office mate at the University of Nairobi, Krishna Maini, who has written an authoritative treatise on East African land law, spent many hours in conversation with me about the fine points of Kenya land law. Finally, I wish to thank my colleague John Campbell, professor of geography, and Larry Mattson for their help in preparing the two maps.

For financial support, I am indebted to a number of institutions: The United States Office of Education, the University of Wisconsin African Studies Committee, the University of Nairobi, and the University of Wisconsin Center System.

I owe a very large debt of gratitude to Crawford Young, my major professor, who provided indispensable assistance at every stage of my research and writing while at the same time giving me the freedom to chart my own course in developing my study.

My student assistant, Kay Schultz, helped in the proofreading. Harrietta Barker, Mary Lou France, and Phyliss Barker Pittman typed parts of my preliminary draft. Sandy Haley typed the final draft promptly and skillfully. Susan Gursky prepared the index.

My wife, Ann, deserves most of the credit for the organization of the bibliography and footnotes and for removing unspecified numbers of misspelled words and incomplete sentences from the final draft. Most of all, she provided understanding and moral support as I labored to produce this study.

With all this assistance, this book should be perfect. It is not, of course, and any errors that remain are my responsibility alone.

LIST OF
ABBREVIATIONS AND TERMS

ADS   Agricultural Development Service of the International Bank for Reconstruction and Development (World Bank) located in Nairobi. It was established to provide advice to the Kenya government on the implementation of agricultural programs in Kenya in which the IBRD has an interest. Established shortly after independence, the ADS is headed by former director of settlement Alexander Storrar and his then deputy director, G. R. Henderson. A number of Europeans in the Department of Settlement joined the ADS when their terms of service expired with the department.

ahoi   Tenants on rural land under Kikuyu custom. Land consolidation crystallized this group into a landless, unemployed class.

AO units   Farms under the Assisted Owner Scheme. This scheme, included within the original program for the World Bank–Commonwealth Development Corporation scheme in 1961, was discarded shortly thereafter because it did not appear to meet the IBRD/CDC specifications and because President Kenyatta considered it to be incompatible with the purposes of resettlement schemes: to help the poor and needy rural Africans by giving them a plot of land. These AO units were to be for farmers with considerable income to invest in very large acreages relative to the other schemes.

APP   African Peoples Party. Fundamentally a Kamba-based party of short duration around the time of independence.

baraza   Swahili term for conference or meeting.

CDC   Commonwealth Development Corporation. One of the lenders behind the low-density scheme. Funded by the British government, it is administered as an independent government corporation. Its current chairman is former Kenya Governor Sir Evelyn Baring (now Lord Howick).

CLB   Central Land Board. 1963–65. Formed to purchase land for the settlement schemes. In theory, operated independently of the regular government administration, in order to prevent political interference in land selection. Composed of representatives of each region and from the national government. In fact, it worked in close harmony with the Department of Settlement.

C of A   Convention of Associations. Once a powerful settler caucus in the inter-war period, it was revived toward the end of the colonial period as a means of helping the European farmers get fair compensation or security for their land during the transfer of power, and to secure the interests of Europeans generally during this period.

EASB   European Agricultural Settlement Board. Established to administer the settlement of European farmers. This board became the organizational basis for the LDSB (Land Development and Settlement Board) which was first charged with implementation of the settlement schemes for Africans.

Emergency   Declared by the governor in 1953 for the whole of Kenya while British troops put down the uprising known as Mau Mau. All African political activity was suspended in the early part of the Emergency (1953–60). The Emergency was as much for African as for European benefit, since most of the casualties arising from Mau Mau were African.

FESU   Farm Economics Survey Unit. A branch of the Ministry of Economic Planning and Development concerned with the collection and analysis of statistics on African farming.

FIP
: Federal Independence party. Formed in 1954 in opposition to the United Country party which favored the "Lyttleton" Constitution. Generally composed of Europeans less favorable to African advances.

githaka
: Principal unit of land tenure under Kikuyu custom.

harambee
: Kenya Swahili word for unity, given prominence by Jomo Kenyatta.

IBRD
: International Bank for Reconstruction and Development. Also known as the World Bank. One of the lenders, along with CDC, in the low-density settlement-scheme program.

KADU
: Kenya African Democratic Union. Formed in opposition to KANU in 1960 under Ronald Ngala and current Vice President Daniel arap Moi. Interested in the welfare of smaller ethnic groups and, in alliance with the New Kenya Party, it advocated a *majimbo* constitution, giving powers to the regions at the expense of the central government. Disbanded and joined KANU voluntarily in 1964.

KALU
: Kenya African Landless Union. Existed briefly during the transfer of power to press the interests of Kenya landless. Essentially a faction of KANU led by and largely composed of Kikuyu.

KANU
: Kenya African National Union. Under President Kenyatta, KANU is the present ruling party of the country. Represents the large Kikuyu ethnic group and, until 1966, the second largest group, the Luo.

KAU
: Kenya African Union. Lineal descendant of the pre–World War II Kikuyu Central Association, it was the main spokesman for African nationalism until it was proscribed in 1952. Led by Jomo Kenyatta.

KC
: Kenya Coalition. Formed by former minister for agriculture and former Legislative Council Speaker Sir Ferdinand

Cavendish-Bentinck. A party of conservative Europeans opposed to the transfer of power, it concentrated on getting the best deal for the Europeans under the circumstances.

KCA Kikuyu Central Association. More militant of two Kikuyu political organizations representing Kikuyu nationalist thinking. Proscribed in 1941.

kipande A fingerprinted employment record required of all Africans until the 1950s. Regarded by Africans as a badge of servitude, since Europeans resisted such a record for themselves. Abolition of the *kipande* became a tenet of African nationalism.

KNFU Kenya National Farmers Union. The main spokesman for European farmers prior to independence, it is now the main spokesman for African as well as the remaining European farmers. Took a particular interest in the provisions of the legislation opening the Highlands to African farmers and in the land-resettlement program.

KPU Kenya People's Union. Formed in 1966 by Oginga Odinga assisted by Bildad Kaggia, Achieng Oneko, and about thirty other members of Parliament who left KANU because KANU had allegedly departed from meeting the objectives and promises of Kenya nationalism. Only seven of the thirty survived the by-election. Represents primarily the Luo and some of the Kamba communities.

LDSB Land Development and Settlement Board. Administered the settlement program during its first two years, 1961 and 1962.

majimbo Means regionalism in Swahili. Advocated by KADU in order to curb the power of the central government in the event that KANU, representing the large tribes, should gain control of the national government after independence.

Mau Mau The name given the rebellion of Africans (1953–60) who were landless, unemployed, and poverty-ridden in Kikuyu country against those Kikuyu who had gained land, education, and a degree of prosperity under colonial rule. Mistakenly conceived as an anti-European movement. Most of the casualties were African.

mbari The kin-based unit of the Kikuyu which held proprietorship over *githakas.*

MEPD Ministry of Economic Planning and Development. Led by Tom Mboya until his death in July, 1969, then by J. Odero-Jowi. Assisted by an influential cadre of expatriates.

NFD Northern Frontier District (or Province). Northeastern Kenya area sparsely inhabited, semidesert in ecology, and peopled in part by Somalis. Kenya engaged in a long minor war with Somali over the status of the region, concluded in 1967. The area remains a part of Kenya.

NKP New Kenya party. Lineal descendant of United Country party of the mid-1950. Formed in 1959 by moderate Europeans Wilfred Havelock and Michael Blundell to advance the cause of multiracialism and counterbalance the nationalism of KANU.

UCP United Country party. Formed in 1954 by Michael Blundell to defend the "Lyttleton" Constitution which contemplated political advances for the Africans.

uhuru Swahili term for freedom.

INTRODUCTION

LAND AND PEOPLE IN KENYA

> Our greatest asset in Kenya is our land. This is
> the heritage we received from our forefathers. In
> land lies our salvation and survival.
> —JOMO KENYATTA, 1964

Land has always been critically important to the well-being of
Kenya. The African people of Kenya have maintained a great emotional and psychological investment in land because land represents
their principal link with revered ancestors as well as being the most
important and tangible *raison d'être* of numerous African ethnic
communities. The depth of this attachment caused land to rival
political independence as the prime focus of African nationalism in
Kenya. The independent African government of Kenya has labored
to divest land of the association with interracial and intraethnic strife
which it acquired during the colonial regime and to make land a
source of common national pride. The government has sought to
make land a symbol of national unity for all the people of Kenya
instead of a symbol of unity for divergent African ethnic communities.

The symbolic uses of land have both reinforced and complicated its political and economic significance for the development of Kenya. Land is the country's principal economic asset, and a very large proportion of her people have obtained their livelihood directly from agriculture. Since industrial development has been limited, an even wider group of people have been indirectly dependent upon a land-based economy for their material well-being. The distribution, use, and tenure of the country's limited reservoir of high-potential agricultural land caused political struggles among European settlers, African communities, and the colonial government throughout Kenya's years as a British dependency. Whichever group controlled land policy governed not only the use and allocation of scarce economic resources but also the authoritative allocation of social values in general.

The political and economic importance of land and conflicts over its use and allocation have been sharpened geographically, since the most important struggles involving land occurred in an area bounded by the eastern highlands and the Rift Valley. In the midst of such political strife, this area also made the greatest contribution to Kenya's economic development. The economic potential and progress in this region served to raise the stakes and to complicate the issues in the three-cornered political contest involving European settlers, African communities, and the administration. The eastern highlands and the Rift Valley areas comprise Kenya's agricultural and political heartland. This heartland has great contrasts in topography, land potential, population densities, and culture. To the east of the Rift Valley lies the homeland of the Kikuyu, who have dominated both the economic and political life of the Africans of Kenya since colonial times. The first great African national leaders—Kinyanjui, Harry Thuku, Koinange Mbiyu, and Jomo Kenyatta—were Kikuyu. Central Province is almost entirely an area of high agricultural potential, and the Kikuyu were the first to experience a major agricultural revolution propelling them into the modern cash-crop economy, just as they had the first and greatest exposure to European civilization and produced leaders of the independence movement. In one sense the progress of the Kikuyu in education, agriculture, and politics has been restrained by the large numbers of people competing for scarce resources. From another perspective, their progress has been enhanced by such population pressures. Numbers have created strength in politics and, after a fashion, prompted agricultural reforms. The Kikuyu have thus always included a disproportionate number of those African peoples who have suffered as well as gained from exposure to colonization and European civilization.

On the western side of the Aberdares mountains lies the vast Kinangop plateau, which rises five to seven thousand feet above sea level. This is a region of mixed agricultural potential and varied history. At the foot of the Aberdares are lands of great agricultural potential, while further west on the plateau farming becomes a much trickier and more uncertain proposition, because it is too lofty and too cold to grow maize. There other crops, such as potatoes, must fill the Africans' subsistence diet. The place names—Ol Kalou, Ol Aragwai, Ol Bolossat—attest the region's precolonial history as Masai range land. European farming on the Kinangop and in the neighboring area of Kiambu, north of Nairobi, caused conflict with the Kikuyu because it seemed to block natural areas of Kikuyu expansion. However, the place names on the Kinangop suggest that much of this land was alienated from the Masai rather than the Kikuyu, a point which the European settlers were fond of making to Kikuyu nationalists in later years. The European farmers did well on the plateau after a fashion, but the success of post-independence smallholder African farming in this area is still uncertain. The Kinangop has been the main area of Kikuyu settlement under the Million Acre Resettlement Scheme, which subdivided and transferred European farms to Africans during the transfer of political power. Settlement schemes on the plateau make up nearly 40 percent of the total acreage covered by the resettlement program.

Below the Kinangop and to the west lies the floor of the Rift Valley, where the Masai shared their pastoral areas with the great ranching estates of Lord Delamere, the now legendary pioneer European settler, and others. North of Nakuru, the informal center of European settler activities, lay the large European wheat farms of

Laikipia. Many of the farms around Nakuru and in Laikipia have remained in European hands to bolster Kenya's economy during the economic and political transition resulting from independence and the Million Acre Resettlement Scheme.

The struggle over land policy resulting from the interaction of political strategies and the quest for rural economic development has been of far greater importance in Kenya's colonial and post-colonial history than the size of the principal geographical area involved would suggest. Land-policy questions have been important in all those areas which were, or became in colonial times, at least partially agricultural as distinct from pastoral economies. But land-policy questions have become intimately involved with national politics, especially in those agricultural regions which experienced not only colonial rule but, more or less directly, European settlement as well. The coastal region is agricultural and has been troubled by land-tenure problems of great complexity. But these problems have not become deeply involved in national politics, in part because Asian and Arab systems of land tenure rather than European systems have been in conflict with African land-tenure systems. The Northern Frontier and Masailand have not been involved in conflict over land because the African peoples of these areas have remained almost wholly pastoral and have not possessed or recognized land with high agricultural potential. The European settlers and the colonial administration took a protective attitude toward them and sought to shield them from invasion by agricultural peoples like the Kikuyu. The peoples such as the Kikuyu, Luo, Luhya, Nandi, Kisii, and Kipsigis who live to the east and west of the Rift Valley have experienced European settlement on their land, especially those east of the valley. They have also become at least partially agricultural either before or since the beginning of the colonial years.

Among the agriculturally oriented peoples whose lands were settled by Europeans, there were and continue to be important differences both in economic posture and in response to European culture. The Kikuyu were among the most aggressive agriculturalists and generally had the most direct experience of European settlement on their land, although some of the most vociferous white settlers were the South Africans on the borders of Nandi and Luhya country. The Luo, Kipsigis, and Kisii were less committed to agriculture than the Kikuyu and experienced the unsettling effects of the European presence to a lesser degree and with less sense of having lost land. On the other hand, the Nandi, the Kamba, and the Kipsigis became significantly more agricultural during the colonial era. Many of the land problems these people experienced were and can still be related largely to their incomplete transition from primarily pastoral to substantially agricultural economic practices rather than to European incursions.

Exposure to European settlement and the structure of traditional African economies are but two among many elements in the social organization, environment, and culture of the African peoples that shaped their responses to colonial and post-colonial land policies. A great deal of important anthropological research may still be done to illuminate the African point of view on land policies in Kenya. However, this study will explain African responses to land policies, not from a cultural standpoint, but rather in terms of the economic and political environment created for African peoples by such land policies. Chapter 1 deals with colonial land policies intended to consolidate rural racial and ethnic compartments and with the unwillingness of the colonial administration to treat land problems related to social change in African reserves. Chapter 2 considers a major pre-independence effort at land reform in the Kikuyu reserves. The remainder of this book examines the development and implementation of programs enabling small-scale African farmers to settle on land previously held by Europeans who wished to leave Kenya prior to independence.

PART ONE

Land and Politics in Kenya:
The Colonial Legacy

Land policies in Kenya have reflected the relative influence of competing constituencies over the authoritative allocation of general social values as well as specific scarce economic resources. They have been the economic expression of prevailing political objectives and strategies.

Land policies and dominant political objectives in Kenya have fallen into two broad categories. First, there have been policies involving land transfer which, from the perspective of Kenya Africans, have served primarily the interests of the British government and/or the Kenya European settlers. Land was transferred to European settlers early in this century to help Britain's Indian Ocean and Suez strategy become economically viable. The same policy also enabled Britain to reward military veterans of World Wars I and II and to provide an escape for others who were dissatisfied with life in Great Britain. Other relatively minor land transfers were conducted by the colonial administration in Kenya within rural areas that remained in African hands. Such transfers, including those recommended by the 1934 Kenya Land Commission, represented an alternative to opening to African farmers the enclave of European farmers created by Britain's original land-transfer policy.

Second, land policies have been directed to the improvement of land use in African and European areas. Such policies have reflected the political objective of reinforcing the status quo and, in particular, of protecting the economic and political position of the European community against African incursion. Between the world wars, land policies in Kenya reflected a misguided attempt to protect African institutions from social change, which in part was forced upon Africans by land-transfer policies and colonization itself. While measures to improve land use in African areas were thus being delayed, Kenya became increasingly dependent upon European farming, as reflected in *de facto* European political preeminence vis-à-vis Africans and Asians. After World War II,

3

the British government, the colonial administration in Kenya, and many European settlers all recognized that existing patterns of social change in African rural areas, both reflected and caused by the disappearance of traditional land-tenure customs among the Kikuyu and other African peoples, endangered the political status quo. Attempts were made to improve the condition of African rural economies within the context of the political status quo established during the inter-war years. The colonial administration sought African adherence to improved methods of land use and cultivation. The political position of the European community, achieved through commercial and agricultural contributions to Kenya's economy, was strengthened by the creation of a ministerial system of government with European representation and by further European settlement. However, such European policies had only limited success, because they did not cope with the basic insecurity among Africans caused by fear of further land appropriation by Europeans and the continuing breakdown of traditional land-tenure rules. Mau Mau was the result, in large part, of that limited success.

During Mau Mau, and under the protection of British troops and Emergency restrictions on African political activity, the colonial administration undertook a gigantic program of land reform in Kikuyu country designed to give Africans individually owned plots with registered titles. This reform was conducted not only to facilitate the introduction of development capital into the rural areas but also to preserve the political status quo by diverting African attention to their own rural areas and away from the "White Highlands." One of the principal objectives was to strengthen and enlarge the corps of moderate, middle-class Africans who would oppose militant African nationalism. Moderate European leaders came to see in these developments the potential for strengthening the political status quo by the creation of a multiracial political alliance of European and African farmers sharing the common objective of rural economic progress. The European leaders urged their constituents to contribute to this coalition by improving their own methods of land use and expanding their production to parallel developments in the Kikuyu areas. The culmination of multiracialism came in the removal of the barriers to African ownership of farming lands in the former White Highlands, after a new British policy of speeding Kenya's independence under an African government had undermined the settlers' political reasons for supporting multiracialism.

Land-transfer policies stimulated the growth of African politics and the development of African nationalism in Kenya. Appropriation of land by Europeans in ignorance and violation of African customs was a direct challenge to Africans. Extensive European farming, however justified on agro-economic grounds, contrasted with intensively farmed African areas to give the Kikuyu, in particular, a sense of relative deprivation vis-à-vis the Europeans and of an alien administration. Overpopulation and limited areas of territorial expansion threatened traditional land-tenure rules within African areas and produced poverty and social insecurity. Such grievances were experienced by African peoples to varying degrees and they consequently had varying degrees of nationalist feeling. Since the Kikuyu experienced such difficulties most acutely, African nationalism became somewhat difficult to distinguish from Kikuyu nationalism. Land loss to Europeans also sharpened specific dreams some African peoples had of territorial expansion and thereby contributed to regionalization of African nationalism as well as to the centralization of African nationalism based on common resentment of the European and colonial presence.

Land-use policies were employed unsuccessfully to change the focus and even counteract the development of African politics by posing economic development as an alternative to political insurgency. As a result, the processes of economic development were to become suffused with political significance. Contributions by Africans to the economic development of Kenya were to become synonymous with political support for the status quo. The Mau Mau Emergency interrupted these developments. The Lancaster House Conference of 1960, which set Kenya on the road to political independence under an African government, destroyed the attempt to achieve the same objectives under the guise of multiracialism.

1

LAND AND THE
COLONIZATION OF KENYA

BRITISH INTEREST IN EAST AFRICA was part of a global strategy
designed to protect British interests in India.[1] According to this
strategy, control of Egypt was necessary to maintain access to the
Suez Canal, and control of Egypt in turn justified control of Uganda
because the Nile headwaters lay there. Initial British expansion into
East Africa came from a different direction, however. The Imperial
British East Africa Company (IBEAC), established in 1888, operated
from a base in Mombasa. In 1889 it moved inland to control Uganda,
and by 1895 the British had established a protectorate there. The
specific political justification for the IBEAC's seeking control of
Uganda was the fear that an expedition led by Karl Peters might
preempt it for the German sphere of influence, a fear largely put to
rest by the Anglo-German Agreement of 1890 which established that
Uganda lay within the British sphere.

The region that was to become Kenya, the land lying between

---

1. Ronald Robinson et al., *Africa and the Victorians: The Climax of Imperialism* (Garden
City, N. Y.: Doubleday, Anchor Books, 1968).

7

Uganda and the Indian Ocean, was important to the British government for two reasons: Britain needed to establish the reality of her
jurisdiction in the area, and Britain wished East Africa to become
self-sustaining rather than a drain upon her treasury. European settlement was employed to achieve these results. The British government was particularly concerned about the economic potential of
Kenya. On the one hand, much of the land lying between Uganda
and the coast did not appear to have much potential for economic
development. On the other hand, while reports by Sir Harry John-
ston, Lord Lugard, and others testified to the presence of some
high-quality land, the British government did not believe that Africans living there would develop such land sufficiently to sustain
economically Britain's political control of the area. Consequently,
when deciding to link the economies of Uganda and the coast by
building a railroad between them, Britain decided that only European settlement could develop the intervening land to a level necessary to provide a prompt and eventually complete return on Britain's
investment in the railroad. The presence of the railroad and a community of European farmers also served to demonstrate British presence and control in the area better than the caravan trade and a few
missionaries would.

Since they were to be the major means of repaying Britain's
investment in the railroad, the European settlers themselves became
part of the imperial investment in East Africa. Between the establishment of the Protectorate of Uganda in 1895 and the creation of Kenya
as an administratively distinct colony in 1920, the dominant concerns
of the British government were to secure administrative control of
Kenya and to encourage European settlement to facilitate its economic development. Land policy expressed both these purposes.
Early colonial administrations considered that "pacification" of the
local African people was necessary to prevent their interference with
the economic development of East Africa. Treaties with the Masai
and armed expeditions against the Nandi, who were interfering with
the railroad, helped to achieve this objective. European settlement
itself contributed to pacification by providing buffer zones on land
disputed by various African peoples. The most important of these

buffers was the area lying to the northwest of Nairobi, including "suburban" Kiambu and all of the Kinangop plateau. To the east and north lay Kikuyu country; to the west and south, the pastoral ranges of the Masai. Other important buffers were established between the spheres of the Nandi and the Luhya, the Nandi and the Luo, and the Kipsigis and the Kisii. The British government assumed control of "unoccupied" land and presented it to European farmers as 999-year leaseholds. The Crown Lands Ordinances of 1902 and 1915 gave the European settlers legal security on their new farms from their own standpoint and from that of the British government. These ordinances, however, went beyond providing legal support for the settlers' presence on allegedly unoccupied land in Kenya, for they purported to make all land in the protectorate the possession of the Crown. Thus the British government sought to pacify the African peoples of the protectorate and to make them tenants-at-will of the British on land which they believed to be their own, in order to provide the foundations for economic development of the area by European settlers.[2]

African insecurity resulted from the British attempt to provide for the legal and political security of the European settlers. Land policy was not the only cause of African unrest. Even before the protectorate had been established and the settlers had arrived, missionaries had been at work in East Africa. Missionary religious and educational projects created a new avenue to social status within African communities and placed the traditional leadership on the defensive. But the British policy of assuming jurisdiction over all African land and allocating significant tracts to European settlers may have done more than anything else to alarm the African peoples of Kenya. No one among them could be certain of the ultimate dimensions of European settlement in Kenya, nor were they assured that the geographical integrity of their various communities would be defended against European incursion. Early administrators like Sir Charles Eliot, the second East African commissioner, were vocal

---

2. Lord William Malcolm Hailey, *An African Survey: A Study of Problems Arising in Africa South of the Sahara, 1956*, rev. ed. (London: Oxford University Press, 1957).

advocates of European settlement. Sir Charles exceeded his authority by encouraging South Africans to become farmer-colonizers of Kenya and by instituting segregation in the Highlands to avoid intrusion by Indian farmers.[3] He also favored interpenetration of African and European settlements because he believed that African peoples would and should become absorbed in a new order wherein European civilization, organization, and interests would be paramount. To achieve this end, he encouraged Lord Delamere and his Planters' and Farmers' Association to seek self-government. African land, the integrity of African communities, African civilization, and the political future of the African peoples—all were endangered by the policy of allocating land to European settlers. The early European settlers did not hesitate to aggrandize their position. Not only did they seek more land at the expense of the resident Africans and control over the political future of the African as well as European peoples of Kenya, but they campaigned for such taxation of the Africans as might be necessary to drive them to seek work on European farms.

The Africans were more than insecure because of European settlement. They were angry that the Europeans resided on what they considered "stolen lands." A great deal of controversy surrounded the circumstances of European settlement in areas bordering on Kikuyu country. The Kikuyu denied that the lands were vacant when the settlers arrived. They argued variously that some of the lands in question were being allowed to lie fallow while their occupiers cultivated elsewhere; that the Europeans took advantage of the traditional Kikuyu practice of making temporary allocations to strangers by assuming permanent possession; and that the Kikuyu were unjustly deprived of their "ownership" of land in the European sense of the word. In addition, subsequent research has suggested that the lands were temporarily vacated because of the spread of an epidemic, thought to be smallpox, in this area at the time European settlement began. The grievances over "stolen lands" were magnified

3. George Bennett, *A Political History of Kenya: The Colonial Period* (London: Oxford University Press, 1963).

several times by the widespread feeling among Africans that the lands remaining to them were not safe from future appropriation or "theft" at the hands of Europeans. The efforts by European settlers to acquire more land and more African labor lent justification to these fears.

Colonization and European settlement provided not only the cause but the circumstances and model for the subsequent development of African nationalism. The loss of land to Europeans and the policies supporting the settlers of the colonial administration and the British government were perhaps collectively the principal cause of African nationalism among the Kikuyu. The creation of the railroad led to the growth of Nairobi as a major city on the doorstep of Kikuyu country that was to become the center of African nationalism in Kenya. World War I introduced Africans from all areas of the country to one another and to European military technology, which they came both to fear and to respect.[4] Finally, European pressure on the colonial administration for land, African labor, and political influence inspired Africans to make their own claims upon the alien administration and provided them with a model for their campaigns. Loss of African land to European settlers was thus largely responsible for the early development of African nationalism in Kenya.

THE CONSOLIDATION OF COLONIAL RULE

The frontier militancy of the small European settler community, the growth of political consciousness in the African community, and the grievances of Indians supported by the Indian government prompted major definitions of colonial policy in Kenya during the inter-war years. The net effect of these pronouncements was a rejection of the ultimate political objectives of the settlers and of the more extreme demands of the other racial communities. At the same time,

---

4. Carl Rosberg, Jr., and John Nottingham, *The Myth of Mau Mau: Nationalism in Kenya* (New York: Praeger, 1966).

these definitions gave only partial recognition of African and Indian grievances. Colonization ceased to be an end in itself, and to that extent the British government and its colonial administration in Kenya departed from the objectives of the settlers. But consolidation of British control over the country stimulated African objections to their colonial status and intensified the African social and economic insecurity which contributed to violent African nationalism after World War II. European development of the country's economy became sufficiently important to the success of this phase of British rule that the settlers were able to achieve considerable political influence although they were not politically paramount.

In 1923 the British government rejected the European settlers' attempt to arrogate political and cultural suzerainty in Kenya to complement their economic preeminence. The so-called Devonshire White Paper (formally titled *Indians in Kenya: A Memorandum*) asserted the British government's own responsibility for the protection and development of the African people and the fundamental identity of Kenya as an African country. Peoples of other races would have their interests protected but not at the expense of Africans.

> Primarily, Kenya is an African territory, and His Majesty's Government think it necessary definitely to record their considered opinion that the interests of the African natives must be paramount, and that, if, and when, those interests and the interests of the immigrant races should conflict the former should prevail. Obviously, the interests of other communities, European, Indian, or Arab, must be severally safeguarded. . . . But in the administration of Kenya, His Majesty's Government regard themselves as exercising a trust on behalf of the African population, and they are unable to delegate or share this trust, the object of which may be defined as the protection and advancement of the native races.[5]

The Devonshire White Paper and subsequent important colonial policy pronouncements concerning land policy attempted to stabilize

5. Great Britain, *Indians in Kenya: A Memorandum,* British Sessional Papers, 1923, Vol. XVIII (4), Cmd. 1922 (London: H.M.S.O., 1923), p. 9.

the political and economic relationships among the various races. But the later pronouncements failed to recognize the social and economic implications of colonial rule and European settlement for the African people, particularly the Kikuyu. Hence, subsequent policies made the European community more indispensable to the colonial regime and therefore stronger, while increasing the social and economic insecurity among Africans that would lead to the violent Mau Mau outburst.

During the inter-war years the Indian community sought and gained an end to residential segregation in the townships, but not in the Highlands where the European enclave remained inviolate. The Indians successfully prevented a ban on further Indian immigration while failing to alter the Colonial Office's preference for communal rather than common roll elections. Common roll elections would have permitted the Indian community to dominate the smaller European community in the Legislative Council. The Europeans no longer held a monopoly of the franchise, but they retained larger representation than the Indian community in the Legislative Council. The African peoples retained a stable position in politics—with little real power. They gained neither representation in the Legislative Council nor an end to forms of racial segregation prior to World War II. The practical effect of these political developments was to deny the European community a political monopoly but to protect its superior position vis-à-vis the other races. Although Kenya was declared to be an African country, no steps were taken to give this practical political meaning.

Successive British commissions were concerned about the unrest centering about the land grievances and problems of the Africans. The Kenya Land Commission, under the chairmanship of Sir Morris Carter, was appointed in 1932. The British Joint Parliamentary Committee had recommended that the commission undertake a "full and authoritative" review of Kenya's land problems, but the terms of reference actually given the commissioners emphasized security for the racial groups and the necessity of making adjustments in their respective reserves in order to increase such security. The commission was also charged to provide land within their reserves sufficient for their economic needs to African communities. The commission heard and received voluminous evidence, the biggest single portion of which concerned the Kikuyu. The commission added 21,000 acres to the Kikuyu Land Unit to remove all claims of right based on possible wrongful alienation. The Kikuyu were allowed 350 to 400 square miles, in addition, to allow for their future expansion—land which the commission found elsewhere than within the White Highlands. The commission denied the illegality of the Crown Lands Ordinance of 1915 and African claims for repatriation of lands based on the contention that this ordinance was illegal.[6] The commission's recommendations strengthened the policy of providing security for all races by reinforcing their separate identities. The commission respected the creation of African reserves already in existence and did nothing to interfere with the consolidation of a European "reserve" in the White Highlands. The creation of reserves and the limited changes instituted on the recommendation of the Kenya Land Commission established a land policy that contemplated protecting African land against further encroachment by European settlers. However, this policy did little to foster either the unity of the African people or their preeminence within what was supposed to be their own country. It thus paralleled developments in the formal political relationships of the races in Kenya.

Inter-war land policy dealt with land problems arising between the races, but in an unsatisfactory manner. The Africans did not like the composition of the board administering the African land units because it was dominated by European settlers and civil servants rather than by the Africans themselves. Africans enjoyed no comparable position on the Highlands Trust Board that administered the European "reserve." Furthermore, the communalization of land tenure in Kenya implied the entrenchment of existing European control over lands which Africans continued to believe had been wrongfully taken from them.

6. Great Britain, *Report of the Kenya Land Commission,* British Sessional Papers, 1934, Vol. X (229), Cmd. 4556 (London: H.M.S.O., 1934), *passim.*

Inter-war land policy did very little to ameliorate land problems within the African reserves, particularly in Kikuyu country. Kikuyu land tenure at the time of colonization was based on the *githaka*, a unit of land controlled by an *mbari* or subclan. An *mbari* traced its descent from an ancestor who had claimed a parcel of land which became the *githaka* of his descendants in the *mbari*. Two fundamental questions were the significance of the process by which an ancestor established his claim to the land and the basis upon which his descendants held it. Kenyatta asserted that the establishment of the *githaka* by the founding ancestor amounted to a "purchase" in the English legal sense and that the descendants collectively managed the *githaka* as a trust on behalf of the founder.[7] At the same time there was evidence in Kiambu, near Nairobi, that individual "ownership" in the British legal sense, as distinct from the trusteeship described by Kenyatta, had begun to emerge. The Committee on Kikuyu Land Tenure in 1929 recognized the *githaka* as the basic unit of Kikuyu tenure, but it also acknowledged the transition in Kikuyu country toward what appeared to be individual "ownership" of land in areas of relatively recent Kikuyu settlement. Not wishing to interfere with the processes of change, the committee declined to demarcate a fixed set of tenure rules which might have eased the insecurity caused by this transition. "In adopting the githaka as a system we do not propose to sterotype the system but we indicate that we accept the process of transition as we find it and intend to direct and control it for the future. We must, therefore, be careful that our method of recognition is not such as to introduce artificial rigidity." [8] The committee left to the discretion of individual district commissioners the decision whether to mark out *githakas* in individual cases. A minority opinion held that the transition to a more individual form of land tenure was already advanced and that rules should be made to govern the system of land tenure, in order to control the possible

7. Jomo Kenyatta, *Facing Mount Kenya: The Tribal Life of the Gikuyu* (London: Secker & Warburg, 1953; New York: Random House, 1962).

8. Kenya, *Native Land Tenure in Kikuyu Province: Report of Committee* (Nairobi: East African Standard, 1929), p. 10.

emergence of classes of privileged landlords and the deposition of tenants *(ahoi)* under customary law whose rights might be extinguished by the assertion of private ownership. The Kenya Land Commission essentially followed the opinion of the Land Tenure Committee majority, though it was more dubious about the legitimacy of the *githaka.* However, the commission did not wish to encourage the hasty growth of individual land tenure, even if desirable in the long run. With no basis for awarding land to individuals or groups within the Kikuyu society, the commission made its awards to the Kikuyu as a whole.

Impotent in the face of changing land-tenure patterns in Kikuyu country, the colonial administration was unable to ameliorate the social distress developing within the Kikuyu reserves. During the inter-war years, population began to grow rapidly in Kikuyu areas. The absence of wars between African peoples and the basic steps taken to give Africans better medical attention are often cited as reasons for the declining death rate and consequent population increases. Increases in the Kikuyu reserves produced overcrowding, because the demarcation of the reserves made new land available only to younger men leaving an overcrowded *mbari* to found one of their own. Changing land-tenure patterns resulted in a tremendous amount of litigation by Kikuyu seeking to establish their rights to land. Overcrowding made the traditional practice of shifting cultivation impossible and resulted in the overuse and depletion of much of the land.[9] Cash crops like coffee were denied to African farmers, and the continuation of regressive head and hut taxes contributed to their impoverishment. The space provided by the awards of the Kenya Land Commission would prove insufficient to affect the generally insecure position of rural Kikuyu. The development of individual land tenure contributed to the growth of a class of landless Africans who had formerly held land as tenants *(ahoi)* and who were repelled by the idea of serving as wage labor for fellow Kikuyu. The unwillingness of the colonial administration to attempt to sort out

9. Eric S. Clayton, *Agrarian Development in Peasant Economies* (New York: Macmillan, 1964), chaps. 1 and 2.

Kikuyu land-tenure rules reflected a general unwillingness or inability to deal directly with the distress caused by social change in the Kikuyu reserves. A similar set of problems occurred in other reserves, especially that of the neighboring Kamba.

The failure to provide measures to increase the productivity of the African reserves made the colonial administration and the country as a whole more dependent upon the European farming enclave in the White Highlands. Where European settlers had once pressed the colonial administration to force Africans to labor on European farms, the poverty of the reserves drove Africans to seek employment on European farms during the inter-war years, despite their distaste for the *kipande* (work record card) which all Africans, and only Africans, were forced to carry, and which consequently became a badge of servitude and inferiority. The European settlers were unable to prevent the introduction of a mild income tax, but the government's technical and administrative services and its provisions for transport and communication vastly favored the European community. Assignment of technical personnel to the African areas to aid their development was frustrated because the government would not attempt to codify Kikuyu land-tenure rules, did not adequately staff the areas, and would not allow Kikuyu to grow coffee as a cash crop. The economic development of the European areas at the expense of the African areas was facilitated by the allowance of free entry and low rail rates for agricultural equipment used primarily by Europeans. The tax revenue of the colony, from which European services came, was disproportionately derived from contributions by African communities. Taxation made even the low wages paid by European farmers attractive to Africans.[10] World War II demonstrated the degree to which the colonial administration had become dependent upon European economic efforts, a dependence the European settlers were able to convert to increased political influence following the war.

10. E. A. Brett, "Economic Policy in Kenya Colony: A Study in the Politics of Resource Allocation," paper presented at the African Institute of Social Research, Kampala, 1964.

ECONOMIC REFORM AND POLITICAL REVOLUTION

Prior to World War II, African political organizations concentrated upon redress of grievances within the existing colonial system rather than upon the achievement of political independence. Harry Thuku organized an East African association in the early 1920s. Missionaries collaborated in the formation of the relatively conservative Kikuyu Association and the Kavirondo Taxpayers Welfare Association. The Kikuyu Central Association (KCA), in which Jomo Kenyatta was a leading figure, was the more aggressive of the Kikuyu political formations in concentrating on the return of "stolen lands" and the representation of Africans in the national government. During World War II, African political organizations were formally suspended, so that grievances over land policy and political representation could not be expressed. The Kenya African Union, formed after the war as a successor to the KCA, was driven to ever-increasing militancy by the failure of the colonial administration to generate the necessary reform of African economic and social conditions or to provide the required increases in political representation for the African people. Mau Mau was the product of this growing African, but primarily Kikuyu, alienation from the existing regime.

Postwar policies emphasized the desirability of economic development in African rural areas with the reality of increased European influence. On the one hand, the British government embarked on a soldier settlement scheme reminiscent of the post–World War I scheme. A substantial number of new European farmers were established under this program, and their presence was to increase the general militancy of the European community in later years.

Europeans achieved positions of responsibility in the national administration during the war. In 1945 Governor Sir Philip Mitchell proposed a semicabinet system of government with some "ministers" to be chosen from outside the civil service on a "representative" basis. The new system was intended to continue the wartime broad-based public support for government activities. Europeans were the principal beneficiaries; Africans gained no ministerial positions until

B. A. Ohanga became minister for community development in 1954. The first African representative on the Legislative Council was not named until 1944. Three more African members were named in 1948. The European community possessed a majority of unofficial members on the Legislative Council, maintenance of which became one of their prime political objectives.

New efforts were made to encourage the economic development of the African reserves. Awareness that fundamental changes in African social and economic structure were preconditions for real progress accompanied the new attention to the needs of the African rural areas. In a 1946 dispatch, Governor Sir Philip Mitchell observed:

> The problem can be stated simply and plainly by saying that an ignorant man and his wife with a hoe are a totally inadequate foundation for an enlightened society, a high standard of living, and elaborate social services, and that unless an adequate foundation capable of bearing these things can be devised . . . a great deal of modern talking and writing about colonial development and welfare is moonshine.[11]

A statement of government policy on land use and settlement after the war indicated some of the motivation behind the decision to open new lands to African development along lines recommended by the Kenya Land Commission. The government had no wish to repeat on these lands the problems already existing in the African reserves. "It can be said with certainty that it is not only useless but disastrous to throw open land for African occupation unaided and unregulated and that it is necessary to establish an organization for the settlement of Africans which will enable them to overcome the difficulties which now face them, including lack of capital, technical knowledge, and mechanical equipment."[12] The government also became concerned about the overcropping and overstocking which had led to serious soil deterioration and poverty, especially in the Ukamba reserve. The

---

11. Kenya, Despatch #44, 1946, p. 1.
12. Kenya, *Land Utilization and Settlement: A Statement of Government Policy* (Nairobi: Government Printer, 1946), p. 5.

paper just quoted suggested that similar problems of inadequate capital and training had led to errors and inefficiency in land development within the European "reserve" (evidence of a tendency to equate European and African economic requirements) despite the difference in prosperity between the two communities.

To realize the necessary social and economic changes in the African reserves, the existing and desirable bases of land tenure in African communities, particularly among the Kikuyu, had to be reexamined. This question had been left unresolved by the Land Tenure Committee (1929) and the Kenya Land Commission (1934). The problem was complicated by the postwar colonial administration's interest in communal and cooperative ventures, which reflected the philosophy of Britain's new Labour government and the influence of Fabian socialism. Such influence seemed to increase governmental indecision regarding changes in Kikuyu land tenure.

> It is doubtful whether we who are ourselves now inclined more to socialism and less towards the Cobdenism of the Manchester school of the nineteenth century have the moral right to destroy this communal feeling and tribal tradition. . . . As far as the Kikuyu are concerned one might go further and say that we have a moral duty not to destroy this communal feeling and tribal tradition.[13]

The crux of the problem was that individual tenure had begun to emerge as the dominant mode of landholding in Kikuyu country. The corollary was that traditional *ahoi* had much less security than under traditional customs, which included a degree of social obligation toward such tenants. To reassert communal tenure in order to strengthen the position of *ahoi* might, in addition to requiring a massive effort, lead to less productive land use. To demarcate individual plots was to preside over the creation of a class of landless ex-tenants.

> The fact is, of course, that whereas the *muhoi* fitted into a working system now that the system has collapsed, he has become an added

---

13. N. Humphrey, "Thoughts on the Foundation of Future Prosperity in the Kikuyu Lands Based on a Review of Some Facts Affecting Agriculture in South Nyeri," *The Kikuyu Lands,* ed. N. Humphrey (Nairobi: Government Printer, 1945), p. 20.

complication. He is merely a man with insufficient land. . . . He is well on his way to becoming a sore on the body politic.[14]

The situation in the African reserves was also complicated by the administration's attempt to move African laborers from European farms to the reserves. The problem of African labor on European estates had come full circle. Tax measures designed to force Africans onto the farm labor market in the early years of European settlement were unnecessary in the late 1920s. In the 1930s the administration wanted to reduce the numbers of African laborers, who had become a drain on the finances of the depression-ridden Europeans. The secretary of state for the colonies felt constrained to ban eviction of any African laborers under the 1937 Resident Labourers Ordinance until land could be found for them in the reserves. In the short term, the settlement of evicted laborers at Olenguruone and in the Yatta produced misunderstandings between the administration and the Kikuyu that contributed to the development of Mau Mau.[15] In the longer term, the attempt to repatriate farmers to already over-crowded reserves—farmers who had lost claims to land there because of their long absence on European estates—contributed to the social and economic insecurity (born of land shortages) in these areas. In the postwar years, the drive to reduce the number of African laborers on European farms was complemented by greater mechanization on European estates, despite official pessimism over the feasibility of such technological change.[16]

The reconstruction of African societies and economies, especially in Kikuyu country, did not occur in a political vacuum. The Kenya African Union (KAU) leadership rejected attempts by the government to improve the African economies by soil-conservation techniques. They opposed the reduction of excess stock in the belief that such improvements might be preparation for further European invasion of African lands or, more plausibly, that they were intended as

14. *Ibid.,* pp. 23–24.
15. Rosberg and Nottingham, *Myth of Mau Mau,* pp. 248–58.
16. Great Britain, Colonial Office, *Survey of Problems of Mechanization of Native Agriculture in Tropical African Countries* (London: H.M.S.O., 1950).

an alternative to recovery of "stolen lands." KAU voiced continued African objections to the *kipande,* taxation policies, the limited educational opportunities for Africans, conditions of African wage labor, and inadequate political representation in the government of the country. KAU's frustration over insufficient and delayed responses to these grievances heightened the insecurity and unrest of African communities within the colonial European-dominated system.

> At present the African lives in fear of bloody wars, and of the police and the intimidation of the European settlers and the government officials. He lives in fear his land that has been left after the robbery of the white man may be taken at the point of a gun; he is insecure while he resides on land that is not recognized by the British as legally his; he is insecure in European employment as he can be discharged at any time; he is insecure in that each employment he has, has not social insurance in any shape or form. In a word, he lives at the present in fear and insecurity.[17]

The "myth" of Mau Mau, Rosberg and Nottingham have concluded, is that it was inspired by a rejection of European civilization in favor of atavism and primitive savagery. This hypothesis has been supported by references to the methods employed by Africans to eliminate their opponents and initiate their followers during the Mau Mau insurgency. Rosberg and Nottingham argue, however, that it was the failure of the colonial administration and the European settlers to respond to the fundamental African insecurity caused by a chaotic transition to modernity that produced Mau Mau. The oath rite, bestial in European eyes, was in the African view a means for reorganizing a Kikuyu society that had been disarrayed by the disappearance of traditional land-tenure customs.

Mau Mau, however, was primarily an African civil war—a hypothesis supported by the casualty figures: Africans rather than Europeans were the main protagonists. This civil war was fought between those Africans who had gained and those who had not gained during the years of European settlement and colonial ad-

17. Tom Mbotela, *Kenya Controversy,* Fabian Colonial Bureau, Controversy Series No. 4 (London: Victor Gollancz, 1947), p. 11.

ministration. Those who had established themselves as landowners and landlords in the reserves or had obtained positions of reasonable security in the modern economy were the targets of those who had not. Among the latter were those tenants who had been displaced by the substitution of individual tenure for communal control over Kikuyu land.

2

LAND REFORM AND POLITICS
OF ACCOMMODATION, 1950–1960

Sixty thousand Europeans cannot expect to hold
all the political power and to exclude Africans
from the legislature and from the Government.
—OLIVER LYTTLETON, 1954

KENYA'S EUROPEAN COMMUNITY and colonial administration saw
in the outbreak of Mau Mau both a warning and an opportunity.
Between 1950 and 1960 the British government conveyed to the European settlers the fear that Mau Mau indicated the end of the degree
of preeminence they had enjoyed since Kenya became a British
colony. By 1950 at least some important figures in the colonial administration recognized the need for comprehensive reform of the
country's economy, especially in the African reserves. The administration took advantage of the removal of Kikuyu political leaders
from Kikuyu country during Mau Mau to institute a revolutionary
reform of land tenure and the rural economy there. Slowly, with

prodding from Great Britain and encouragement from the colonial administration, the European community recognized that more intensive development of those areas of the economy where its influence was dominant was a precondition for its continued leadership of the country. The Europeans also began to understand that accommodation of the objectives of African nationalism, such as greater African elected representation in the Legislative Council and removal of racial barriers to African farming in the White Highlands, was essential if the post–Mau Mau restoration of African nationalism was not to submerge completely the political status quo in which the Europeans enjoyed a preeminent political, economic, and social position.

There were, during 1950–60, some colonial government reforms that have had a profound bearing on the processes of nation-building in Kenya since independence. The agrarian reforms are the basis of the present government's rural development strategy and objectives. The experiment in multiracial politics probably helped prepare the European community for the transfer of political power that was to follow, even though it experienced very great strains during the transfer and afterward.

The greatest importance of the reforms was in their influence on the style of politics. Because a major purpose of the agrarian reforms was to counteract militant African nationalism, the processes of rural economic development were to become suffused with political content. Since the multiracial experiment was premised on acceptance by farmers of both races of the importance of striving for economic development within a framework in which European political influence would continue to be very strong, the political overtones of economic development as well as multiracialism itself appeared profoundly conservative to African leaders when they reappeared on the scene. These leaders were thus, to some extent, alienated from measures to reintroduce African politics and to open the White Highlands to African farmers, and from the whole process of rural economic development undertaken during the decade. The processes of economic development and defense of the political status quo became identical, and the first elected African leaders consequently distrusted and were alienated from both, although they could not easily oppose the results achieved.

ECONOMIC DEFENSE OF THE POLITICAL STATUS QUO

The campaigns of the Kenya African Union helped to produce the administration's drive for an economic development program in defense of the political status quo. KAU maintained its assault on the injustices of the existing distribution of land not only in Kenya but in London as well. The Kenya African Union was behind the campaign of the Congress of Peoples Against Imperialism (CPAI), which was directed primarily at members of the British Parliament.[1] The congress composed a petition in 1952 which Fenner Brockway subsequently presented in the British Parliament. The petition claimed that African squatters on land in the White Highlands had no security, that Africans had been crowded onto poor land, and that they were driven to seek employment in the towns. The petition alleged further that the best land had been taken for Europeans, that Africans had not been compensated for the land taken for European occupation, and that the Europeans had not made full use of their land. The congress argued that the Native Lands Trust Ordinance and the Crown Lands Ordinance, which together governed the division of rural land between the races, should be replaced and that no more Europeans should be allowed to farm in Kenya. Finally, the petition demanded that agricultural training and credit should be given to Africans and that Africans should be allowed to elect members of the Legislative Council.[2]

One major reason for the emergence of a policy favorable to fundamental transformation of the African rural areas was the new recognition, by the colonial administration and the European set-

1. Carl G. Rosberg, Jr., and John Nottingham, *The Myth of Mau Mau: Nationalism in Kenya* (New York: Praeger, 1966). The petition was reported in the *East African Standard* on January 25, 1952, and presented to Parliament by Fenner Brockway on July 15, 1953.
2. *East African Standard,* January 25, 1952. Reproduced as Appendix I of *Opportunity in Kenya,* Fabian Colonial Bureau, Research Series No. 162 (London: Victor Gollancz, 1953).

tlers, of a need to direct the attention of Africans away from recovery of the White Highlands. At the same time, the Europeans slowly became aware of the need to justify their continued leadership of the country in terms of their capacity to produce economic and social progress for Africans as well as for themselves. Governor Sir Philip Mitchell in 1951 requested a royal commission to examine the state of the African economy and to recommend ways to deal with the pressing and acute problems being faced by Africans in their reserves: serious population congestion, insecure land tenure, and the inability of small-scale family farmers in the African reserves to preserve the land or achieve yields above bare subsistence. The governor offered his own analysis of the problems the commission would be examining.[3] He attacked Africans' idea that recovery of all or part of the White Highlands would relieve distress in their reserves. He argued that a policy of transferring European land to Africans would infringe the historically valid claim the Europeans had to the land. He argued also that such a policy "would be not only an act of gross and indefensible injustice but of egregious folly." [4] The "folly" lay in part in the allegedly erroneous hypothesis that a significant amount of land in the White Highlands was undeveloped or underdeveloped by Europeans. Since the amount of such land was considered to be insignificant by the administration and the European community, there could be no economic justification for turning over any of the Highlands to Africans. An even more important aspect of the "folly" of such a land-transfer policy lay, however, in the implicit failure to recognize that the inefficiency of African agricultural economic practices was the prime cause of rural African social and economic troubles.

> The cause of the problem lies far deeper, in the basic agricultural and economic defects of African tribal practices, and the poverty

3. Kenya, *Correspondence of the Governor and the Secretary of State on the East Africa Royal Commission on Land and Population in East Africa* [Kenya No. 193 Lyttleton to Mitchell, November 16, 1951; Despatch No. 109 (September 11, 1945); Sessional Paper No. 8 (1945); Despatch No. 44 (April 17, 1946); and Despatch No. 98 (June 2, 1950)], issued November 16, 1951.
4. *Ibid.*, p. 6.

of much of the land, and the solution must be sought further afield than the next door European farm. If the problem is to be solved it must be realized that an emotional and political approach to the problem can achieve nothing. . . . It is necessary to devise measures which will turn the people concerned from bitter preoccupation with the real or imaginary past to a hopeful and happy enthusiasm for the future, be it in farming, industry, transportation, the public service, or any other means of earning a good living.[5]

Finally, the governor maintained that not every African was suited to becoming an enterprising farmer in the cash economy. "Not everyone," he reasoned, "in any country has the means, desire, or capacity to become successful farmers—these considerations override any incidental aggravation to congestion caused by immigrant farmers." [6]

Sir Philip Mitchell's statement to the secretary of state for the colonies revealed the fundamental premise of economic and social reforms initiated during the decade that followed: land-use reform leading to enhanced economic development and social progress was to be instituted as a reinforcement and justification for the political status quo. Reform of land use would serve as an alternative to reform of land distribution—which would have signified recognition and accommodation of one of the most important objectives of African nationalism in Kenya. The political attack mounted by the African nationalists on the Europeans in their rural bastion would be turned aside by a concerted attack on the problems of economic development. The increased development of the country's economy would relieve the congestion of the rural reserves by providing jobs outside the rural areas for Africans, while development of the re-

---

5. *Ibid.*, p. 8. The first resettlement schemes for Africans in the White Highlands were to be placed on land underdeveloped in relation to its "agricultural" potential. Their existence constitutes an admission by the Kenya government that the European enclave had not fully developed the land in its possession. See, further, Kenya, *Unalienated, Undeveloped, and Underdeveloped Land* (Nairobi: Government Printer, 1960). This was a report commissioned by the government arising out of a Legislative Council motion of June 19, 1959, inquiring into the amount of unused and underused land in Kenya. Its conclusions were that, while there was little high-quality unused land, there were opportunities for more intensive profitable development of land in all areas.

6. Kenya, *Correspondence.*

serves themselves would bring a measure of prosperity to Africans who remained on them. Such enterprises, rather than changing the White Highlands from a racially exclusive farming enclave, would absorb the attention and efforts of people who would otherwise have engaged in attacks on the political status quo symbolized by the presence of the White Highlands. Economic development processes themselves were to become identical with political processes leading to reinforcement of the status quo rather than to political change. Oliver Lyttleton, the secretary of state for the colonies, expressed broad agreement with Mitchell's arguments.

The European community also believed that economic development of the African reserves should be encouraged, but within a political and social context that would be not only preserved but reinforced.

The Kenya Electors Union (KEU) argued in its 1949 manifesto that the European settlers were "anxious to avoid the too hasty destruction of indigenous institutions and social usages. These are being destroyed fast enough, and we see a serious danger that if they are not upheld social discipline will be jeopardized before new social organizations, customs and sanctions have rooted themselves." [7] The European leaders knew well enough that unregulated change was occurring in the African reserves and that social disorder would be the most likely result, but they preferred an attempt at arresting the process of social change to any attempt at encouraging new institutions compatible with the direction of social change in the reserves.

The strategy of encouraging African economic development as a means of preserving and reinforcing the political status quo did not initially include measures to reform African land tenure. In asking for the royal commission to suggest guidelines for the reform of African economies and societies, the governor expressed interest in land consolidation because some African communities, in parts of Kikuyu country, were known to be engaging in voluntary exchange of land fragments through sales leading to enclosure of con-

---

7. Kenya Electors' Union, *Kenya Plan* (Nairobi: Kenya Electors' Union, 1949), p. 4.

solidated landholdings.[8] The governor believed that this process might deserve the encouragement of the colonial administration once all its consequences could be perceived and assessed. On the other hand, when the senior appointed African representative in the Legislative Council took the initiative in asking the colonial administration to establish and recognize land titles in the African areas, suggesting that failure to do so was responsible for the frustration leading to Mau Mau, the chief native commissioner responded that the absence of such titles had not prevented Africans from selling land or deprived them of the protection of the Native Lands Trust Ordinance.[9]

LAND REFORM AND MULTIRACIALISM

Mau Mau and the declaration of a state of emergency by the new governor, Sir Evelyn Baring (now Lord Howick), provided the necessary catalyst for the serious implementation of the developing strategy of combining economic reform of African areas with revision of the political status quo. The return to power in Britain of Winston Churchill's Conservative party increased the receptivity of the colonial administration to the idea of favoring individual, as distinct from some form of collective or communal, land tenure, although it remained anxious about the consequences of individual tenure in African areas.[10] The strategy of villagization employed in Kikuyuland to isolate insurgents from the loyalists and the absence of KAU leaders from the political scene provided the opportunity to reform Kikuyu land tenure systematically. Moreover, the neces-

8. Kenya, *Correspondence.* Rosberg and Nottingham, *Myth of Mau Mau.* Interview with H. E. Lambert. See also M. P. K. Sorrenson, *Land Reform in the Kikuyu Country* (Nairobi: Oxford University Press, 1967).

9. *East African Standard,* November 28, 1952.

10. Mitchell said, in his Despatch No. 240, 1951, of a trend toward consolidation of individual land holdings: "This is a tendency with which the Government should certainly not interfere, except with great caution and when it is entirely sure of its ground; indeed the view may well be taken that encouragement should be given to it, for it is in line with general agricultural policy" (p. 12). Interviews with Lord Howick and R. J. M. Swynnerton, October, 1965.

sity of bringing a substantial number of British troops to Kenya to repress Mau Mau made the new government, and particularly its colonial secretary, considerably less sympathetic to the political status quo. Baring and some of the more moderate members of the European settler community undertook to support increased political partnership of the races as the means of protecting the European political position in the country from any precipitate changes of colonial policy in London. The strategy of redefining the political status quo while encouraging African economic advancement had two components: the consolidation and registration of individual landholdings in Kikuyu country; and the development of multiracial politics. While African nationalism was held in check during the early years of the Emergency, which lasted from 1953 to 1960, these components operated largely independently of one another. When African nationalism began to reappear in the later 1950s, the components merged into a reasonably coherent and comprehensive strategy.

Land Consolidation. Two of the most fundamental obstacles to the development of the rural economy of Kikuyuland, especially, were the fragmentation and dispersion of landholdings and the inability of Kikuyu, because they did not have individual legal title to their holdings, to offer their land as security for development loans. Patterns of inheritance in Kikuyu tradition were such that individuals tended to inherit land in chunks dispersed over fairly wide areas. Some individuals inherited as many as twenty or thirty separate parcels. Efficient development of crops or of livestock was nearly impossible under such conditions.

As early as 1932 the Department of Agriculture had favored the idea of land consolidation and registration of individual titles.[11] But the department had to subordinate its views to those of the leaders of the colonial administration, who feared the consequences of encouraging individual land tenure.

11. Eric S. Clayton, *Agrarian Development in Peasant Economies* (New York: Macmillan, 1964), chap. 1.

Between 1952 and 1953 the administration's policy on land-tenure reform in African areas underwent a sharp reversal, in part because African farmers had themselves taken the initiative. In a few districts the "chiefs" had on their own embarked on a process of exchanging fragments in order to gain consolidated holdings. For the next two years the government did not interfere with this process or attempt to oppose it. In 1955, the colonial administration endorsed land consolidation and asked for funds to hasten the process officially along with funds to complete military operations under the Emergency.[12] In the interim, land consolidation gained a measure of more or less open support from a number of local administrative officials in Kikuyu country.[13] The change of view came from two sources—the administration and the Department of Agriculture. The administration began to recognize that land consolidation was an asset because it could be employed to reward the loyalty of those Kikuyu who allied themselves with the colonial administration against the Mau Mau insurgents. Land consolidation became an essential element in the government's campaign to create a stable middle class of politically conservative Kikuyu who would become a counterpoise against the future reemergence of militant nationalism, especially among the Kikuyu. A district commissioner in Fort Hall wrote that it was "important to seize the opportunity of rewarding loyalists by giving them larger and better holdings. . . . If we are to keep them on our side," he cautioned, "and to reward them for their outstanding work, at the same time showing the rest that Mau Mau does not pay, we cannot do better than to help them with their land." Another hoped that the land-consolidation scheme "will change the face of Kikuyuland and bring into being a middle class of Kikuyu farmers who will be too busy on their land to worry about political agitation." The administration also came to believe that the economic development resulting from land consolidation would lead to the creation of a sufficiently buoyant rural economy to absorb landless Kikuyu, including thousands of Kikuyu repatriated from Tanganyika (as it

12. Interview with Lord Howick, October, 1965.
13. Sorrenson, *Land Reform,* chap. 7.

then was), the European Highlands, and other areas of Kenya.[14] The creation of a strong rural Kikuyu economy would enable other areas to escape Mau Mau by ridding them of Kikuyu labor. No one wanted potential Mau Mau instigators in his vicinity.

A second reason for the encouragement of land consolidation and the consequent development of individual land tenure came from the Department of Agriculture. While the administration as a whole was acquiescing in the emergence of voluntary processes of land consolidation in Kikuyuland, the Department of Agriculture was making a forthright and comprehensive plan for the development of African reserves.[15] The plan, which subsequently bore the name of R. J. M. Swynnerton, the assistant director to the minister of agriculture, was devised in great haste, at least in part because the prospect of thousands of unemployed Kikuyu returning to their homeland from Tanganyika and other areas of Kenya worried the colonial administration. It was necessary to provide for their employment and well-being as well as for the Kikuyu already present whose loyalty needed to be secured.

One of the main elements in the Swynnerton plan was a land reform which would remove the communal control of land tenure, consolidate the creation of a landed and a landless class, and risk the possibility of African indebtedness resulting from individual ownership and control over the land. The result of communal control over land tenure in Kikuyuland had been inheritance by Africans of widely separated fragments of land, making economic development inefficient if not impossible.

> In the past Government policy has been to maintain the tribal system of tenure so that all the people have had bits of land and to prevent the African from borrowing money against the security of his land. The result is that there is no agricultural indebtedness by Africans to other races. In the future, if these recommendations [of

14. *East African Standard,* February 13, 1953.
15. Kenya, *A Plan to Intensify the Development of African Agriculture in Kenya* (Nairobi: Government Printer, 1955). Correspondence between Cavendish-Bentinck and Swynnerton, October 16, 1963, ARG 32/2.

the Swynnerton plan] are accepted, former Government policy will be reversed and able, energetic or rich Africans will be able to acquire more land and bad or poor farmers less, creating a landed and a landless class. This is a normal step in the evolution of a country.[16]

Although the governor and others were still fearful of the consequences of such a sudden *volte face,* the adoption of the Swynnerton plan committed the government to a change in philosophy if it really meant to bring about economic progress in African areas. To insure the loyalty of Kikuyu and other Africans uncommitted to Mau Mau, the government could not afford to delay implementing the plan.

The Swynnerton plan committed the government to four important policy stances arising from the recognition and encouragement of individual land tenure in Kikuyu country. First, the government moved to diminish the reliance of Africans upon their traditional institutions for social regulation and cohesion, looking to more specific economic relationships to provide at least a partial substitute. The plan recognized that initially those who had been absorbed on the land as tenants under traditional Kikuyu land-tenure rules could be displaced. The government was very concerned that these people be reabsorbed successfully, and it believed that they would become employees of those who obtained larger and more consolidated units under the new system. The government thus contemplated that the specific relationship of employer and employed in modern economic institutions would replace the more diffuse relationships obtaining in the landlord-tenant relationship found within traditional Kikuyu society.[17] Second, in creating a landless class and a landed class, the government opened up the possibility that both groups might be reintegrated not within their traditionally defined ethnic communities but with their counterparts in society at large.[18] The proponents of multiracialism were, in part, to base their incipient social order on a common interest of both European and African landlords in

16. Kenya, *A Plan,* p. 10.
17. *Ibid.*
18. See Great Britain, *East Africa Royal Commission, 1953–1955: Report,* British Sessional Papers, 1956, Vol. XIII (397), Cmd. 9475 (London: H.M.S.O., 1956). See also chap. 3, *infra.*

economic development and a common system of land tenure. On the other hand, the presence of a presumably very large landless class, partially created by land consolidation, would later drive the Europeans to seek a land resettlement program in the White Highlands under which the landless could purchase subdivided farms and the Europeans could leave the country with some portion of their capital. Third, the Swynnerton plan countenanced a new emphasis on agricultural solutions to Kenya's development problems. The discussions about caring for the landless class of Kikuyu centered on ways and means of absorbing them within the rural economy; possible urban commercial or industrial solutions were not actively considered. Fourth, the Swynnerton plan initiated a change in government policy on agricultural credit for Africans. The government implicitly seemed to accept the possibility that the substantial economic benefit to the country arising from increased African agricultural production might lead to substantial indebtedness on the part of the new Kikuyu smallholders.

One important economic consequence of the Swynnerton plan was to place Central Province, the Kikuyu homeland, in a favored position vis-à-vis other regions and peoples. With individual tenure and registered landholdings, the Kikuyu had mortgagable assets to offer as security for agricultural development loans. In other areas, such as Nyanza, where the large Luo community lived, individual land tenure was delayed because of traditional customs. In the coastal region, delay occurred because the confused inherited patterns of land tenure had not been sorted out. Thus, in addition to the political stake in the future of the country which the Kikuyu gained by virtue of their numbers and early intensive exposure to European colonization, they acquired an important economic stake in Kenya through being the primary beneficiaries of a major pre-independence agrarian revolution.

The Swynnerton plan was designed to develop the African agricultural economy not only for its own sake but also to serve the political status quo in two distinct ways. The plan tried to demolish again, on economic grounds, the arguments of African leaders for more land, especially when such arguments threatened the European settlers' tenure in the White Highlands.[19] Swynnerton argued that there were no large unoccupied, highly productive areas in Kenya remaining to be settled by Africans. The White Highlands were not mentioned by name, but by implication African claims to allegedly unused productive areas of the Highlands were dismissed as unfounded. The possibility of irrigating large semiarid areas of the Northern Frontier District were dismissed as a relatively unproductive and unprofitable use of scarce development funds.[20] Furthermore, apart from aiding existing resettlement schemes in African areas under the previous ten-year program, no emphasis was given to the idea of resettling people from areas of dense population in less populated areas. The plan's emphasis was on the "intensification" of African agricultural development. Its basic argument was that most of the potentially good agricultural land was under reasonably beneficial occupation, and therefore no legitimate economic purpose would be served by changing the occupants. The claims of African nationalists to "stolen" and/or unused land in the White Highlands were, by strong implication, rejected on economic grounds.

Second, the Swynnerton plan reinforced the status quo by outlining ways in which the agricultural development of African areas might build a class of politically contented rural citizens who could be accommodated safely in the existing order. The plan argued that Africans should begin to assume responsibility for their own economic development at the local level on both political and economic grounds. On the latter, Swynnerton wrote, "Ultimately appreciation of the insistence on sound cultural practices, on plant sanitation, cooperatives, marketing, and so on, must come from large groups of progressive African farmers having their own representative bodies as is now the case with the European agricultural industries." [21] There would be exceptions to this principle where the productivity of lands was being permanently endangered, where large government investments had to be protected, or where industries were endan-

19. Kenya, *A Plan,* par. ii.
20. *Ibid.*
21. *Ibid.,* par. 12.

gered by trade recessions or pestilence. Swynnerton argued that "the greatest gain from the participation of the African community in running its own agricultural industries will be a politically contented and stable community." [22] He thus foresaw that the agrarian revolution that would ensue, given the implementation of his plan, would produce an alternative to the KAU route to social and political leadership of the African communities. Not only land consolidation, in and of itself, but the whole process of agrarian development in Kikuyuland and in other African areas would produce the kind of leadership upon which moderate Europeans and relatively foresighted colonial administrators might rest the responsibility of maintaining a multiracial society.

Two other factors facilitated the implementation of the Swynnerton plan as well as land consolidation in Kikuyu country. Until 1951 the Kikuyu had been denied the opportunity to grow coffee. Europeans feared that, if Kikuyu or other Africans grew coffee, it would be of lower quality and would harm Kenya's position in the world market, and that Africans' inadequate supervision of the crop would lead to the development of coffee berry disease or other maladies that might spread to the coffee crops under European cultivation. Allowing Africans to grow coffee met a long-standing demand of the nationalists while facilitating agricultural development. Furthermore, the process of villagization in Kikuyu country during the Emergency was opportune for the Swynnerton plan. The purpose of villagization was to isolate loyal Kikuyu from the insurgents. It was also hoped that such villages would produce secondary, agriculture-related industries in which landless Africans could be employed. These villages proved temporary and many of them have disappeared since the Emergency. Those that remain have not realized all that was hoped. However, after congregating people in villages, the government could re-plan the countryside without regard to existing homestead boundaries and hasten the process of land consolidation.

Land consolidation, registration of individual titles, and Swynnerton plan measures to increase the development of efficient cash-

22. *Ibid.*

crop farmers combined to transform the Kikuyu countryside in the latter half of the 1950s. Both the pace of consolidation and the growth of the agricultural economy in Kikuyuland surpassed the expectations of the most optimistic government personnel. The most tangible and significant result of the agrarian revolution has been the enclosure and consolidation of individual landholdings and subsequent registration of title. At the end of 1959, 1,314,658 acres of land had been consolidated.[23] Of this area, 820,049 acres were in Central Province, while an additional 350,594 had been consolidated in Nyanza. In Central Province alone, 117,746 freehold titles had been issued. Subsequent farm planning had been undertaken on 13,644 farms in Central Province and 2,512 in Nyanza. By the end of the decade considerable progress had been made toward meeting the Swynnerton plan's proposals for phased increases in cash-crop development.[24] The acreages for pyrethrum and coffee were met and surpassed respectively, while the growth of tea lagged somewhat behind the target figure. Major increases in cash-crop production were recorded by about 1960, increases which can almost certainly be attributed largely to land reform and government assistance in cash-crop development. Pyrethrum production leaped from 40,000 tons in 1954 to 184,000 tons in 1960 and 359,000 tons in 1964. Coffee production grew from production worth £172,000 ($481,600) in 1954 to £2,247,000 ($6,291,600) in 1960 and £5,366,000 ($15,024,800) in 1964. Smallholder production as a percentage of total production in these areas rose from 9 percent in 1954 to 23 percent in 1960 and 30 percent in 1963. One important consequence of the agrarian revolution in central Kenya during the years of Mau Mau was to make smallholder production a significant factor in the agricultural economy of the country.

Multiracialism.   While the agrarian revolution progressed according to a political strategy that essentially endorsed the status quo,

23. Hans Ruthenberg, *African Agricultural Production Development Policy in Kenya 1952–1965* (Berlin: Springer-Verlag, 1966).
    24. *Ibid.*, pp. 8–12.

the British government, its colonial administration, and a segment of the European community began to design a political and constitutional structure within which African political activity could be accommodated when Emergency restrictions were relaxed. The development of a politics of accommodation included not only provisions for increased African participation in the Legislative Council and gestures intended to improve race relations but discussion of the possibility of ending the racial exclusiveness of the White Highlands and allowing qualified African farmers to purchase farms there. The architects of "multiracialism" founded their movement on the premise that the beneficiaries of assistance to African rural economies and those Africans included in national political activity on the basis of a restrictive franchise would develop interests similar to those of the more moderate members of the European community. They hoped and believed that multiracial politics would develop upon the foundation of a common effort to further Kenya's economic development and that the Africans would identify with a multiracial effort at nation-building in Kenya as an alternative to restoring African nationalism to full vitality.

The European community became divided between those who saw merit in policies designed to improve the lot of the African peoples—such as the Swynnerton plan, land consolidation, and increases in the number of appointed African representatives on the Legislative Council—and those who were primarily concerned with protecting European interests and inclined to oppose anything that might suggest weakening European leadership and influence. The experience of some European settlers in World War II may have influenced many of them to take the former point of view. Sir Michael Blundell, who was to lead those Europeans favoring multiracialism, observes in his memoirs:

> The older ones, who had not served in the armed forces in the war, really wished to maintain the political and economic status quo and were more attracted to the simple doctrine of opposition to the Government. The younger ones were much more conscious of African feelings and sympathetic to their political advance, and saw

ahead to the days when they might be governing themselves, even if the vision was far from clear.[25]

Europeans who came to Kenya after the war were building their homesteads and farms in order to repay substantial debts incurred for that purpose, and were concerned that political change not endanger their investment before it had begun to yield net profits. They opposed the multiracial policy. Europeans who had settled there before World War II, while not necessarily out of debt, had farms or businesses that were going concerns, helped considerably in many cases by having produced for the war effort.[26] They favored multiracialism.

The outbreak of Mau Mau and the declaration of the Emergency by the new governor, Sir Evelyn Baring, led the British government to put the European settlers on the defensive. The secretary of state for the colonies, Oliver Lyttleton (now Viscount Chandos) left the Europeans in no doubt about the impact of Mau Mau on the British government's colonial policy:

Sixty thousand Europeans cannot expect to hold all the political power and to exclude Africans from the legislature and from the government. The end of that will be to build up pressure which will burst into rebellion and bloodshed. You are suspicious and critical of what you term in a pejorative sense "colonial office rule." When as a result of over conservative and traditional policies you provoke an explosion, you are not slow to ask the British Government and the Colonial Office, which at other times you attack, for troops, aeroplanes and money to suppress a rebellion. I warn you, that one day you will be let down and therefore besides force, which must now be used and which we will provide, you must turn your minds to political reform and to measures which will gradually engage the consent and help of the governed. The security of your homes, the security of the money, and hard work, and skill which you have lavished upon your farms and the industries which you have begun to build, cannot rest upon battalions of British troops. I

25. Sir Michael Blundell, *So Rough a Wind: The Kenya Papers of Sir Michael Blundell* (London: Weidenfeld & Nicolson, 1964), p. 84.
26. Based on interviews with a number of European members of the Legislative Council during this period.

may or may not have principles concerning democracy to reinforce these arguments, but I am not going to display them. I am at this moment confining myself to hard facts and to your material interests.[27]

The British government allowed the European community time to prepare for African political advances by promulgating a new constitution, bearing Lyttleton's name, in 1954, in which the principle of parity between European representation and representation of other races combined was maintained in the Legislative Council. There was also an informal understanding that further constitutional changes would be delayed until 1960, an understanding which became known as the "standstill policy." With the imminent retirement of Winston Churchill as prime minister and a new general election due in Great Britain within a year, the European settlers could have derived only limited satisfaction from the promise of a six-year moratorium on further constitutional changes. Prior to the implementation of the new constitutional arrangements, Lyttleton's predecessor, James Griffiths, in authorizing increases in Legislative Council membership while maintaining the parity principle, had warned the Europeans not to consider the parity arrangements sacrosanct. He said: "I must not be taken as accepting the view that the maintenance of parity between the European members, on the Unofficial side of the Legislative Council, is essential any more than I am accepting during this interim the other views and proposals put before me." [28] Among these other proposals was an African one for the addition of twelve more African members of the council. The price of denying this request, although one African position was created on the Executive Council for the first time, may have been to sacrifice the last opportunity of preventing the eruption of Mau Mau from the ranks of KAU. The award of a lone Executive Council position was not sufficient to induce KAU to participate in the

27. Viscount Chandos, *Memoirs* (London: Bodley Head, 1962), p. 398.
28. Statement by the secretary of state, May 31, 1951, reproduced in Fabian Colonial Bureau, *Opportunity in Kenya*, p. 45.

subsequent conference on future constitutional changes which Lyttleton had suggested.[29]

The 1954 "Lyttleton" Constitution made no change in the composition of the Legislative Council and permitted the continuation
of the parity principle. Its major change was the adoption of a full
ministerial system of government to replace the membership, or
semiministerial, apparatus. The award of six ministerial positions to
Europeans under the new arrangements did not satisfy the Europeans any more than the one African position had appeased the
Africans. The European community considered that the constitution
had been imposed, forgetting that previous attempts to establish
constitutional changes on the basis of interracial negotiations had
not been successful. This alleged imposition strengthened the militancy and oppositional spirit of many Europeans and led them to
demand more local control of policy in Kenya at the expense of
London and more regional control of policy within Kenya. The
Europeans generally did accept the application of the parity principle
to the appointment of unofficial Legislative Council members to
ministerial positions, though many resented the appointment of two
Asian members. The single African minister, B. A. Ohanga, was
generally accepted, perhaps in part because his Ministry of Community Development was concerned primarily with purely African matters. Another African and two Asians joined the government bench
as assistant ministers or parliamentary secretaries.

The Lyttleton Constitution was also important because it
prompted some members of each racial community to support the government and cooperate in the development of colonial policy. On the
other hand, it preserved the political status quo in important respects,
not only by maintaining the parity principle in the Legislative Council but by forbidding any minister to propose land legislation affecting the rights of any other group. Multiracialism was to be fostered

29. Mr. Fenner (now Lord) Brockway insists even today that opportunities for gaining
the participation of KAU in constitutional discussions were not fully exploited and that he
had the confidence of the KAU leaders sufficiently to have effected such participation. See
his *African Journeys* (London: Victor Gollancz, 1955).

within a framework that retained large elements of the status quo.

Notwithstanding the elements of continuity in the new constitution, and perhaps because many Europeans sensed the impermanence of their political influence in the administration of the country, the new arrangements touched off an intense and angry debate over the principles of multiracialism which the new constitution seemed to exemplify. Michael Blundell, almost immediately after joining the government as minister without portfolio, founded a political party with a view to supporting the multiracial principles of the Lyttleton Constitution.[30] His United Country party (UCP) was promptly challenged by the birth of the Federal Independence party (FIP), which in general sought to establish provincial autonomy in policy-making as a bastion against the colonial administration in Kenya as well as the British government, both of which it believed to be unduly infected with multiracial heresies.[31] A third force in European politics consisted of those who were critical of the formation of parties of any persuasion, believing parties to be bad tactics for the European community to follow, since a European community divided in politics was a weakened European one and such weakness could open the door to greater political influence by representatives of other racial communities. But the division of European political opinion may have been inevitable, since the structure of the constitution, in creating a number of European positions in the "cabinet," had deftly forced a choice between attempting to ride the tiger of African political advances and caging it.

The United Country party was one of the key elements in the new political configuration, for its avowed purpose was not to behave as political parties usually do—i.e., to seek executive and legislative power, divide spoils, score points on the opposition, or discipline followers—but to persuade the European community of the rightness and sensibleness of multiracialism and thereby to broaden the base of support for the Lyttleton Constitution. Its purposes were "to promote racial cooperation based on a common loyalty to Kenya

30. The United Country party (UCP) was formed in July, 1954.
31. The Federal Independence party (FIP) was also formed in July, 1954.

and to the Crown, to support the government by a coalition of the three races as a contribution to the stable development of the country, and to encourage and guide the economic, social, and political progress of all its peoples." [32] Blundell and Wilfred Havelock, as leaders of the new UCP and ministers in the new government, were critical liaison men between the colonial government and the mass of European settlers, most of whom did not share these leaders' moderate views. The party's main sources of strength were in the Rift Valley and in Nairobi. These areas were the strongholds of Blundell and Havelock, and it is very possible that much of the support the party built for the new order was based on personal loyalty to one or both of them as well as to the principles involved.

Obtaining political support for the new constitution within the European settler community was only one task in the assignment of building an environment within which the principles of the new political arrangements could take root. The other tasks were the creation of machinery within which African political organizations could safely be restored and the establishment of a program for social and economic progress in the country that would generate support for the new politics. The latter objective had a double focus: stimulating greater and more efficient economic contributions from the European farmers; and providing for economic development and social change for the African peoples.

The government initiated the revival of African politics in 1955. District political associations were permitted to allow African political spokesmen to organize for the first African elections, to be held in 1957. The government actively enforced the restriction of each African political party to a single administrative district. Meetings of leaders of district associations were proscribed, addresses to a given district political association by leaders of another were barred, and the government acted under pressure from European politicans to prevent the burgeoning trade union movement from yielding a *de facto* political party.[33] The Kenya Federation of Labor (KFL), for

32. July 16, 1954, policy statement of the UCP published in the *East African Standard* on that day.
33. Tom Mboya, *Freedom and After* (London: André Deutsch, 1963), chap. 2.

example, narrowly escaped proscription for venturing into what the government believed to be national political activity.[34] Despite restrictions, the associations which grew up in Nairobi and Mombasa as well as the development of the KFL served as valuable surrogates for national political organizations, since they established interethnic group relationships that would be vitally important when Africans were to assume real leadership of Kenya. On the other hand, the restriction of African political activity to the district level resulted in the emergence of political groups representing only one ethnic group in the majority of cases, while European and Asian parties were able to reinforce racial or communal solidarity by organizing all their kinsfolk throughout the country on a national basis. The local African political associations survived, were eventually represented by a region-oriented national party, the Kenya African Democratic Union (KADU), and were partly responsible for the divisiveness that strained the later Kenya African National Union (KANU), which was determined to forge national unity out of diverse ethnic groups.

The character of restored African politics was affected by the government's attempt to establish a close relationship between the effective political community, those in society with some minimal direct participation in the process of determining the authoritative allocation of social values, and the community of those who were making effective contributions to nation-building in Kenya. Nation-building in this context meant the process of building the social and, particularly, the economic infrastructure of the country and the deemphasis of broadening political participation among Africans. The government deputized W. F. (later Sir Walter) Coutts, sometime district commissioner in Kikuyuland and later Kenya chief secretary, to develop recommendations for African voter qualifications in the 1957 African elections.[35]

The qualifications entitling Africans to vote were possession of property, a given level of income, a minimum age, public or military

34. *Ibid.*
35. Kenya, Sessional Paper No. 39 of 1955–56.

service, and education. The government changed from three to two the number of such requisites needed for the award of a vote. Africans possessing more than two of these qualifications gained as many as three votes. The justification for establishing these requirements revealed the extent of the government's departure from the policy of strengthening traditional African societies against the forces of modernity, the policy that delayed needed African land reforms for so many years.

> The chief reason for the Government's acceptance of the Coutts principle of a standard [voting qualification] above the minimum [universal adult suffrage] is that African communities in this country show a difference in education, in social and material development, in political experience, and in knowledge of the outside world, which separates the people concerned not by a generation, but by hundreds of years, and the government is convinced that before an African can be expected to play a proper part in helping to guide the affairs of the Colony, he must be accustomed to the exercise of individual responsibility and have at least some conception of the modern world and some recognition of the problems which confront us.[36]

Of the multiple franchise arrangement, the chief secretary observed:

> The Government is firmly of the opinion that those who have contributed a greater share to the welfare of the state or who are particularly well qualified to play a part in public affairs, should have greater say than those who can command nothing more than minimum qualifications.[37]

The government thus appeared to recognize and even encourage African progress in the "modern" ways to which the Europeans were accustomed. It wished to reward contributions to the development of the country, and in proportion to the magnitude of such contributions to nation-building. Consistent with this view, the government awarded the franchise to members of the armed forces in World War II whose military service might have cost them their education and

36. Kenya, Legislative Council, *Debates,* LXVIII (1956), 200.
37. *Ibid.*

also to those who had developed their land sufficiently to earn the requisite income but who might have missed the opportunity to gain a primary education and had not yet received title to their land. Those who had participated in land consolidation and Swynnerton plan programs were not forgotten, though the elections may well have come too early for many of those whose economic position had been improved by the agrarian revolution to meet the income qualification.

Government policy stood in contrast to colonial policy in West African countries, which weighted representation in national assemblies in favor of tradition-oriented peoples considerably closer to the date of independence.[38] To a degree, the tendency of district parties to reinforce ethnic divisions was counterbalanced by the franchise restrictions, which emphasized the political importance of those who, by virtue of involvement in the processes of nation-building, might have been assumed to have risen above such parochial considerations.

The developmental premise of multiracialism linked the constitutional and the economic aspects of the response to African nationalism, and Mau Mau in particular, which together composed the strategy of political accommodation of Africans based upon their involvement in nation-building. The political principle behind the Swynnerton plan and land consolidation, that political leadership of the country should be in the hands of those who contributed to the economic development of the country or other aspects of nation-building, was extended by the Coutts proposals to the sphere of formal political activity. Those who were to become community leaders by virtue of their roles in the country's social and economic infrastructure were to be the leaders or to influence heavily the choice of leaders who would determine public policy. While the government was creating electoral machinery for the benefit of African nation-builders, it developed an eighteen-point plan in 1954 to guide nation-building efforts, a plan which would shortly become the basis for the government's endorsement and encouragement of land

38. *East African Standard,* July 9, 1954.

consolidation in Kikuyu country and elsewhere. It extended the economic development begun in Kikuyuland to all areas of the country, European and Asian as well as African. The government viewed this eighteen-point program as a broad attempt to make full use of the political standstill in being until 1960. Its fundamental argument was that development could not be curtailed simply because of the Emergency. Land-use measures necessary to increase the productivity of the land were to receive high priority, while measures to improve the efficiency and productivity of European farming were also to be enacted. Policy in these areas was to be guided by the Troup report on the economy of the European White Highlands and by the Swynnerton plan for the African reserves. In addition to developing the entire economy of the country for its own sake and as a basis for political accommodation of Africans in a multiracial order, the eighteen-point plan had the major purpose of providing for the reabsorption of Africans displaced in one way or another by the Emergency. Industrialization was promised as a means of providing employment for a growing labor force. Education of all varieties was to be encouraged. Measures were to be taken to improve the well-being of the population at large by means of better health facilities, progressive wages and working conditions for labor, and modern housing facilities designed especially for Africans with limited incomes.

The response to this plan indicated better than the program itself its political significance. The Kenya Electors' Union condemned the plan as a "thinly veiled effort to approve influences hostile to European settlement in Kenya." [39] Some members of the KEU thought they perceived evidence of "supine acceptance of dictatorship from the United Kingdom Parliament." [40] In their view the eighteen-point plan would simply negate efforts to bring the Emergency to a successful conclusion if it merely resulted, as the KEU predicted, in increased loss of confidence in Kenya on the part of the European community as a whole. The KEU believed it held a right to a govern-

39. *Ibid.*
40. *Ibid.*

ment program centered on the needs of the European settlers. "If Kenya is to survive towards a western and prosperous way of life, it will only do so by the united efforts of the Europeans. The government must realize this and not seek to estrange European support." [41] Overemphasis on developmental contributions by the Africans was, for the KEU, a kind of racial appeasement. They desired that guarantees of the English language, English civilization and culture, and the racial sanctity of the White Highlands be vouchsafed to them by the government.

The United Country party of Michael Blundell issued its statement of policy the same month as the eighteen-point plan appeared.[42] Its principles were support for the multiracial constitution, economic development efforts by all races, African political and economic advancement, and the building of a multiracial nation generally. There was little difference between the programs of the UCP and the Council of Ministers. The KEU accepted the Lyttleton Constitution only on a provisional basis, to see if it would work, while the UCP, as one of its critics noted, presumed its success and sought to make that presumption self-fulfilling. The KEU believed that European interests were placed in jeopardy by the eighteen-point plan, while the UCP said in effect that what was good for Kenya was good for the European settlers.[43] Blundell and even his future and much more conservative political adversary, Cavendish-Bentinck, felt compelled to dispel publicly the fear expressed by the KEU and its sympathizers that the new emphasis upon African economic development and social progress might imply greater concern by the government for African than for European interests.[44]

The real meaning of the eighteen-point program to the European community was a new emphasis by the colonial administration, supported by Blundell and the UCP, that European as well as African farmers would be required to justify their place in the new multiracial order. One of the most significant products of the eighteen-point

41. *Ibid.*
42. *Ibid.,* United Country party's policy statement, July 16, 1954.
43. S. G. Ghersie argued in this way in the *East African Standard,* July 16, 1954, which adopted a similar stance, editorially.
44. *Ibid.,* August 6, 1954.

plan was the Agricultural Ordinance of 1955.[45] This ordinance, which had been in preparation for several years, was a collation of existing agricultural regulations reinforced by measures for government enforcement and appeals procedures for farmers affected by such regulations. It remains the foundation of Kenya's agricultural policies to this day. Its purpose was to achieve efficient and productive farming in Kenya by farmers of all races by preserving soil fertility, providing means whereby the land would yield the optimum productivity, and providing a system of price guarantees that would shield farmers against losses from causes outside his control and guide him in determining the acreage to be alloted various crops. While the bill was intended for the entire agricultural community of Kenya, there was a scent of European orientation about its organizational provisions, many of which applied only to European farmers. The ordinance established a series of provincial and district agricultural committees to be appointed from lists of persons recommended by the Kenya National Farmers Union (KNFU), then almost exclusively European. The farmers themselves would elect members of the committees according to KNFU recommendations and screened by the Ministry of Agriculture. These committees were to assist the ministry in maintaining standards of agricultural production and in maintaining communications between farmers and the ministry on problems of agricultural policy and practices. No longer could farmers have the option of farming or not farming according to efficient procedures that would conserve the land and maximize its productivity. Failure to conform to ministry directives for the preservation or development of the land would result in the ministry's doing the necessary work at the farmer's expense. The expense would then become a lien on the farmer's property. The European orientation of these measures was confirmed by the recognition in the ordinance and in its presentation to the Legislative Council that the bill was not fully applicable to African farmers. African farmers did not in a great many cases farm the twenty-plus acre allotments with which the ordinance was concerned, African farming customs and prob-

45. Kenya, *Revised Edition of the Agriculture Ordinance, 1955,* No. 8 of 1955, incorporating all amendments made before July 1, 1961 (Nairobi: Government Printer, 1961).

lems differed, and most African farmers were not eligible for the
price guarantee and acreage allotment of the bill.

The Europeans panicked at the new ordinance. Cavendish-
Bentinck, the minister for agriculture, had to defend the ordinance
against the allegation that it placed new restrictions on the European
farmers rather than codifying and enforcing old ones.[46] On the other
hand, the chief European architect of Kenya's multiracial order,
Michael Blundell, viewed acceptance of the ordinance by the Europeans as the indispensable precondition for the settlers' continued
enjoyment of their privileged economic and political position. He
told a meeting of one of the settlers' associations:

> I do not believe there is any necessity for Europeans to have any
> feeling of insecurity but it is necessary to accept the measures to
> ensure the land is farmed efficiently on Western standards. Unless
> you are prepared to accept some measure of securing proper devel-
> opment then I do not see how paper promises of any kind can
> guarantee you long term security of tenure.[47]

Blundell believed that the European position in Kenya would have
to be supported by solid contributions to Kenya's economy, just as
Africans were to earn their right to participate in the multiracial
political and social order by virtue of similar contributions.

The African members of the Legislative Council endorsed the
eighteen-point program and expressed the belief that it was a harbin-
ger of better times to come when all members of the multiracial
society of Kenya could feel confident that they had equal opportunities to play effective parts in the national government.[48] The African
council members promised support for measures aimed at ending the
Emergency as long as measures were taken simultaneously to treat
African farmers on the same terms as other farmers and to provide
opportunities in commerce and industry for Africans. They argued
that fair procedures for the conduct of forthcoming African elections

46. *East African Standard,* October 29, 1954.
47. *Ibid.,* August 20, 1954.
48. *Ibid.,* July 9, 1954.

would provide a good weapon for anti–Mau Mau Africans to use against the insurgents.

MULTIRACIALISM, AFRICAN NATIONALISM, AND LAND REFORM

Shortly before the Royal Commission requested by Governor Mitchell reported in June, 1955, its most far-reaching recommendation had been anticipated by a prominent back-bench member of the Conservative party in the House of Commons. In January, Cuthbert (later Lord) Alport told the House of Commons that the White Highlands was a "political and economic anachronism." There was, he argued, "no security for either race while they remain separated in their respective enclaves without contact." [49] He suggested that all land should be held on tenancy from the government and that tenancies should be allocated without regard to race. He insisted that the Europeans must support multiracialism and reconsider their views on land policy in order to ensure their own survival. Once again the Europeans were admonished to change their strategy in their own self-interest.

A meeting of European settlers at the Nanyuki Sports Club, called to consider this forthright attack on what they believed to be their fundamental interests, complained that Alport's remarks were at variance with assurances given the settlers by the Colonial Office in the past regarding their enclave.[50] The argument that changes in colonial policy about the White Highlands, as well as with respect to political change generally, were breaches of faith was to become the basic European position over the next decade. Alport's attack was too much even for the United Country party, which noted that thousands of Africans were employed by Europeans in the White Highlands and expressed the fear that Alport's statements might have represented the views of Alan Lennox-Boyd (later Lord Boyd), who had recently become colonial secretary.[51]

49. *Ibid.*, January 21, 1955.
50. Kenya Electors' Union in *ibid.*, February 18, 1955.
51. *East African Standard*, February 25, 1955.

The three European ministers were asked by their constituents to resign their ministerial responsibilities should there be any tampering with the White Highlands during the time allotted for the standstill policy.

Kenya was thus forewarned when in June the report of the East African Royal Commission found the maintenance of both tribal and racial land barriers to be incompatible with the development of a modern economy.[52] The commission noted the demands expressed in the last KAU land petition and also the bitterness caused by the juxtaposition of broad, extensively farmed European lands and intensively farmed, overcrowded African lands. It argued that the Europeans themselves had not found the security they sought in the Highlands Order-in-Council. Said the commission: "Nothing is more clear in Kenya today than the failure of the measures instituted by the Kenya Land Commission [the 1934 Land Commission] to give the Europeans the sense of security which was their expressed object." [53] The commission observed that European farmers already had legal security individually for their farms and argued that it should be preserved and defended. It recommended the creation of machinery for leasing land to would-be land proprietors that would operate free of racial or tribal biases. It did not believe that claims disposed of by the 1934 Kenya Land Commission should be revived and recommended, but rather that Africans with farming ability should be allowed to possess land in the Highlands, so that a single rural economy could be created.

> We think that there is no hope of progress in Kenya except by its development as an integrated economic unit. . . . By the present policy of exclusive tribal reservations, and under the various obligations by treaty, agreement and formal declaration . . . Kenya, in particular, has been divided into a number of watertight compartments, none of which is, or can be made, economically self-sufficient and the frustrations of the last twenty years have been largely due to failure to recognize that fact. . . . Policy regarding the tenure and disposition of land should aim at individualization of land ownership and mobility in the transfer of land which, without ignoring

52. Great Britain, *East Africa Royal Commission Report*, chap. 6, par. 19.
53. *Ibid.*, par. 18.

existing property rights, would enable access to land for economic use.[54]

"Watertight" rural compartments, both racially and ethnically defined, were thus at variance with the individualization of landowner-ship and ability to sell and otherwise dispose of land that the administration had begun to accomplish in Kikuyuland during the Emergency. The assault on the Europeans' cherished White Highlands was the logical conclusion, in the commission's view, to the processes of land consolidation and registration of individual title begun in the name of the political status quo and encouraged by the new philosophy of multiracialism. The commission gave substance to the worst fears of right-wing Europeans, who saw in African progress a challenge to manifestations of their racial "superiority."

The KEU and UCP had already expressed their reactions to the commission's major recommendation in replying to Alport. L. R. M. Welwood, one of the European ministers, thought the report a "curiously ruthless document." [55] A London correspondent observed that the general reaction was one of pretending nothing had happened.[56] Most Europeans, he found, thought that the proposals would never be implemented and would, in any event, founder because the Africans themselves did not wish to remove barriers separating their various ethnic communities any more than the Europeans wished an end to their racial enclave. The African trade union movement and the political associations of Africans in the cities were the major challenges to this argument, since they had demonstrated some capacity to work together without regard to ethnic differences. However, the European community was clearly worried. The Federal Independence party condemned the report as positively dangerous. Many European former politicians remember anxious and frequent meetings called to devise responses to the assault on their position.[57] Even the governor, Sir Evelyn Baring, replying for the Kenya gov-

54. *Ibid.,* par. 7.

55. *East African Standard,* June 24, 1955.

56. Report by Gordon MacLean, No. 10094, August 9, 1955. No record of publication. Found in the files of the *East African Standard.*

57. Interviews with Havelock, Cavendish-Bentinck, Blundell, and other European political leaders.

ernment, lectured the British government on the realities of attempted rapid change in Africa and the need for patience. Citing Scripture, he wondered whether the changes that were occurring and which the Royal Commission had encouraged were any measurable improvement for the ordinary Africans.[58] However, the views of the commission probably helped move the government to final endorsement of land consolidation and individual title registration in December, 1955. Certainly it provided the initial impetus for measures to end racial land barriers, accomplished by legislation introduced in late 1959.[59] The governor, once convinced that the new policy was necessary, spoke out for it frequently, and Blundell led the European moderates in identifying with what they came to believe were essential changes from the standpoint of their own interests.[60]

The African elections of 1957 produced a group of African Legis-

58. Baring's comments were directed particularly to the commission's alleged intention to change traditional African customs in the interests of greater economic development and prosperity. But the application of the following comments was to racial as well as to tribal land barriers:

"In Africa patience is an essential quality of Government. And although we accept these changes must be made, whether or not the transformation will make the African a happier man is a matter for conjecture; for the circumstances of modern life involve not only the privileges but also a degree of responsibility which is likely to seem burdensome at first. This transformation from group to individual responsibilities can hardly do other than intensify the personal loneliness and isolation of the African emerging into modern life. The alleviation of this loneliness is a problem to which we are well alive; but it is a problem which has again and again confronted western man over the centuries. 'The troubles of our proud and angry dust are from eternity and shall not fail.'

"For these reasons, although we accept that many of the protective restrictions must eventually be removed, there are many steps which cannot yet be taken. It would, for instance, be most injudicious for the Kenya Government to try to move faster than public opinion allowed toward breaking down tribal and racial boundaries, particularly those boundaries which distinguish the various areas of land assigned to separate communities and separate tribal groups." Great Britain, Colonial Office, *Despatches from the Governors of Kenya, Uganda, and Tanganyika and from the Administrator, East African High Commission, Commenting on the East Africa Royal Commission* (London: H.M.S.O., 1956), pp. 3–4, pars. 10–11.

59. Within a year of the publication of the Royal Commission Report, the European Elected Members went to work to hammer out a new policy on land tenure which led to their support of the bills to open the Highlands.

60. E.g., *East African Standard,* March 27, 1959 (Speech to Royal Agricultural Society of Kenya), and July 6, 1956. Blundell's speech at Nakuru was reported in *ibid.,* November 1, 1957.

lative Council members who successfully ended the standstill policy on political changes well before 1960, the appointed year for its review. Of the incumbent African nominated members of the Legislative Council, only Daniel arap Moi, now vice president of Kenya, survived. He was joined by seven other new African leaders, most of whom were to become prominent members of the African government after independence. Moi was to become vice president succeeding Oginga Odinga, who was elected from Nyanza to represent the Luo people—the second largest African ethnic group in the country. Five others were to become ministers after independence. The eight newly elected African representatives immediately agreed to advocate an end to the continued reservation of the Highlands for Europeans only, racially segregated schools, the Lyttleton Constitution, and restriction of the franchise for African adults. They knew their objectives were substantially beyond those most European leaders were prepared to support. "It was obvious," Tom Mboya noted later, "that our presence there [in the Legislative Council] was only to add color." The African members resolved, therefore, not to accept ministerial positions until steps had been taken toward meeting their demands.[61]

The African elected members focused on the number of African representatives on the Legislative Council. Strikingly, the European members voluntarily agreed to increase the number, thereby relinquishing the principle of parity which they had defended for the past ten years. The African members rightly claimed that they had effected an end to the Lyttleton Constitution by making increases in the number of African representatives without corresponding increases in the number of European members, their price for accepting ministries. Lennox-Boyd, the new colonial secretary, came to Nairobi in late 1957 to establish a new constitution, which confirmed the end of parity by awarding six additional seats and one new ministerial position to the Africans. As a counterpoise he added twelve Specially Elected Members who would be chosen by the Legislative Council and would require the support of members of

61. Mboya, *Freedom and After,* pp. 119–20.

more than one racial group. In addition, Lennox-Boyd created a
second chamber, a Council of State, whose purpose was to examine
the legislation of the Legislative Council for possible discriminatory
provisions and remove them if found. These safeguards appeared to
employ the multiracial ethic as a counterweight to increasing African
influence in the government.

Under the "Lennox-Boyd" Constitution, the Legislative Council
completed the achievements of the multiracial movement by enact-
ing measures confirming individual titles to Africans who consolidated their landholdings and by opening the White Highlands to
competent African farmers. While confirming the existence of a class
of landowning Kikuyu with access to the multiracial order, these
measures crystallized the position of a landless class. They placed
the Kikuyu in a unique and favored position vis-à-vis other African
peoples, though some of the other African communities—notably
the Luo—did not immediately recognize the advantages conferred
by registered individual titles. In the process of consolidating and
registering individual titles, efforts were made to protect the interests
of those Africans who were in detention or fighting on the side of
the Mau Mau insurgents. But injustices did occur. The entire task
had to be done again in Fort Hall District because of irregularities.
And some Kikuyu on the side of Mau Mau did lose land. In each
of these ways, land reforms undertaken to support the multiracial
political and social order risked the polarization of African society
between those who did and those who did not participate in and
benefit from the reforms. Just such a polarization contributed to the
outbreak of Mau Mau in the first place. In many respects, multiracial
politics purported to confirm that polarization.

The Landed. The Native Lands Registration Ordinance of 1959
enabled Africans with consolidated holdings to receive full title to
their land.[62] It emerged after lengthy consideration of the problem
of determining whether and how African holdings could be properly

62. Kenya, *Native Lands Registration Ordinance of 1959,* Ordinance No. 27 of 1959, pp.
199–270.

interpreted in English legal terms. The main task confronting the Working Party on African Land Tenure, on whose recommendations the ordinance was written, was that of insuring that no new rights were created.[63] They sought to do so through recognizing individual tenure before it had fully and naturally evolved. The ordinance was to apply only in those areas where private, individual tenure—in approximately the English legal sense—had emerged. The Kikuyu were to be the principal beneficiaries at that time. Precautions were taken so that the issuance of individual title did not influence any local arguments over ownership of the land in question, because once titles had been recognized no arguments over claims on the land prior to the issuance of the title were to be honored. To be certain that no land disputes would be swept under the table by the issuance of title, the working party established that "the essence of the system which we propose is that ownership is established by proving long occupation to the satisfaction of the traditional land authority.[64] Subject to this self-imposed limitation, the working party expressed the desire that confirmation of individual titles proceed as rapidly as possible to fulfill the objective of a uniform land-tenure system for all of Kenya.

In addition to determining ownership claims, the working party found a number of thorny problems in establishing a land-tenure system based on registered individual ownership. One problem was to determine the rights of sale. On the one hand, the working party observed that there were traditional prohibitions against outright sale to members of other African societies within some communities. To recognize these prohibitions would have been to open the door to suits based on racial or ethnic discrimination in sales and would have defeated the objective, enunciated by the Royal Commission, of taking land policy beyond the reach of racial or ethnic politics and prejudices. In most Western countries racial barriers to the sale of land arose after the idea of private ownership of property had been established—the reverse of what occurred in Kenya. On the other

---

63. Kenya, *Working Party on African Land Tenure* (Nairobi: Government Printer, 1958).
64. *Ibid.*, p. 19, par. 49.

hand, full recognition of the right of new owners to sell their land raised the possibility of small African farmers' encumbering their land and eventually losing their titles. The working party observed: "It has been proved in many countries that the surest way to deprive a peasant of his land is to give him a secure title and to make it freely negotiable." [65] To meet these difficulties the working party proposed the creation of a set of land boards, one purpose of which would be to regulate interracial land sales. They would act to prevent the creation of too many co-owners, oversee and perhaps prevent land sales between persons of different African ethnic groups, and prevent a newly created landowner from selling without considering the interests of other members of his family. In effect, the working party recommended and the statute enacted limitations on the right of sale by the creation of land boards and delegated to them the resolution of difficulties on a case-by-case basis.

Another problem was presented by inheritance of consolidated and registered land. The absence of restrictions on inheritance would have resulted in the participation of a great many people in the legacy and possibly also a recrudescence of the fragmentation which the process of land consolidation was intended to correct. Restrictions on the right of a landowner to convey his property to his descendants would, in addition to diminishing the significance of his ownership rights, present him with an embarrassing choice of who, among his offspring and wives, would succeed him on the land. Finally, the legislation departed from the English standard of primogeniture to the practice of permitting as many as five heirs, and efforts were to be made to prevent fragmentation.

Finally, those Africans who held land as *ahoi* under traditional Kikuyu custom had to be considered. To reduce the numbers of Kikuyu with no access whatsoever to ownership of land, the Native Lands Registration Ordinance, on the recommendation of the working party, provided for the creation of special rights of tenancy with the same degree of permanency in law as under traditional Kikuyu rules. These provisions did not by any means eliminate landlessness

65. *Ibid.,* p. 45, par. 101.

or unemployment among the Kikuyu, nor did they prevent the new owners from adopting a somewhat less charitable attitude toward the tenants. Given the opportunity to achieve individual ownership, the opportunity to obtain loans for the economic development of farms, and the responsibility of repaying those loans out of profits, owners were inclined to view tenants as economic liabilities rather than as social responsibilities.

After hesitation, the colonial administration and the moderate members of the European community began to campaign for support to end racial, if not inter-African, ethnic land barriers. The governor publicly ridiculed the idea of watertight economic compartments preserved by racial and ethnic land barriers.[66] Michael Blundell argued within the European Elected Members Organization for the adoption of a multiracial point of view on land policy.[67] As chairman of the European elected members subcommittee on land policy, he prepared a memorandum which basically followed the argument of the East African Royal Commission while deferring to the fears of less moderate European members.[68] He argued that there should be freer exchange of land in the interests of fuller economic utilization, although not at the price of sacrificing the protection afforded more "backward" peoples by the colonial administration. At the same time, the memorandum recommended that land should be vested in African ethnic communities and individual races in order to prevent domination of one race or ethnic group by another. Cleverly, Blundell invited the confidence of both moderate and conservative European leaders. The moderates were pleased at the proposal to permit interracial or interethnic land sales, provided only that the purchasers demonstrate a capacity for competent farming. The more conservative members believed the vesting of land in individual communities and the creation of boards to oversee interracial land transfers would discourage African purchases of land in the White Highlands.[69] The Council of Ministers, led by Chief Secretary Walter

66. *East African Standard,* July 6, 1956.
67. Unnumbered documents of the European Elected Members Organization. Private files of Sir Wilfred Havelock.
68. *Ibid.*
69. *Ibid.*

Coutts, Blundell, Wilfred Havelock, and other moderates in official as well as nonofficial circles, began to discuss means of bringing multiracial principles to bear upon land policy. The result of these various efforts was the introduction of an ordinance to end the racial exclusiveness of the White Highlands toward the end of 1959.[70]

The ordinance eliminated any further racial restrictions on land sales. Restrictions could be imposed only to prevent quality land from going to persons not equipped to farm it efficiently or productively. A Land Control Board was established, supported by divisional and regional boards, to administer land transfers between races so that they were consistent with the economic health of rural Kenya and not reflections of residual race prejudice. Critics observed that the ordinance struck at race prejudice while ignoring similar prejudices between African communities. Many of these critics, however, would have preferred that even this first step in the direction of placing land tenure on economic rather than social prejudice foundations had not been taken.

Blundell insisted that European farmers in the Highlands be given the option to convert their leaseholds from the Crown into freehold tenure over a period of years.[71] Amendments were subsequently introduced to lengthen the time and reduce the price of such conversions. Blundell and other European leaders believed this option to be consistent with the objective of placing land tenure on a common basis throughout the country. Freehold tenure was considered possibly more secure against any further changes in the government's land policy arising from increasing African participation in political decision-making. European farmers with private, freehold tenure similar to that possessed by Africans would derive security from the fact that any governmental policy directed at European freeholders by an African-dominated government might arouse fears among Africans who possessed freehold rights. The option for European leaseholders to convert to freehold seems to have been created in part out of recognition that within less than a year the term for

70. Kenya, Colony and Protectorate, *Land Tenure and Control Outside the Native Lands,* Sessional Papers No. 10 of 1958–59 and No. 6 of 1959–60.
71. Interviews with Baring, Blundell, and Havelock.

what was to have been a six-year standstill on constitutional changes would expire. Increased African participation, of uncertain proportions, was expected after that date.

The Landless. In addition to establishing a class of rural landholders, the most certain and immediate consequence of land consolidation and the registration of individual titles was the isolation of a landless class of Kikuyu. Land consolidation did not necessarily create landlessness, much less unemployment, among the Kikuyu, but it did certainly crystallize the position of those without solid claims to land and without means other than farming of obtaining a livelihood. In fact, land consolidation did not increase the size of this class as much as it might have because the colonial administration, and Governor Baring in particular, resisted the attempts of the Agriculture Department to prevent Africans with unprofitable landholdings from returning to their plots at the end of Mau Mau hostilities. Nevertheless, those who were tenants *(ahoi)* in a great many cases became dependent upon wage employment rather than farming for their livelihood.

The size of the landless class depended on a number of considerations. One was the financial ability of the new title-holders to employ labor, and their willingness to employ outside labor rather than utilize family manpower. On the other hand, prospects for rural wage labor depended upon the willingness of potential laborers to work for employers of their own ethnic group. Many Kikuyu found this degrading. The Kikuyu were restricted in seeking employment by regulations governing their migration to and from major cities like Nairobi and by the unwillingness of other ethnic groups and European farmers in other areas of Kenya to employ large numbers of them. The provisions of the Native Lands Registration Ordinance governing inheritance and tenants, and the attitudes of the new owners toward such tenants, affected the size of the Kikuyu landless class. There was some early evidence that deaths of title-holders were not faithfully reported, to postpone determination of who would inherit land. In the absence of a complete field examination, it is difficult to determine how persistent or widespread these practices have become. Finally, the numbers of landless were swelled by the return of thousands of Kikuyu formerly employed on European farms and in Tanganyika and the failure of European farmers to reemploy many of these laborers when Emergency restrictions were eased. The tendency of European farmers to mechanize their operations on grounds of efficiency and because they believed politicians were pressing African laborers to demand higher wages helped to increase the size of the unemployed, landless Kikuyu group.[72] Many of the laborers dismissed from European farms during the Emergency were believed to have joined the Mau Mau insurgents in part because they had lived outside the Kikuyu reserves for so long that they were unable to assert successfully any claims to land under traditional rules.

The precise number of landless Africans without any means of employment but farming has never been known with any degree of accuracy in Kenya. This is paradoxical, since land hunger has been one of the most persistent and fundamental causes of both economic and political insecurity in the country. The key to the paradox lies in the uncertain relationship between landlessness and unemployment. The 1960 report of the Commission on Unemployment headed by F. C. Dagleish emphasized the existence of underemployed persons, i.e., those who are not fully dependent upon wages for a livelihood but who are unable through self-employment or wage labor on or off the land to engage in productive full-time labor.[73] Although land consolidation helped to clarify and separate the landed and the landless classes in the Kikuyu rural economy, not all of those who became landless subsequently became either completely unemployed or fully employed as wage labor. The commission estimated that there might have been at the time approximately 309,000 Kikuyu alone in the working-age group. Of these, 123,000 or 40 percent could be described as fully self-employed on economic holdings as a result of land consolidation. Of 184,000 possible work-seekers, the commis-

72. Kenya, Land and Agricultural Bank, *Annual Report, 1961* (Nairobi: Government Printer, 1962), reports from individual districts 13 to 34.

73. Kenya, Colony and Protectorate, *Survey of Unemployment* (Nairobi: Government Printer, 1960).

sion estimated that perhaps 120,000 Kikuyu were wage-earners outside the reserves in the cities or on farms outside Central Province.
Thus there may have been about 65,000 landless Kikuyu either
unemployed or underemployed in 1960. But the extent of their destitution could not be assessed accurately because of the phenomenon
of underemployment.

Despite uncertainty over the numbers of landless and unemployed Africans, their existence in substantial numbers was accepted
in all political circles. The Dagleish Commission recommended further emphasis on agricultural development in the reserves. The commission considered that land consolidation might eventually turn a
labor surplus into a labor shortage and that the pool of landless and
unemployed Africans existing at the time would be reabsorbed as
wage labor in the rural economy. Agricultural and administrative
personnel recorded their belief that further land consolidation and
cash-crop development might provide employment for an additional
400,000 males. In addition to increasing the opportunities for wage
employment through agricultural development, the commission believed that the failure of Africans to seek out existing employment
opportunities contributed to the degree of unemployment and landlessness. In the commission's view, greater emphasis on the value
of manual labor in primary education, greater urbanization, and
unequal population distribution contributed to this phenomenon.
The commission believed that higher wages would be desirable in
order to stabilize the urban working force but expressed reservations
about the capacity of the urban economy to generate enough employment to absorb the labor surplus. It did not even consider the possibility of population redistribution—an indication that even in 1960
not everyone was prepared to abandon the limitations imposed by
racial and ethnic land barriers.

The government accepted the commission's view that the key to
relieving unemployment lay in agricultural development of African
areas rather than in further development of the urban economy:
"The unemployment at present manifested in the settled areas is
essentially a projection of this larger problem of underemployment
in the African land units and arises in the main from the growing

desire of Africans to enter the wage earning sector of the economy." [74] The government thus argued that underemployment was in part a state of mind resulting from Africans' exposure to the modern economic system, which made African employees less satisfied with subsistence living than before. The government also sought to protect the White Highlands from more intensive development, meaning more African employees in the European enclave, by arguing that unemployment of Africans must be solved by the further agrarian development of the African reserves.

The government did realize that it was urgent to relieve unemployment and that traditional customs, which often softened the impact of rural unemployment, could not be relied upon to provide a full or rapid solution to the problem:

> This question of traditional customs and so on softening the position of unemployment could not be expected to be a real safeguard. Therefore, we must not lay a lot of hope on that. . . . As the Sessional Paper [based on the Dagleish Report] makes clear this situation is unlikely to last and there is little consolation to be derived from it. The provision of opportunities for full employment must be the first concern of any government. It is vital for the social and economic welfare of all its peoples that the problem should be solved. [75]

The government appeared to recognize that unemployment might lead to a recrudescence of Mau Mau or similar insurgency, but it also argued that political stability would have to be restored before the economic development necessary to relieve unemployment could be generated. In 1960 the government was still concerned with maintaining and justifying measures enacted during the Emergency to enforce stability as well as to provide for economic development which might diminish threats to political stability.

The African representatives in the Legislative Council did not like the government's proposed solution to African unemployment,

---

74. Kenya, Colony and Protectorate, Sessional Paper No. 10 of 1959–60, p. 5.
75. Statement by R. G. Ngala, minister for labour, in Kenya, Legislative Council, *Debates,* LXXXVI (1960), 1183.

although they did not quarrel with the results achieved by land consolidation and cash-crop development. Daniel arap Moi and Jeremiah Nyagah, moderates representing smaller African ethnic groups bordering on Kikuyuland, deplored the government's adoption of a long-range solution to African unemployment when the presence of an unemployed class was an immediate and urgent problem requiring effective short-term as well as long-term solutions. Odinga, representing the Luo people of Nyanza, accused the government of indifference to the problems of the landless and unemployed and argued that land consolidation was designed to create and assist a class of African landlords who would cooperate with the Europeans and ignore the masses.[76] The government did in fact seek to create a class of African landlords, but it hoped to avoid the creation of a countervailing landless class by encouraging African landowners to employ wage labor in the development of their farms. However, Odinga's credentials to speak for the disinherited were somewhat weakened by the fact that he himself had consolidated his very extensive landholdings and was therefore a beneficiary of the policy he attacked. Finally, Tom Mboya, whose principal constituents were in Nairobi and in the Kenya Federation of Labor, attacked the government's rural solution to unemployment. He did not believe that moving the urban unemployed to rural areas would improve their employment prospects:

> These people who have got used to urban life are no use being sent back to the rural areas. They are no use to themselves. They are a nuisance in those areas when sent back to the rural areas. . . . Solving the unemployment problem is not going to stop the movement because all you will have done is to take away the problem from this area and put it in that area.[77]

The colonial administration believed that taking the problem out of the cities and putting it in the countryside might, on the contrary, be a solution. With emphasis given to rural development, the urban

76. *Ibid.*, p. 1192.
77. *Ibid.*

unemployed might find work in the rural areas. Dispersed there, they might cause less political trouble for the government than if concentrated in a few urban areas. Simultaneously, this policy would reduce the constituency of Mboya, who had become a respected but irritating thorn in the administration's flesh. Despite changes leading to the end of the racial exclusiveness of the White Highlands and rapid political advancement of the African peoples, the government overrode African objections to its policy for coping with the economic and political danger posed by landlessness and unemployment and continued the policy of the past decade by relying upon the development of the reserves rather than that of the White Highlands or the cities.

The Crisis and Legacy of the Passing Order. The dilemma for the representatives of African nationalism in the Legislative Council was whether and to what extent they should identify themselves and their cause with the achievements of the multiracial order at the expense of those Africans who had not been the beneficiaries of reform between 1950 and 1960. The dilemma was of greater significance in Kenya than in other African countries, where the representatives of African nationalism were faced with a similar problem in deciding when and whether to join the government in the last years of colonial rule. Because of Mau Mau, the leadership implications of the decision in Kenya were more complicated. Since independence was not yet in view, the implications for Africans' progress toward governing their own country were more difficult to assess. The movement for a multiracial order presented a positive and possibly plausible alternative, or threat, to independence under an African government. Finally, African nationalists' approach to land reforms undertaken in the spirit of multiracialism had important and relatively long-term significance vis-à-vis several basic decisions: acceptance or rejection of European economic and social institutions and norms; acceptance or rejection of increases in the polarization of rural African societies between landed and landless; and the choice of whether African nationalism in Kenya would be identified with those who had achieved the long-held nationalist objective of security of land tenure or with those who had not yet gained this blessing. Maneuvering by both European and African leaders on these questions occurred against the background of uncertainty over what changes would be instituted when constitutional discussions were again held in 1960.

One of the main concerns of the representatives of African nationalism in the Legislative Council between the elections of 1957 and those of 1961 was to prevent divisions from occurring within their ranks over multiracial initiatives backed by the colonial administration and moderate Europeans. The advocates of multiracialism intended to create such divisions by building an alliance between Europeans and Africans of moderate political views against conservative Europeans on the right and African nationalists on the left. The promulgation of the Lennox-Boyd Constitution posed a dilemma for the African legislators because it gave with one hand and took away with the other. It gave Africans an end to the parity provisions, but it created Specially Elected Members and the Council of State as checks on the ranks of members of the council elected from constituencies among whom Africans were now more influential. In part the dilemma was created by the fact that the Legislative Council itself was the only national platform for African political leaders as long as the Emergency restrictions on political parties covering more than one administrative district prevailed. However, the major issue was whether African members of the Legislative Council should agree to stand for election to the Specially Elected Member seats. Eight Africans finally did stand and were called "traitors, quislings, and black Europeans" by Mboya and the press. Foolishly, from its own point of view, the colonial administration prosecuted the African elected members for their language as a conspiracy against law and order. Conspiracy charges were dismissed, fines for defamation were imposed, and the African elected members were enabled to help their own cause by making a *cause célèbre* of the whole matter—with administration assistance.[78]

Revelations in 1958 and 1959 concerning the government's treat-

78. See George Bennett, *A Political History of Kenya: The Colonial Period* (London: Oxford University Press, 1963).

ment of Africans in the Mau Mau detention camps provided an issue around which all African legislators could make common cause. Reports of severe mistreatment fed African nationalism and led Oginga Odinga to refer to Jomo Kenyatta, detained in 1953 for leading Mau Mau as president of KAU, as the father of Kenya African nationalism. All the African group in the Legislative Council paid homage to Kenyatta as the symbol of the nationalist cause. Europeans were shocked at the very mention of Kenyatta's name by African elected members, since Kenyatta was synonymous with Mau Mau for many of them. The new publicity for Kenyatta raised the question of the African council members' own relationship to the imprisoned leaders of KAU. A number of the members themselves feared Kenyatta because they feared the Kikuyu and Mau Mau. When the first interviews with Kenyatta were permitted shortly before his release in 1961, they were agreeably surprised to find him a man of moderation. Until that time, however, both his political views and his health were unknown quantities because nobody had been in touch with him. These considerations, leading the African members to limit their identification with him and others in detention, were counterbalanced by more persuasive reasons to increase their identification with Kenyatta and his collaborators. Except for Mboya, none of the Africans in the Legislative Council had enjoyed any opportunity to build allegiances outside his own district and his own ethnic community, while all communities could identify with Africans imprisoned by colonialists. In addition, there were numbers of imprisoned leaders of KAU from the Luo and other African communities whose following could not be ignored by representatives of these other groups in the Legislative Council. Finally, the name of Kenyatta and the cause of the detained leaders afforded a rallying and unifying issue for the African members. Eventually, Kenyatta's release was to become the single most important issue to at least one of the two major African political parties before and after the 1961 elections.

In the months prior to the Lancaster House Conferences, multiracialism continued to plague the cause of African nationalism and to divide its ranks. In 1959 Blundell gave up the Ministry of Agricul-

ture, which had been his responsibility since 1955, to form a new
multiracial party, the New Kenya party (NKP), which portrayed
itself as an alternative to the racialism represented not only by more
conservative Europeans but also by those reviving African nationalism. It advocated substituting a nonracial quest for economic development in place of racial politics, and it sought to make contributions to the development of a viable national economy and social
structure an alternative criterion to advocacy of nationalism or racialism for determining political influence. The implications of such
a policy were to suffuse the processes of economic development with
political significance by making them an alternative to extensive
changes in the relationships of the races in formal processes of political decision-making. Blundell spent the summer months prior to the
Lancaster House Conference campaigning in England to rally support for his party's philosophy in British political circles. Alan Lennox-Boyd, the colonial secretary, was a firm friend of the European
moderates. Before he left office, he endorsed the multiracial approach to Kenya politics and emphasized that political and property
rights for all would need to be respected before further constitutional
advances could occur. Blundell claimed to have found other influential members of the Conservative party equally sympathetic. Indeed,
years later, after Kenyatta's government had won the approval of
those in the British government concerned with overseas policies,
a number of these Conservatives expressed admiration for Blundell
and his cause.

    An additional threat to nationalism was posed by an incipient
division in the ranks of the African elected members between those
who sensed that the smaller ethnic groups which they represented
might be in danger of domination by the larger groups in an independent state, and those, like Mboya, Odinga, and Gikonyo
Kiano, who advocated a more militant attack on the existing political
order and who happened to represent larger constituencies. This
division was undoubtedly strengthened considerably by the policy,
when African political parties were allowed to be revived, of restricting each of them to one district only. This cleavage was patched up
before the Lancaster House Conference, and Ronald Ngala, a repre-

sentative of one of the small communities, was chosen to lead the united African delegation. But the same division was to reappear and lead to the creation of two national political parties after the Lancaster House Conference. One, the Kenya African National Union (led by Odinga, Mboya, and later Kenyatta), advocated a strong central government. The other, the Kenya African Democratic Union (led by Ngala and Daniel arap Moi), represented the small ethnic communities that sought a degree of regional autonomy to protect themselves from the larger communities such as the Luo and Kikuyu.

The decade of political and economic reforms linked together under the banner of multiracialism has had a lasting impact on the character of political leadership in Kenya. The attempt to create an alternative leadership cadre to that which included KAU leaders detained during the Emergency did not succeed. The idea, for instance, that cooperative societies might provide experience and institutional support for a more conservative political elite has not been realized because the cooperatives themselves have yet to become viable enterprises. They have not succeeded in managing their members' affairs to the satisfaction of the government or the members themselves. Individually they have been too small to provide a real basis for leadership. Experience with the cooperatives in the settlement schemes offices will not become an avenue to community leadership until these management problems have been resolved. The real local leadership, even during the height of the agrarian revolution in Kikuyuland, was elsewhere. F. P. B. Derrick, in his analysis of Kikuyu politics in 1960, observed: "The leaders of public opinion will nearly always be found to be members of local or district councils and it is clear that these will yield an increasing influence as long as Africans are in a minority in the central government." [79]

The architects of reform in the 1950s did not anticipate that those Africans who led the nationalist cause after 1957 would themselves become a part of the rural middle class they sought to create. Presi-

---

79. Unpublished manuscript among materials of the Rhodes Library colonial records at Oxford University being compiled by J. J. Tauney.

dent Kenyatta, Odinga, and other leading figures (including Mboya before his death) in the present government of Kenya have become substantial landholders. Many of them have even gained plots for themselves or their relatives in the settlement scheme program since 1961, although these plots were generally intended for indigent Africans. Instead of creating a leadership elite to counterbalance the nationalists, the architects of multiracialism established reforms that enticed the nationalists to become identified with the landed class and the processes of economic development they sought to foster. Whether or not these processes of identification are the cause, the present Kenya government has emphasized the processes of rural development in much the same manner as the Swynnerton plan did. The present government has also in the process deemphasized further participation by more people in political decision-making. The long-term impact of multiracilism may have been that economic reforms generated by it, and consequent deemphasis of further political development as such, have become the nation-building model for the independent African government. Such identification by leaders with the land and policies oriented to further rural development attest not only to present economic realities but also to the continuing emotional and psychological attachment of African people to their land.

The short-term impact of multiracialism was to alienate the African leaders from the reforms because they seemed to represent the entrenchment of the European community. Mboya observed:

> It is unfortunate that most of the changes were not encouraged earlier because it can now be argued that it is the outbreak of Mau Mau which has resulted in creating this attitude toward African problems. This contention is intensified because even the most liberal of the European leaders continue to pledge themselves to defend the sanctity of the White Highlands, to maintain separate schools and hospitals, and to maintain European domination in the Legislative Council basically unchanged.[80]

80. Tom Mboya, *The Kenya Question: An African Answer* (London: Fabian Colonial Bureau, 1956), p. 16.

The end of racial parity in the Legislative Council seemed to open the door to the leaders of African political opinion in the council and was thus counted a victory by the African elected members. But the demise of the White Highlands as a racially exclusive entity, because it was accomplished under the banner of multiracialism and because it helped only those who had become wealthy farmers under land consolidation and the Swynnerton plan, was not seen by African politicians as a vindication of the nationalist objective of recovering "stolen lands." Multiracialism had thus succeeded in alienating those who spoke for Kenya African nationalism from land redistribution. The alienation of African nationalists from their own cause of recovering "stolen lands" was to have a profound impact on the transfer of political power and nation-building under an independent African government after 1960.

PART TWO

*Land Resettlement
and Nation-Building*

The transfer of political power in Kenya from the colonial administration to an independent African government occupied a unique place in the processes of decolonization that occurred throughout much of Africa shortly before and after 1960. This distinctive transfer of political control over the country's destiny was influenced by a peculiar combination of circumstances: Mau Mau, the reforms of the previous decade undertaken in the name of multiracialism, and the continuing importance of the European community in the political and economic life of Kenya. The most unusual circumstance of the transfer of political power in Kenya was the simultaneous decolonization of the White Highlands and the return of this land to Africans. The parallel processes of transferring both political power and a significant degree of economic power to Africans were to have a decisive influence upon each other.

The most important product of the transfer of land and political control in Kenya, apart from the creation of an independent African government, was the Europeanization of both processes. Although the return of "stolen lands" in the White Highlands had been one of the most important objectives of African nationalism, the process of Africanizing the White Highlands was undertaken on European terms and with European interests given foremost consideration. The economic importance of the White Highlands gave the departing European farmers leverage in the processes of transferring political power to an African government. Although Europeans in Kenya were shocked at the prospect of independence under an African government, their leaders were able to influence the transfer of power to their advantage at the expense of the incipient African government and its constituents.

The processes of economic development were allegedly threatened by the processes of political change both during and after the transfer of political power. European settlers were able to use the threatened decline of the country's economy arising from cessation of development in the White Highlands as a means of persuading the colonial administration and the British government to guide the transfer of political power without sacrificing European essential interest. The negotiation of the first scheme to resettle Africans in the White Highlands, replacing European farmers, was jeopardized by anxiety on the part of the World Bank (IBRD) and the Commonwealth Development Corporation that political changes might threaten economic productivity and their investment in the settlement program. The second resettlement scheme, under which a million acres of European farmland in the Highlands were to be subdivided and resettled by 30,000 landless, unemployed Africans and their families, was not in itself expected to contribute much to the economic development of Kenya. Rather, its objective was to remove the political pressure posed by the army of landless and unemployed, so that the government and the country could subsequently give full attention to programs that would encourage economic development. The new African government then decided that the rural economy, on which the country was to remain primarily dependent, would henceforth be guided by policies similar to those enunciated in the Swynnerton plan and implicit in land consolidation during the 1950s, because of the conspicuous economic progress achieved. Land redistribution under the resettlement program was then to be deemphasized, because it had served the interests of political change, dominated by the European community, rather than economic development.

The problem for the independent government has been to rid the processes of nation-building of the legacy of European influence. This has not been easy. Both further land redistribution and emphasis on broadening participation in the processes of political decision-making have been discarded as viable nation-building objectives in favor of more land consolidation and economic development, in large part because the former policies were made to serve European purposes during the transfer of political power. However, the juxtaposition of land development and land distribution, with emphasis on development, has exposed the government to the charge that it has abandoned an important tenet of African nationalism in favor of policy developed under European-colonial auspices in the 1950s. Defense of the present policy by Europeans and by American advisors in Kenya obscures the fact that security of tenure and economic progress in the African areas were also objectives of African nationalism. Deemphasis of land redistribution has left the Highlands as much an economic and political anomaly in African hands as it was formerly a racial and political anomaly under European control. The processes of economic development tend to become synonymous with political processes, because economic development is considered an alternative to activation of formal political institutions. Thus those outside the processes of economic development may also be driven to political alienation from a government they believe to be building upon the record of the multiracial movement of the 1950s rather than upon the objectives of African nationalism.

3

LAND AND EUROPEANIZATION OF
THE TRANSFER OF POWER

KENYA IN 1960 was better prepared for continued development of her agriculture-based economy than for a relatively rapid transfer of political power to an African government. This was quite satisfactory to the moderate Europeans who had sponsored the movement for a multiracial political and economic order during the 1950s. The prominence of Europeans and European ideas in the development of Kenya in the 1950s resulted from Mau Mau and the consequent severe limitations on African political activity after 1953. African participation in Kenya politics was thus delayed in part because there were no African political parties at the national level to insist upon it. The generation of Africans that would provide the political leadership of independent Kenya had less time and opportunity to gain experience in organizing political structure than many of their counterparts elsewhere in Africa. Great responsibility for the furtherance of African political interests lay with the few African members of the Legislative Council, especially those who served from 1957 to 1961.

The Lancaster House Constitutional Conference in early 1960 established political independence under an African government as an immediate objective of colonial policy in Kenya. At the outset of the conference, Iain Macleod, who had become secretary of state for the colonies, announced the Conservative government's aim was for Kenya to be "a nation based on parliamentary institutions on the Westminster model and enjoying responsible self-government." [1] Both the proposal that Kenya become independent under an African government and the stated intention of the colonial secretary to achieve this result within the near future came as a surprise to all the Kenya representatives at the conference, and all political parties had to reconsider their objectives and tactics. The African leaders, united behind Ngala, had demanded the conference as a condition of their continued participation in the Legislative Council. However, they had not expected immediate majority rule or the promise of early independence. These grants, made before they had been de-manded, presented a problem, for the African leaders were thereby deprived of the issue that was most likely to unite African political movements and leaders. They had to mobilize a movement to insure that the path to independence would not be delayed beyond what was promised.

Both the United party, which replaced the Federal Independence party as the main conservative European political organization in the late 1950s, and the New Kenya party of Michael Blundell had objected to holding the conference. They feared that political changes not to their liking might result from its deliberations. How-ever, neither expected such fundamental changes from the confer-ence. The United party refused to accept the conference report. After the conference, the more conservative European political leaders derived their influence more from the economic importance of their constituents in the White Highlands than from their position in the

1. Great Britain, Colonial Office, *Report of the Kenya Constitutional Conference Held in London in January and February, 1960,* British Sessional Papers, 1959/60, Vol. X (891), Cmnd. 960 (London: H.M.S.O., 1960).

formal political sphere. After hesitation and considerable misgivings, the New Kenya party accepted the conference report. The moderate European settlers subsequently demonstrated a willingness to participate in the government of Kenya during the transfer of power, wherever they could. Thus they were able to restrain somewhat the polarization of the races resulting from the transfer. However, the NKP paid a heavy price in terms of support within the European community for its decision to support the political changes. Its rejection by much of the European community was symbolized at Embakasi Airport in Nairobi when its delegation returned after the conference. Blundell was condemned by a European woman as Judas Iscariot and thirty pieces of silver were thrown at his feet. Blundell replied that he would be in Kenya long after she departed.[2]

The nature and pace of political advance in the multiracial countries of East and Central Africa posed a double problem for the British government. Any pattern of constitutional and political advance, or the lack thereof, risked provoking the European minority or the African majority, respectively. As Macleod explained:

> In the Northern Rhodesian Constitution, the British Government wanted to see a period of increased African participation in a government in which the Governor held the final say, prior to the inevitable movement toward self-government and so to independence. Anything less would have provoked an African uprising, anything more an explosion from the Europeans.[3]

The moderate stance of men like Michael Blundell and Wilfred Havelock was of the utmost importance, for they and their followers represented the potential bridge between the Africans and the more unreconciled Europeans. Macleod explained: "Blundell makes it clear that I pressed him very hard. Of course I did. He was the key to the New Kenya Group and the Group was the key to the success of the Conference."[4] Additional factors influenced Macleod's judg-

---

2. Sir Michael Blundell, *So Rough a Wind: The Kenya Papers of Sir Michael Blundell* (London: Weidenfeld & Nicolson, 1964), p. 283.
    3. Iain Macleod, "Blundell's Kenya," *Kenya Weekly News,* March 27, 1964, p. 10.
    4. *Ibid.*

ment. He was moved by evidence of atrocities and mishandling of prisoners in the Emergency detention camps, the pace of political advance in West Africa, the cost of the colonies to a British government in serious economic straits, and, possibly, American influence in favor of decolonization. An important consideration was the hypothesis, supported by the colonial secretary, that the strategy of limited political and economic aspirations of Africans in the name of multiracialism in the previous decade could become the foundation for a smooth transfer of power to an independent African government.

The most important feature of the Lancaster House Conference political settlement was an African majority in the Legislative Council, with lowered African voting requirements and reserved seats for the racial minorities. Under the new constitution there was to be a Legislative Council of sixty-five members, fifty-three of whom were to be elected on a common roll in which all races participated and twelve of whom were to be national members chosen by the other fifty-three after the election. The national members were to play the same role as the Specially Elected Members under the Lennox-Boyd arrangements. Twenty of the fifty-three common roll seats were to be reserved for representatives of the minority races, although all races were to vote for these members. For those seats reserved for representatives of the Europeans, Asians, and Arabs, there would be primary elections to insure that candidates chosen at the regular election by voters would have a certain minimum level of support within their own racial communities. The limits of the franchise were widened substantially beyond those employed in 1957. Any literate person forty years of age or earning £75 ($210) per year or more was to be allowed to vote. For the first time, the Council of Ministers was to consist of a majority of members chosen from among the African members of the Legislative Council. Europeans were to be given three ministries and the Asian members one. The elections under the Lancaster House Conference agreement were not held for over a year after the conference ended. Not only was African control of the government delayed, but the elections themselves were set up to favor the needs of the European community and, particularly, the interests of the more moderate Europeans. The reservation of twenty seats to the minority races meant that one African party would have to win all the remaining constituency seats to be sure of controlling the Legislative Council. The requirement that representatives elected from those twenty constituencies demonstrate support from more than one race favored the moderate Europeans over their more conservative adversaries.

Land resettlement was the price of European accommodation of the political changes, which included not only an African majority in the Legislative Council but the relaxation of Emergency restrictions on African movement and political activity. Blundell says that measures under which Africans would be enabled to succeed Europeans on farms in the Highlands was the condition of his party's acceptance of the conference decisions. "Eventually the decision was made to accept, provided that the African Elected Members agreed to work in the new government which would be formed and Her Majesty's Government made funds available for education and the purchase and development of land in Kenya." [5] The Colonial Office at first said that Kenya could have funds for either education or land reform but not both. Blundell records that he visited the Colonial Office during the conference to persuade its parliamentary under-secretary, Lord Perth, that £5,000,000 ($14,000,000) was needed for land resettlement and that this should be granted in addition to, rather than in place of, development assistance for other projects. He told Perth: "It's a government of the patricians for four years and then the plebs are in and we must prepare for it." [6] Perth was said to have agreed somewhat sadly. Land resettlement was designed to help the European community prepare for independence rather than to realize the historic objective of Kenya African nationalism for the recovery of the White Highlands. The European moderates were of sufficient importance to the British government in its plans for the transfer of political power to an African government that Blundell was able to strike this bargain with the Colonial Office.

5. Blundell, *So Rough a Wind,* pp. 275–76.
6. *Ibid.,* p. 276.

The European moderates' decision to seek the land-resettlement program represented the beginning of a dilemma which the independent African government would inherit: whether to use scarce available economic assistance from Great Britain and elsewhere to counterattack potential immediate threats to political stability or to invest such funds and manpower in programs that might add greater strength to the economy and perhaps thereby reinforce long-term political stability. Blundell, more than most of his colleagues in the European community, tried to take the long view but found himself arguing for a program to meet a particular and pressing short-term problem for political stability posed by the unsettling effects of the transfer of power. The leaders of the future African government would have preferred to delay any such program of resettlement until after independence, but they acquiesced in the use of development funds to provide economic underpinning for the transfer of political power. At the earliest opportunity, they returned to the long view: investing in economic development to promote social benefits and political stability, maintaining the latter in the short run by other means.

The problem of allocating economic aid was the corollary of a similar dilemma in the political sphere. During the 1950s communal elections, racial land barriers, and Emergency prohibitions on African political activity had served as surrogates for fundamental long-term solutions to Kenya's problems of race relations, national integration, and political stability respectively. The decisions taken at Lancaster House not only precipitated a series of short-term problems connected with transferring political power to an African government but removed Emergency restrictions, which allowed avoidance of long-term problems as well.[7] On the one hand, the lifting of Emergency restrictions on movement and political activity by Africans entailed the progressive release from detention of those arrested for alleged participation in Mau Mau, the relaxation of restrictions

7. See, for example, the debate on the ending of Emergency restrictions (Kenya, Legislative Council, *Debates* [1960], LXXXI, 210 ff.). Also see the debate on the Detained and Restricted Person (Special Provisions) Bill (*ibid.*, LXXXIII [1960], 1336 ff.) and on the Preservation of Public Security Bill (*ibid.*, LXXXIV [1960], 1225 ff.).

on movement across district borders particularly in Kikuyuland, and the end of compulsory villagization. On the other hand, the end of the Emergency also meant the re-formation of African national parties for the first time since 1952. The transfer of political power thus coincided with the removal of barriers to the development of national consciousness and participation in national politics by the mass of the African peoples. The ending of communal elections forced the racial minorities to think in terms of real cooperation with the African peoples if they were to maintain any influence in national politics. There had been no chance to develop such relationships before the process of reversing the existing power relationships between Africans and the European minority began in 1960. Finally, racial land barriers were on the way out before the Lancaster House Conference began, but the initiation of the transfer of power came before this long-term step toward national integration had been fully realized.

The attempts of the Kenya government to deal with both long- and short-term economic and political problems confronted the existing African leaders with a difficult dilemma of their own: whether or not to participate in the government between the Lancaster House Conference and the elections that would implement its principles. The problem arose from the creation of four African positions in the Council of Ministers following the Lancaster House specifications. Cooperation with the outgoing government was desirable if the African leaders were to have any influence on long-term measures the government might take to rebuild political and economic order in Kenya. Too close cooperation with the regime, however, might weaken these leaders in the eyes of the newly enfranchised African rank and file, who might not appreciate the reasons for cooperation with the colonial government. If the African masses were to be mobilized in support of independence and an African government, then opposition to the existing colonial regime would have to be maintained. In the end, the African elected members, who had maintained a fair degree of unity at Lancaster House, took both sides of the issue. Musa Amalemba, who had agreed to stand for election as a Specially Elected Member and subsequently to accept a ministry, stayed as one of the four African ministers. Ronald Ngala, Masinde Muliro, and Taita Towett finally agreed to join him in the government, while Mboya and the others remained in opposition. Mboya claims this arrangement was by agreement among all the leaders, yet those who joined the government were later among the more conservative of the African leaders.[8]

The Lancaster House Conference created a crisis of confidence in the European community concerning their future in Kenya. Its impact was most sharply felt in the functioning of the agricultural economy, where European influence was particularly strong. The impact of the political decisions taken at Lancaster House upon the European contribution to the rural economy was immediate, but the full effects of political change there were not felt until several months later. Kenya's Land and Agricultural Bank put the problem in this way:

> The year 1960 was an average one for the Kenya farmer and while prices on the whole were satisfactory, the good economic prospects at the commencement of the year did not come up to expectations owing to the drought and the unsettled political atmosphere. Many farmers have adopted a short term policy on planning, and development of farms has generally been at a standstill. Confidence in the industry has reached a low ebb but it is pleasing to note that there remains quite a number of farmers determined to carry on in spite of difficulties.[9]

Unemployment was substantial but not sharply increased from the levels of the two previous years. Political change had resulted in an economic decline whose consequences were yet to be felt.

The impact of political change on European economic confidence in the future of Kenya became a political issue that competed with measures to implement African political advance for center stage in the political theater. European moderates argued with European conservatives over Kenya's future from the European perspective.

---

8. Tom Mboya, *Freedom and After* (London: André Deutsch, 1963), pp. 128–29.
9. Kenya, Land and Agricultural Bank, *Annual Report, 1960* (Nairobi: Government Printer, 1961), p. 1.

Group Captain L. R. Briggs, leader of the conservative United party, expressed the view that "the outcome of this [Lancaster House] conference [was] a death blow to the European community in Kenya." [10] The more European conservatives decried the impact of political change on their position in the country, the more likely it was that such pessimism would be reflected in further deterioration of the rural economy caused by European farmers' inactivity. Recognizing this relationship, European moderates attempted to maintain political confidence in the country and counteract the economic deterioration, a strategy consistent with their pre–Lancaster House roles as advocates of political and racial cooperation in the common enterprise of economic development. Blundell said after the conference: "There remains a challenge and a revolution in our thinking which we have got to make in our country on our return. I am certain that together we can meet the challenge and achieve that revolution in our thinking and make a success of the country." [11] R. S. Alexander (member of the New Kenya party, leading businessman, and former Nairobi mayor) urged the appointment of a commission to assess the condition of the economy. The purpose of the commission would have been to prevent false assertions about the deteriorating condition of the economy from becoming self-fulfilling. He opposed the inauguration of settlement schemes because he believed them to be overly expensive palliatives for short-term manifestations of failing confidence in the economy rather than means to long-term economic development and improved race relations:

> There must be answers concerning this vital question of the moment of land use and settlement schemes, because in much of what is said there is far too clear an indication that too many people instead of thinking of underwriting land values or having genuine resettlement schemes have far more in mind the need of an evacuation fund and it is with an evacuation fund that we in this colony must have nothing whatsoever to do. . . . We must be certain . . . that farm lands that are producing exportable surpluses are not turned into

10. *East African Standard,* April 22, 1960.
11. *Ibid.*

farming that is purely subsistence agriculture, because that surely is the quickest and most insidious way to national bankruptcy.[12]

The issue of European confidence in the economy, or the lack of it, and what measures were needed to bolster it, drew attention away from the fact that resulting unemployment brought poverty and insecurity to a great many rural Africans. Tom Mboya joined the argument on the side of the European moderates, attempting to further the division between them and the conservatives. He argued in support of Alexander:

> Those European settlers who are talking in terms of repatriation or of evacuating money are a liability to this country. The sooner they leave the better. Those Europeans who have the courage of their convictions and who really talk in terms of Kenya as their country and have no other loyalty can stay here and they have a future, and we are prepared to say so.[13]

The threat to the economy posed by the actions of European farmers and the words of their conservative spokesmen tended to forge an alliance between some prominent African leaders and European moderates. Both European moderates and African leaders like Mboya preferred at this stage to think in terms of the long-run condition of the economy rather than in terms of the relationship between European contributions to African unemployment and landlessness and the historic concerns of Kenya African nationalism. Ironically, it was the chief secretary, Walter Coutts, who observed the connection between the present signs of economic decline and the crystallization of a landless, unemployed class of Africans during the Emergency years: "My own belief is that we have got apparent unemployment with us for a very specific reason, and that is that because of our control of movement during the Emergency . . . an increase of population has been obscured." [14]

The connection between political change and possible economic

12. Kenya, *Debates* (1960), LXXXIV, 81.
13. *Ibid.,* p. 84.
14. *Ibid.,* pp. 87–88.

decline stimulated by anxious European settlers created an important problem for the African leaders with respect to land policy.
Further mobilization of the newly enfranchised Africans in support
of nationalism and the prospect of political independence would
heighten European fears and economic decline, strengthening European demands for land-resettlement schemes to save themselves at
the expense of the economy. Such schemes would then become a
responsibility of the future African government which that government might find politically difficult to honor, since the resettlements
had served European rather than African interests. Failure to mobilize African political consciousness might tempt the colonial administration to delay independence or grant it on unfavorable terms as
well as stimulate others to challenge the African elected members'
leadership. However, land resettlement favorable to Europeans
might have reassured European farmers sufficiently that African
leaders could have waited to frame their own land policy until after
independence. The African elected members were divided. At a
November, 1960, press conference Mboya and James Gichuru
refused to declare their views on land policy or the problem posed
by the European farmers. Odinga, however, was prepared to take
the traditional nationalist position. "The settlers," he declared,
"must realize that the land they are farming is not their property." [15]
But public indecisiveness and/or disagreement among African leaders fanned European fears as much as a forthright hostile attack on
their position.

THE DECOLONIZATION OF THE WHITE HIGHLANDS

The decolonizing of the White Highlands went on in 1960 on
terms favoring the continuation of multiracial policies, advocated by
European moderates and the colonial administration in the 1950s,
rather than on terms dictated by the historic objectives of African
nationalism in Kenya. An earlier bill opening the White Highlands

15. *East African Standard,* November 21, 1960.

to African farmers had been withdrawn for reconsideration because portions of it were unsatisfactory to the Kenya National Farmers Union (KNFU), representing European farmers. A revised ordinance was introduced in June, 1960, along with legislation providing for the resettlement of Africans on farms European settlers wished to vacate. This ordinance represented the product of Blundell's insistence at the Lancaster House Conference on British support for such legislation as the price of European moderates' agreement to the conference decisions. The negotiation and implementation of this legislation were complicated because the exigencies of political change appropriate to the transfer of power dictated changes in the structure of the program. World Bank and Commonwealth Development Corporation support for the program was predicated on multiracial assumptions in the original structure of the program. (These negotiations will be examined in chapter 5.)

The colonial administration's withdrawal and subsequent reconsideration of the bill opening the Highlands to African farmers reflected the fact that the multiracial principles of the bill were designed to serve European interests as much as or more than those of Africans. When the legislation was first introduced, the Kenya National Farmers Union vigorously criticized a number of its provisions as opposed to European interests. It believed that the grace period during which European farmers could decide whether to convert from leasehold to freehold was not long enough. It objected to the conversion price's being set at twenty years' rent, which it considered excessive. Indirectly, the KNFU criticized the whole purpose of the bill to put land tenure on a common basis throughout the country by noting that the bill allowed differences in tenure practices between African communities to continue. The colonial administration withdrew the bill and reintroduced it with a five- rather than a three-year grace period and a conversion price set at eighteen rather than twenty years' rent.

Despite its limited application and the administration's deference to the European community, Wilfred Havelock, as minister for local government and lands, introduced the bill as a "new policy [which is] the portal to a new Kenya where farmers of all races will be able to work as good neighbors, helping each other and increasing the prosperity of the nation. This is something that has never yet been done in Africa." [16] Months after the Lancaster House Conference determined that Kenya would shortly be an independent country under African rule, moderate Europeans still saw the future of the country in multiracial terms under which European farming could continue to prosper. Havelock underscored two principles behind the bill: that land should be an economic asset developed as such without regard to race; and that "the government will do all it can to help everyone who is determined to stay in Kenya and to face and overcome the problems of the future." [17] It was assumed that African leaders would support land legislation premised on the objectives of multiracialism.

Allowing Africans to buy land in the Highlands was by itself not sufficient to accomplish racial integration in the agricultural economy. Most Africans with the ambition and the necessary educational qualifications and experience to take over the farms lacked the capital to do so. Consequently, during the same debate Bruce McKenzie, the minister for agriculture, introduced the first resettlement program.[18] As outlined by McKenzie, it was in part a progress report on negotiations with the British government for financial assistance in implementing the program and in part an outline of the kinds of programs that he thought necessary. The purposes of the land-resettlement schemes as he saw them were (1) to maintain and develop Kenya's land, which was and remains its main source of wealth; (2) to establish confidence in Kenya's economy on the part of farmers of all races; and (3) to relieve certain social problems in the African areas. Like Havelock, McKenzie assumed that "the overwhelming majority of the farmers of the European and Asian communities will wish to remain in the country and to continue to make their irreplaceable contribution which they now give to our economy." [19] The land-resettlement schemes, like the legislation ending the exclusively

16. Kenya, *Debates* (1960), LXXXVI, 31 ff.
17. *Ibid.*
18. *Ibid.*, pp. 35 ff.
19. *Ibid.*

European enclave in the Highlands, reflected the continuation of multiracial principles despite the impending transfer of power to an African government, as did the continued presence of European farmers, their cooperation with Africans in common economic endeavor, and the absence of artificial barriers to communication between the races.

There were five different types of resettlement proposed, designed to accommodate five different kinds of interests and requirements. The first and most important was the so-called Yeoman Farmer Scheme, which purported to be for members of any race but "in practice there can be little doubt that the vast majority of the people who will benefit from these schemes to be included in the program are those African farmers with proven knowledge of modern farming principles and £200 of capital to invest." [20] However, only a small number of African farmers could meet even these minimal financial requirements. The most likely beneficiaries were tenants of European farmers in the Highlands and those who had already benefited from the Swynnerton programs a few years earlier. Another class of settlement was to be undertaken by European farmers especially for the benefit of their tenants. The resources would be provided from private and commercial sources, with the government overseeing the operations to protect the tenants' interests. Several schemes in this group were proposed to McKenzie, and many were found to be so patently rigged to enrich the retiring farmer and prolong his position as a country squire that very little came of them. One high official in the Ministry of Lands and Settlement later admitted that McKenzie thought the principal advantage of this category of resettlement was that the minds of otherwise politically troublesome European settlers were occupied in dreaming up proposals. On the other hand, some European farmers turned over their farms to their tenants on their own initiative and achieved handsome results while helping African farmers to prosper and develop a stake in the new Kenya. One such noteworthy scheme was developed by Peter Marrian, sometime president of KNFU and assistant minister for lands and

20. *Ibid.*

settlement. The third kind of resettlement involved the use of Land Bank funds to provide loan capital for land purchase and development, the intended effect of which would be to maintain the market for land, a major concern of the European farming community. A fourth program enabled Africans to buy large farms from Europeans on very nearly the same terms that the European farmers themselves had acquired land on their arrival in Kenya. This was a program for the minute minority of African farmers with the money and experience to manage a large farm and to pay off a long and heavy mortgage. Finally, 60,000 acres were set aside for 4,500 poor African families. This so-called Peasant Scheme was designed to help the losers in the scramble for land and access to the modern economy. McKenzie expressed its purpose in these words: "We must not ignore the needs of others who, possibly through no fault of their own, have not succeeded in establishing a position in life, who possibly have no land at all or at best a small strip which is barely capable of providing even subsistence for the man and his family; and who finally probably possesses neither the skill nor the education nor the inclination for urban life." [21] The point of this program was not merely humanitarian. "They present an urgent problem which is primarily a social one, but which also inevitably impinges upon security. . . . We all know . . . only too well that a large class of this type of person exists in the colony today." [22]

These proposals for land resettlement were particularly significant for two reasons. First, in terms of the purposes they were intended to serve and of the institutions through which they would be implemented, they presumed an essential continuity with the past rather than a break with the older order. They were conceived in the spirit of multiracialism, which now was aimed at retaining the confidence of European farmers as well as including Africans in the political and economic development of Kenya. The encouragement of European farmers to devise private resettlement schemes, the use of the Land Bank which had previously served primarily European

21. *Ibid.*
22. *Ibid.*

financial needs, and the use of a European Agricultural Settlement Board style of organization all presupposed institutional continuity with past ventures in agricultural development. McKenzie did state that changes in the organization of agricultural administration proposed that year by a commission under the chairmanship of the late Sir Donald MacGillivray would take place.[23] But the general tenor of the commission's recommendations was that existing agricultural organization should be unified and streamlined, eliminating parallel organizations designed to serve formerly racially exclusive farming areas. McKenzie did not propose, and the MacGillivray Commission did not recommend, a complete redesigning of the institutional structure used in previous settlement programs to take account of the financial resources, education, experience, and type of farming to be done by the new African settlers. The unspoken assumption was that African farmers would be integrated with the ongoing system of agricultural administration. Also, and perhaps surprisingly, nothing was said about turning over the administration of agriculture or of settlement to Africans in particular. An African politician might have gained the impression that resettlement was a piece of agricultural surgery, a kind of transfusion performed by Europeans and colonial civil servants upon the European economy in which African farmers would be the passive beneficiaries.

Second, in view of the knowledge that the numbers of landless and unemployed persons in the country were dangerously large, it is noteworthy that the resettlement program included only a token scheme to accommodate such persons. The impending transfer of power had thrown the European community and its leadership into great turmoil; yet no very substantial efforts were made to deal with the problem of landlessness and unemployment that could have driven the African leaders to the extreme positions and actions that the Europeans so greatly feared and expected. In retrospect, such a limited accommodation to the needs of the rural African disinherited, coming so soon after the Emergency in which they had perhaps

23. Kenya, *Report of the Committee on the Organization of Agriculture* (Nairobi: Government Printer, 1960).

suffered the most and during which many had retained an indispensable loyalty to the alien government, proved to be the major shortcoming of this first settlement program. The main reason for the deficiency appears to have been the government's determination that the program contribute to the maintenance and further development of the economy rather than accommodate subsistence-level farming. The landless and the unemployed were generally presumed to lack the knowledge and certainly the resources needed to undertake modern farming, and the government did not want to delay inception of the program until they could be suitably equipped. In short, the program for the unemployed and landless was intended as a token of government sympathy that might yield some favorable side effects in maintaining civil security; but land policy as a whole was to be oriented toward economic growth, the interests and capabilities of those who already possessed land, and long-term increases in political stability and national integration.

The African elected members responded variously to these land reforms reflecting the problems which the reforms presented in preparing for the transfer of political power. From the economic perspective, the reform measures made good sense. A future African government could not object to inheriting a strong economy. This view was taken by Ngala, Masinde Muliro, Gikonyo Kiano, and Jeremiah Nyagah. All were to become ministers in future African governments. They noted, however, that a future African government might wish to undertake different and more extensive land reforms. Odinga took the position that land reforms would have to be undertaken in the future by an African government reflecting the wishes of the African people. The corollary was that the present colonial administration enjoyed no competence to engage in any pre-independence land reforms. He argued that the only purpose and objective of these present measures was to entrench European interests, however moderate the ideological superstructure:

> They [the Africans] do not consider that the Kenya Government is competent [as presently constituted] to make a policy which is going to affect land because they regard the land as their sole prop-

erty and as their property they must have full say on it. Any government which shall have a say on the land will have to be the government which they choose themselves and the government which is responsible to them.[24]

According to Odinga, the real purpose of the reforms was to allow panic-stricken European farmers to leave Kenya with their capital. "They cannot expect that when they go . . . from this country that they will receive compensation for the land and that the land should be considered their property." [25] He thus took the fundamental position of Kenya African nationalism: land in Kenya belonged to Africans. No Europeans and no alien administration had any right to take important decisions regarding its disposition. Odinga's position on land questions was to cost him a ministry in the coalition government formed after Kenyatta's release. As vice president in Kenyatta's government after independence, he was to become estranged from that government over its alleged failure to reflect the concerns of pre-independence African nationalism, especially land policy. Strikingly, Daniel arap Moi, who led the opposition Kenya African Democratic Union, made much the same point. He argued that these land reforms were only partial and that their intent was to preclude a future African government from conducting land reforms in its own way. "Some people seem to be misled to think that the Kenya Highlands are being opened. . . . In actual fact, Sir, it is being opened and then tightened up properly, which would mean that it would be impossible to undo these things unless one goes to a court of law to challenge the titles." [26] Moi did not contemplate wholesale seizure of European land in defiance of existing legal standards. He was struck by the intent of the proposed reforms to tie the hands of a law-abiding future African government. Moi was to succeed to the vice presidency shortly after Odinga departed to form the opposition Kenya People's Union (KPU).

Tom Mboya, who was to become the principal organizer of

24. Kenya, *Debates,* LXXXVI (1960), 63 ff.
25. *Ibid.,* pp. 60 ff.
26. *Ibid.,* p. 166.

KANU and (after independence) minister for economic development, revealed the full complexity of the African dilemma in re-
sponding to these reforms. He recognized and rejected a major
assumption in the program: that the economy of the country needed
to be preserved by protecting the position of European farmers in
the White Highlands. He questioned the assumption "that Kenya's
economy would break down and run into chaos the moment you
interfere with the Europeans or displace them." [27] But this observa-
tion carried the implication that the condition of Kenya's economy
was significant to him. Defense and promotion of the rural economy
without deference to European farmers was later to provide a justification for an African government to channel rural development
funds into former African reserves at the expense of moves to develop an African economy in the Highlands via land redistribution.
Measures to Africanize the White Highlands were distasteful because to Africanize them was to appear to serve European interests,
given the prominence of European demands for such programs and
the evident purposes behind them. On the other hand, Mboya recognized that such reforms constituted an assault on African nationalism and the people on whose behalf it was to be advanced. Rhetori-
cally, he inquired:

> Would it be fair for our people to interpret this move as an attempt
> to accelerate these measures and bring in legislation before the con-
> stitutional changes take place? . . . I believe that as an outgoing
> government it should have taken into account the need to restrict
> its activities to such short term measures as are consistent with its
> present life. . . . [I] am not trying to suggest that the next Govern-
> ment of Kenya will be out to destroy everything that has been done
> in the past, but I am prepared to state that the next government may
> find some things done today to be totally inconsistent with its own
> thinking on the question of the development of the country.[28]

At the same time, he deplored the tokenism of the whole program,
since a 120,000-acre program could not begin to cope with the needs

27. *Ibid.,* p. 78.
28. *Ibid.,* p. 80.

of Kenya's African landless and unemployed. He opposed the reforms not because of what they accomplished but because the wrong government was undertaking them in order to serve the wrong interests. Both before and since independence African leaders have had to choose between measures that were intended to serve both departing Europeans and landless Africans and measures, based on Swynnerton plan reforms of the former African reserves, that served remaining Europeans and landed Africans. The combination of moderates who developed multiracial policies before 1960 and conservatives who forced extensive resettlement programs after 1960 insured that the land policy of African national leaders would serve the interests of Europeans as well as Africans, no matter whether they chose the path of land-use reform and development or land redistribution and development. Before independence the dilemma of the leaders of African nationalism was enhanced by the problem of deciding whether to encourage the outgoing government to undertake reforms or not and whether to associate the African people with them or not. The views of the principal African nationalist, Jomo Kenyatta, could not be employed to resolve these dilemmas because he was still detained incommunicado for his alleged role in leading Mau Mau.

The African leaders in effect acquiesced to multiracial influence in land policy as well as in the government, to insure that the end of the transfer of power, political independence, would not be delayed. Africans gained a majority of seats in the Legislative Council and in the government, but only under conditions that made cooperation with members of the other races essential. Refusal to accept this *quid pro quo* would have jeopardized prompt independence under an African government. The Africans accepted these 1960 land reforms because not to do so might have provoked a serious decline in the economy and consequent unemployment owing largely to the policies of worried European farmers. Such economic difficulties might also have delayed independence. At least one leading Conservative party spokesman on African affairs believed that land reforms should be completed before independence. The World Bank and the Commonwealth Development Corporation, who financed the first settlement program, agreed that African refusal to contemplate immediate land reforms might have undone the compromise under which land resettlement and the transfer of political power proceeded simultaneously.

THE 1961 ELECTION: THE INFLUENCE OF KENYATTA

Between 1960 and 1961 national African political parties were permitted to form and to operate within a political environment in which the colonial administration and moderate Europeans retained the initiative. The 1961 elections allowed the full expression of African nationalism and the politicization of the African peoples. The elections were significant not only because they permitted African parties to assert their views free of dilemmas posed by moderate European-colonial administration legislative initiatives but because expression of KANU's views provoked a variety of responses from Africans as well as Europeans.

The elections were structured so that the African party which gained a plurality of seats would be required to work with other African parties or parties representing other races if it wished to form the government. Twelve of the sixty-five seats were to be chosen by the winners of the other fifty-three, and twenty of those fifty-three were reserved for representatives of the minority races. In addition, an important feature of the election was the percentage of votes required for those twenty seats in primary communal elections in order to go forward to the final elections where all races would participate. The Lancaster House Conference report said that candidates in those constituencies must have "support within their own communities." The Working party, composed of the chief secretary and the minister for legal affairs—both civil servants and European —assumed that such candidates must have "*substantial* support within their own communities." [29] The higher the percentage of the total vote required the more likely it would be that the other races

29. Kenya, *Report of the Working Party Appointed to Consider Elections under the Lancaster House Agreement* (Nairobi: Government Printer, 1960).

would have only one candidate in the regular election. The lower the percentage, the greater the likelihood of a choice of candidates. In the European constituencies, the issue was whether to encourage choice between moderates and conservatives by the voters of the other races or accept the preferences of the European community itself. The more choice permitted the other races in these reserved-seat constituencies, the more the Europeans could be compelled to accept a measure of multiracialism by sharing with other races the choice of their representative.

The government decided on a figure of 25 percent and stood firm against the arguments of the Europeans, including Blundell, for 30 or 33⅓ percent and the African appeals for a figure closer to 10 percent. The more conservative Europeans recognized that, given a 25 percent requirement, they might not be able to prevail against the moderates in the reserved-seat constituencies and that Europeans would be compelled to share the choice of their representatives with voters of the other races. Their departure from the sphere of formal politics was symbolized by the resignation of the Legislative Council speaker, Sir Ferdinand Cavendish-Bentinck, who had held that position since leaving the Ministry of Agriculture in 1955. He objected to the alleged failure of the new electoral system to accommodate the interests of Kenya's racial minorities, and he felt, in consequence, that he could no longer preserve his impartiality as speaker. Very soon thereafter, he became the leader of a new conservative European party, the Kenya Coalition (KC).[30] Lacking any real influence in formal politics, the KC attempted to speak independently for the economic and social interests of European farmers and to exert leverage on the formal political sphere from outside by raising the specter of further deterioration of the economy caused by anxiety-stricken European farmers. The Federal Independence and United parties had been genuine political parties seeking influence in the theater of formal political decision-making; the Kenya Coalition more closely resembled a pressure group acting on behalf of a powerful economic group.

30. He was particularly distressed at the adoption of the 25 percent primary requirement.

Two features in the conduct of the election were particularly significant for the future development of African politics in Kenya. The absence of strong national direction in the campaign by either KANU or KADU meant that the views expressed in their respective manifestoes were perhaps more indicative of the attitudes of a small circle of national leaders than of the rank and file of either party. Inability of the national leaders to give direction to the selection of candidates in individual constituencies meant, conversely, that constraints upon the leaders of the two major parties in negotiating with each other, with the representatives of the European and Asian parties, and with the colonial administration, were less severe. This relative freedom of negotiation would work to the advantage of the colonial administration, suggesting terms for the formation of coalition governments after the election.

Second, the absence of major policy differences between the two parties and the rather clean division of support between them along provincial boundary lines suggest reasons for both the appeal and the impermanence of *majimbo* (or regionalism). The approach of independence made the smaller ethnic groups fear that they would be dominated by the larger ones, and they sought protection in the form of regional autonomy, or *majimbo.* Not the least of the causes of their fear was the possibility that land-hungry Kikuyu in Central Province might spill over into the territorial spheres of influence of smaller African societies. On the other hand, the absence of major policy differences between the two parties, apart from the question of *majimbo,* suggested that if and when KANU stilled these anxieties the barriers to a merger of the two parties would not be too great. The land-resettlement schemes played an important role. The imminent departure of the European settlers would remove buffers between many African peoples, contributing to their fears of each other. The creation of extensive resettlement schemes, in which land-hungry and unemployed members of larger African societies were absorbed, removed one threat to the territorial integrity of the smaller African societies.

KANU made the release of Jomo Kenyatta the overriding issue in the 1961 election and was ambiguous on other policy questions because of uncertainty about his views as well as internal divisions among its principal leaders.[31] Both parties agreed that Kenyatta and the other detained nationalists should be released, but KANU was the more insistent of the two parties, threatening not to join the government after the election unless and until he was released. KADU leaders expressed concern about the possible emergence of a "Kenyatta cult" among KANU supporters, even though they said they also wanted him released. On the need for increased and expanded educational facilities, greater employment, higher standards of living, and vigorous agricultural and industrial development, the two parties were in close agreement.

The main difference in the published platforms and public utterances of the African parties' leaders was one of emphasis. KADU gave considerable attention to the importance of guaranteeing individual human rights, while KANU emphasized the preeminent importance of rapid economic, social, and political change. This difference of emphasis was reflected in their respective approaches to the subject of land reform in Kenya. Both parties considered that land reform should be an essential element in Kenya's future nation-building program. However, KADU stressed the importance of adequate compensation for expropriated land, while KANU addressed itself more specifically to the problem posed by land allocated to Europeans and emphasized that the British government should assume responsibility for the predicament in which the European settlers fancied they found themselves. KANU tended to look at the possible economic costs of land transfer to a future African government and not at the benefits of such a program that would accrue to European settlers. Neither party gave so much attention to the role of a land-reform program in relieving unemployment and landlessness among Kenya's newly enfranchised African citizens.

KANU's land policy comprised four main tenets, on each of which there was significant ambiguity. KANU accused the government and a section of the European community of using land policy

31. George Bennett and Carl Rosberg, *The Kenyatta Election: Kenya 1960–1961* (London: Oxford University Press, 1961).

as a means of harassing the Africans' progress toward independence. "Even today a section of people in Kenya would go to any extent to use the land question, in the form of assurances of title, etc., as a stick with which to beat the African leader on his path to freedom." [32] KANU insisted that land reform should be the responsibility of the independent African government and not that of the colonial administration, which was using land reform against the African national leadership. The party argued, on the one hand, that reforms were necessary because of past injustices wrought by the Carter Commission and the land hunger and general suffering, within the African reserves, to which the commission's decisions had contributed. On the other hand, KANU did not specify very clearly the nature of the land reforms it intended to undertake; and while deploring the condition of landlessness caused by colonial policy, KANU stopped short of declaring that land should be bought or taken from the Europeans to be given to landless and unemployed Africans. KANU was concerned about the health of the economy as a whole as well as about the welfare of those who had not gained a livelihood from the economy or shared in its development. "Resettlement will, then, be KANU's foremost problem: resettlement not at the cost of the high standard of agriculture already attained, but definitely at the expense of absentee landlordism, of individuals owning large square miles while neighboring African people jostle in small areas." [33]

A second problem for KANU's policy planners came in assigning priorities between the claims of squatters already resident in the Highlands on European farms and those of landless and unemployed persons in the African reserves. KANU promised to sort out the problems of the squatters but did not indicate whether they or landless persons in the African reserves would get first consideration in the resettling of land vacated by departing European farmers. [34]

KANU supported the policy of land consolidation and registra-

32. *The KANU Manifesto for Independence, Social Democracy and Stability* (Nairobi, [1960]), p. 17.
33. *Ibid.*, p. 15.
34. *Ibid.*, pp. 15–16.

tion but did not want to force such processes on unwilling peoples. "Consolidation of land can play an important role in raising the production of farms. KANU believes, however, that its government cannot be dogmatic as to which type of consolidation is suitable for the whole of the country." [35] For a strongly nationalist party opposed to *majimbo* in the later development of its policy, such solicitude for the integrity of ethnic groups was noteworthy. The unhappy experience of the Luo with initial attempts at consolidation and registration in the middle 1950s and/or some embarrassment on the part of the KANU leadership in coming to terms with an apparently successful colonial government development program contributed to KANU's attitude toward consolidation and registration.[36] The colonial government's reform had occurred without the cooperation or concurrence of many KANU leaders who were in detention at the time, yet opposition to past or future programs of a similar nature would have flown in the face of the historic concern of nationalists in Kenya for security of tenure for African peoples and would in any event have created more chaos than it would have relieved. In the related question of the security of property rights under future African governments, KANU's attitude was also ambiguous. "In other words KANU at present cannot commit any future government to the principles of compensation, although the principle of fair and just compensation in the course of such reforms [as the future government might undertake] is accepted." [37] KANU faced a clear dilemma: to have guaranteed land rights and compensation in the event of expropriation would have been to appease the European settlers and would possibly have provoked unrest among some rank-and-file Africans and their spokesmen; but not to have promised

35. *Ibid.,* p. 16.
36. The Luo people constituted one of the biggest groups of supporters for KANU. The party's first vice president, Oginga Odinga, was a Luo. He had indicated considerable opposition to consolidation, despite having enclosed and consolidated his own extensive land holdings. In the middle 1950s efforts were made to consolidate Luo land along lines similar to those successfully initiated in Kikuyuland. The response was unfavorable owing to a mixture of inadequate preparation, difference in land rights and their evolution between the Kikuyu and the Luo, and differences in the attitudes of the peoples involved.
37. *KANU Manifesto,* p. 17.

security of property rights might have antagonized those Africans who had gained individual land titles during land consolidation and registration in the 1950s. Such Africans' ability to contribute to the treasury of KANU could not have been forgotten.

Finally, KANU was embarrassed by its dependence upon the British government to underwrite the assets of European farmers who felt threatened by the advent of an independent government headed by Africans. KANU insisted that any land-stabilization program to secure the value of European farms must be entirely the responsibility of the British government, which had in the first place encouraged the settlers to come to Kenya without consulting the African peoples. Unless Africans were to be given the land free, there was a danger that land transfer, which was the particular interest of the departing European farmers, might leave independent Kenya with a class of debt-ridden peasant farmers. Not to have had such a program, however, would have left the new African government with a politically anomalous European farming enclave on which the country might still be economically heavily dependent. On the other hand, without a program of land transfer or stabilization of land values, many thousands of landless and unemployed Africans would have constituted a nearly irresistible demand upon the new African government to institute and finance its own land-transfer program, summarily seize European farms, or risk political instability during lengthy court proceedings to acquire control of European land. However distasteful it was, KANU as well as the Kenya Coalition needed the British government to provide funds that could enable European farmers to sell their assets and leave the country.

In the European constituencies, the New Kenya party argued for a politically stable, economically progressive Kenya, which could occur only through political and social cooperation between Europeans and Africans. This was a warning to both the conservative Europeans and the Africans concerning the inevitability of African political advance, and the importance of the European contribution to the economy, respectively. The NKP retained the option to cooperate with one or more of the African parties or the more conservative Kenya Coalition. Consistent with this stand, the party took an equivocal position on the release of Kenyatta—although the moderates feared Kenyatta as much as the conservatives, not to mention the followers of KADU. The Kenya Coalition, on the other hand, burned its bridges and remained unalterably opposed to Kenyatta's release. It demanded that attention be given to questions of economic development more than to matters having to do with political change and the transfer of power—reflecting its unreconciled position vis-à-vis the formation of an African government.[38]

THE AFTERMATH OF THE 1961 ELECTION: NATIONALISM AND THE RESPONSES

The results of the spring elections of 1961, and the subsequent refusal of the governor, Sir Patrick Renison, to release Kenyatta, produced a deadlock in post-election negotiations to form a new government. KANU won two-thirds of the votes cast in the common roll elections but gained only a plurality of seats in the new Legislative Council. KADU and the minority parties representing Europeans and Asians won the rest, except for a sprinkling of independents. The procedures for elections in the reserved-seat constituencies favored the NKP over the Kenya Coalition. In the primaries, where only Europeans were voting, all nine KC candidates survived, with 60 percent of the votes. Only four of the nine NKP candidates survived, and the party as a whole gained only 22 percent of the votes cast. In the common roll election in these constituencies, KANU decided that it preferred the ambivalent moderates of the NKP to the uncompromising conservative KC candidates. Four of the five remaining NKP candidates were thereby enabled to survive by impressive majorities, while only three KC candidates were victorious. Blundell, who had barely gained the necessary 25 percent in the primary against Cavendish-Bentinck in the Rift Valley constituency, won handsomely in the common roll election.

KANU's decision to back the moderates was one of the earliest

---

38. See the Kenya Coalition manifesto, *East African Standard,* December 2, 1960.

instances where Odinga was in a minority within his party. Odinga preferred to back Cavendish-Bentinck and the Kenya Coalition candidates, because their position was less ambiguous and they had not supported the multiracial policies of the past decade. J. M. Kariuki, in writing of his experience as a Mau Mau detainee, indicated that he and many of his compatriots felt a similar distrust of Blundell, the NKP, and their intentions.

Renison had announced shortly after taking office a year earlier that he would not release Kenyatta because here was "a leader unto darkness and unto death." [39] African leaders of both parties had expected that the generally peaceful conduct of the election, the great majority of popular votes polled by KANU (which had announced that it would not join the government until Kenyatta's release), and the preference of both parties that he be released would bring a concession from the governor. Apparently unmoved, Renison announced only that Kenyatta would be moved from distant isolation in Lodwar to the somewhat more accessible Maralal. After the formation of a government, not before, political leaders and others would be permitted to reestablish contact with him. But no release would be considered before the government had not only been formed but was functioning effectively. KANU fulfilled its promise not to join the government under such conditions, a decision which was to affect significantly the course of the transfer of power and the early years of independence.

The political impasse between KANU and the governor was made possible by two factors: the relatively weak legislative position of KANU despite its demonstrated vote-getting capacity; and the governor's determination that steps to protect the minorities who were well represented in the Legislative Council must precede further political advance. KANU was virtually prevented from gaining a majority of the Legislative Council seats because of the provisions for reserved seats and national members. Furthermore, both in the top leadership of KANU and at the grass roots, there was visible evidence of less than complete unity. Finally, KANU's leadership

39. *East African Standard,* May 11, 1960.

was inhibited from taking any action to form a government because those who led the party into the government might have been accused of attempting to bid for power at Kenyatta's expense. Such inhibitions affected KADU as well as KANU, for KADU ministers Ngala and Taita Towett were both moved to resign from the existing government in disapproval of the governor's position. Rosberg and Bennett conclude that "while leaders and factions could still maneuver for positions from which to assert power, had any attempted to fully assume it, they would have been accused of arrogating to themselves the mantle reserved for Kenyatta." [40] By preventing Kenyatta's release, the colonial governor denied the vast majority of African people a government led by the chief symbol and proponent of their nationalism. Without Kenyatta, both parties, but particularly KANU, felt inhibited in forming a government in which the views of the majority of the African people would be represented in effecting the transfer of political power.

After Kenyatta's transfer to Maralal, he and the governor engaged in what amounted to a public debate over the future course of the transfer of power. During this debate, the governor made it clear that protection of the rights of individuals and of the minorities was the precondition for further progress toward independence. Kenyatta held his first press conference in April, following the election. He attempted to allay the fears of the minorities while indicating that political independence under an African government should precede measures, such as land reforms, which the minorities believed to be in their interests. He said he opposed violence, that he was never a Communist, and that he would leave his political future up to the African people. He believed that the Lancaster House Constitution had served its purpose and that discussions should be held with a view to taking further steps toward Kenya independence. He urged political unity among African leaders and said nothing to undermine the refusal of KANU to form a government. Efficient European farmers would be welcome to continue their operations under an African government. Land reforms could wait, he said,

40. Bennett and Rosberg, *Kenyatta Election*, pp. 79–84.

until after independence, since those Europeans who made themselves useful need have no fear for their security. His pronouncements on land policy should have been encouraging to European moderates, for they reinforced the arguments Blundell had made since the mid-1950s: that the key to European security lay not in controlling the political processes but in rendering indispensable contributions to the development of Kenya's economy.

Renison did not agree that the Lancaster House Constitution had outlived its usefulness; he felt it was necessary in order to engineer an orderly progress toward independence that would take into consideration individual liberties, the stability of the economy, and the interests of racial and ethnic minorities. He said: "The abandonment of such a planned approach [toward independence as contemplated in the Lancaster House Conference of 1960] could lead to a landslide in which the rights of individuals, minority tribes and communities, together with the administrative and economic structure of Kenya would be in danger of being overwhelmed." [41] The real issue between Kenyatta and the governor was not any explicit disagreement over policy, but whether an African government under Kenyatta and representing the majority of the African voters could be trusted to protect the economic and political needs of racial and ethnic minorities as it promised. The governor did not appear to believe it could, and thereby committed himself to the formation of a minority government. KANU and Kenyatta would later join this government on the minority regime's terms rather than their own.

The new government was a coalition of parties representing a minority of the voters in the 1961 election, augmented by nominees appointed by the governor. Ngala had visited Macleod in London following the All African Peoples Conference in Cairo. Apparently on the colonial secretary's suggestion, Ngala and KADU were persuaded by the governor to enter into the formation of a government. The NKP had indicated during the election that it would participate in the post-election government if asked, because it believed European political cooperation with Africans to be desirable and essential

41. *East African Standard,* April 15, 1961.

from the standpoint of race relations and the economy. Deserting KANU, which had supported European moderates in the election, the NKP agreed to join KADU in the government along with a majority of the newly elected national members, representatives of the Kenya Indian Congress, and European and African independents. The minority coalition was still short of the members necessary to control the Legislative Council. Consequently, Renison nominated eleven new members of the council whose support for the coalition enabled it to govern.

The new government did move first to meet the principal demand of the majority African party. In connection with KADU's agreement to form the government, the governor announced that his administration would build a house for Kenyatta in his home district in preparation for his eventual release. Subsequently, several men who had been tried and detained at the time of Kenyatta's arrest were returned to their homes, and, finally, in August Kenyatta himself was released. Shortly thereafter, K. K. Njiiri of KANU resigned his Fort Hall seat for Kenyatta, who was duly elected to the Legislative Council virtually without opposition. During this process of reinstating Kenyatta in public life, KADU and KANU had made attempts to reconcile their differences and present a united front to Britain and the colonial government. In July a joint party statement was issued in which KANU and KADU agreed that land titles should be respected and that rapid strides should be taken toward independence. Another joint conference in August was less harmonious and contributed to KADU's interest in *majimbo,* according to Michael Blundell.[42] Nevertheless, the dialogue between KADU and KANU was maintained well enough for KANU to join the government in November, when new constitutional talks were in prospect.

The minority coalition government simultaneously turned its attention to the requirements of its constituent minority communities. These requirements included financial assistance for Kenya's economy, in which the Europeans had a particular interest, and the

42. *Ibid.,* August 25, 1961.

development of constitutional proposals to protect African as well as European and Asian minorities against the excesses that some of them feared would result from an African government representing the largest African communities.

The revival of the economy commanded first priority. The majority of the European community, especially the farmers, had little real voice in the new coalition government, since the Kenya Coalition was on the opposition benches. Unable to express themselves through normal political channels, the European farmers made their point by bringing their sector of the agricultural economy to a virtual standstill. Given the farmers' uncertainty about their future under an independent government, it was natural for them to omit any longer-term planning investment for their farms and to concentrate largely upon short-term requirements. The consequences were described in the 1961 Land Bank annual report.

> The year under review has been one of the most difficult within record. Drought and Army Worm infestation in the early months of the year during the planting period followed at the end of the year by floods creating extensive damage have proved disastrous for many farmers especially those mainly dependent upon cereals. Owing to the unsettled political atmosphere the short term planning policy mentioned in the previous report continues as farmers are unable to gauge the future security of tenure. Numerous farms are now being placed on a care and maintenance basis, capital and development expenditure being almost at a standstill. There is little activity in land sales except under government settlement schemes.[43]

The economic instability associated with political uncertainty was, as in 1960, compounded by difficult growing conditions. The report indicated clearly, furthermore, that land-resettlement schemes were the chief means available for maintaining land values, which in turn was one key to the willingness of European farmers to continue to invest in their property. Land resettlement schemes could not remove European uncertainty about future prospects for European

43. Kenya, Land and Agricultural Bank, *Annual Report, 1961* (Nairobi: Government Printer, 1962), p. 1.

farming in Kenya, but they were essential in the process of coun-
teracting the near-cessation of land sales and the collapse of land
values which were the reflection of the European farmers' crisis of
confidence.

Leaders of all parties had shown concern for the maintenance
and further development of the economy. Consequently, the cessation of investment and development in the European agricultural
sector constituted as much of a demand upon the government as
would have occurred had the Kenya Coalition been in KANU's
position as the plurality party in the Legislative Council. As a result,
Blundell, who resumed the Ministry of Agriculture portfolio in the
new government, entered into negotiations in Britain for further
funds for land resettlement beyond those provided in the recently
concluded agreement with the World Bank and the Commonwealth
Development Corporation. In November the British government
agreed to provide funds for an additional 12,000 African families to
be resettled on formerly European farms.[44] These were to be families
with fewer educational and financial qualifications for modern farming than those on the schemes financed by loan funds from the World
Bank and the Commonwealth Development Corporation. The new
settlers would be placed on smaller plots capable of providing a
smaller net income. Finally, the departing European farmers were
to be paid for their farms with a 50 percent down payment and the
remainder in three equal installments. Previously, they had been paid
one-third at the outset and the remainder in seven installments. A
great many of the European farmers were heavily in debt because
of investments in developing their farms, and they required payment
quickly to liquidate their debts and have the capital necessary to
make a new start elsewhere. Given the widespread belief within the
European community that the British government had broken long-
standing promises, especially to the farmers, by agreeing to start
Kenya on the road to independence, some wondered if an African
government would insist on the new farmers' repaying their loans

44. *East African Standard,* September 8, 1961. Negotiations to accelerate the payment to
the European farmers of the full amount from the sale of their farms were completed in
November.

and if the British government would continue to honor its financial promises if the loan repayments were not forthcoming.[45]

While the release of Kenyatta was being effected and new land-resettlement schemes were being undertaken to counteract the economic consequences of the European farmers' crisis of confidence in the future of Kenya, the major European and African political parties and their leaders began to consider their approaches to future negotitations in London on further steps toward independence. The provisions of a new constitution under which Kenya would achieve independence, and the consequences of the transfer of political power for the economy, particularly the European farming sector, were the two principal issues. The issues upon which the KADU-NKP coalition seized and those which the Kenya Coalition, the Convention of Associations, and the Kenya National Farmers Union pressed on the British government betrayed the fact that all were speaking for minority interests in general or for particular minorities. The KADU platform, which appeared in October, 1961, emphasized the following points: the need to enshrine basic human rights in a written constitution; the importance in particular of respecting other than property rights and titles; the necessity of providing constitutional guarantees of fair compensation in cases where property might be taken over by the government; "cooperation" among the peoples of all areas; an independent judiciary; and, above all, loyalty to the state through loyalty to the region in which one lived.[46] KADU leaders argued that a regional or federal structure for a future constitution was the essential foundation for personal freedom. In a later position paper that appeared shortly before the 1962 Lancaster House Conference, KADU made it clear that respect for property rights and provision for fair compensation in the event of expropriation should apply not only to individual but to tribal rights as well.[47]

45. The Convention of Associations, once a powerful settler caucus in the days of the first Lord Delamere and now reestablished, published a brochure quoting statements from Lord Elgin in 1908, Lord Milner in 1921, and Winston Churchill in 1922 to statements as late as April, 1959, by Mr. Lennox-Boyd indicating the importance of the European community to Kenya and the British commitment to that community. Iain Macleod was said to have indicated, in the British Parliament, that these undertakings still stood.

46. *East African Standard,* October 20, 1961.

47. *Ibid.,* February 2, 1962.

KADU's emphasis on regionalism, or *majimbo,* with which the party was to be primarily identified, did not appear in KADU's campaign platforms or in the major public utterances of its leaders during the 1961 campaign. The idea was, therefore, born sometime between the election and KADU's October statement of views. There are conflicting explanations of the origin of *majimbo.* Tom Mboya blames the idea on the European members of the 1961 minority coalition government.[48] Michael Blundell says that the concept arose in response to KANU's mood in the joint party talks in August. He describes KANU as having been in a "dictatorial and difficult mood; they seemed obsessed with the fact that they were the majority party and arbitrary demands were the order of the day."[49] Another explanation, offered by one KADU Legislative Council member, was that his party's stance reflected the rise of ethnic feelings and that *majimbo* was necessary in order to reassure the smaller African communities. This tallies with observations made in other African countries during the last months preceding independence.[50] As noted earlier, KADU was initially composed of political alliances based upon the Rift Valley and the Coast Provinces; the 1961 elections suggested that KADU's main strength lay in these two areas and that in the future it might be able to control local politics there. These explanations are mutually compatible. Collectively they suggest that tribal feelings as well as unrest in the European "tribe" indicated to both the European and the African leaders in the coalition the wisdom of provisions for some autonomy for regions or provinces in the new constitution; that these feelings were exacerbated by fear of Kenyatta and of the largest African communities represented by KANU; and that the distribution of political influence among KANU and the coalition partners in the 1961 election indicated the plausibility of *majimbo* as a defense against KANU and Kenyatta after independence.

48. Mboya, *Freedom and After,* p. 86.
49. Blundell, *So Rough a Wind,* pp. 298–99.
50. For example, David Apter, *The Political Kingdom in Uganda* (Princeton: Princeton University Press, 1962).

The Kenya Coalition and the Convention of Associations employed the power of the European farmers, which they rather than the NKP represented, as a weapon in their battle to secure, in the forthcoming constitutional discussions, recognition of individual land titles and fair compensation in the event of expropriation. The KC argued for security against indirect as well as direct expropriation, claiming that possible failure of the new government to provide minimal social services would expropriate the European farmers by taking away much of the sale value of their property.[51] The coalition tried with some success to persuade the African parties, the colonial administration, and the British government that, if its demands were not met, its constituents would leave Kenya immediately and wreck the economy in the process.

> It is too often taken for granted that he [the settler] is prepared to stay here whatever the circumstances. This is certainly not true; many are already leaving and large scale migration schemes are being considered. The settled European population is small and there are underpopulated countries which are only too ready to welcome migrants.[52]

The KC argued that, to prevent the departure of European farmers and the scrapping of at least the agricultural economy, a land-stabilization fund was needed that would permit farmers who wished to

51. Correspondence between Iain Macleod and Cavendish-Bentinck. See also, a Memo on Land Titles and Allied Subjects based on Conference of Convention of Associations, July 31, 1961. Cavendish-Bentinck to Macleod, August 21, 1961: Will Her Majesty's Government "stand financially behind the victims of any such act of expropriation or such other circumstances as may destroy the whole basis of European settlement?" Macleod and the under secretary of state, Hugh Fraser, both indicated support of European obligations to the annoyance of African leaders (*East African Standard,* May 25, 1961). Macleod replied to Cavendish-Bentinck on July 24, 1961, as follows: "Let me say at once that H.M.G. entirely accept it that it is their duty to seek to receive an acceptance of its obligations by the successor government. . . . The continued protection of fundamental rights in property will inevitably be an essential part of any further discussions on further constitutional advance in Kenya. . . . I believe that the importance of this point is now fully recognized by responsible African leaders in Kenya." The African leaders were in general agreement that Macleod was deceiving the settlers by pretending to give assurances that could come only from African leaders and, in particular, from Kenyatta.

52. Correspondence between Macleod and Cavendish-Bentinck.

leave Kenya to realize the full value of their farm properties and that would at the same time protect the sale value of farms for those who wanted to stay and see how things worked out under an African government. In its words: "The underlying motive is to make land saleable." [53] The coalition did not initially approve the land-resettlement program, not only because of its allegedly inadequate scope but also because its purposes were different from the land-stabilization proposal. The latter would permit European farmers to sell when and if they wished, while the resettlement schemes enabled the farmers to sell and leave only if their farms were found suitable for smallholder settlement schemes for African farmers and did not permit them to hedge their bets against future political developments. The European community was concerned about its collective future under an African government and also about the willingness of its members to act as a unit. One European fear about the decision to permit European farmers to acquire freehold title was that, in getting away from the prospect of remaining leaseholders under an African government, some European farmers would be willing to sell to Africans and end the racial exclusiveness of the Highlands. The land-resettlement schemes opened another division in the European community between those who wanted to sell and leave the country and those who would prefer to stay past independence, if possible; and resettlement forced those who were uncertain to make a choice before independence rather than permitting them to "wait and see."

In correspondence with the Colonial Office, the Convention of Associations also reflected the KANU idea of waiting until after independence to carry out needed land reforms. The convention threatened that their members would leave immediately if steps were not taken by a given date to relieve the European farmers' distress. "Unless some immediate steps are taken, a great number of farmers will [set] 31 December, 1962, as the last possible date they can stay in the country and will take action to salvage whatever they can." [54]

53. *Ibid.*
54. Letter of C. O. Oates (chairman of Convention of Associations) to Hugh Fraser (under secretary of state for the colonies), May 5, 1961.

They alleged that the British government had broken promises to the European community by ignoring the provisions even of the Lancaster House 1960 Constitution, which itself constituted a breach of previous assurance, as demonstrated by the so-called failure of the British government to take care of the economy and move deliberately rather than precipitately toward independence.

KANU's main problem, at least from the standpoint of the party's moderates, in defining its position prior to the coming constitutional discussions, was to maintain the integrity of its nationalist position and to find means of keeping its ranks united and its followers involved. At the same time, KANU leaders needed to go part way to accommodate the European settlers to prevent them from bequeathing the independent African government a seriously weakened economy. KANU also could not ignore the African landless and unemployed. The KANU leadership needed to differentiate KANU from the other parties while at the same time avoiding the appearance of being merely an opposition party. Failure to achieve the first objective might have meant that sections of KANU would cross the floor to join the coalition government, which KADU had thought might result from its agreement to join the government; failure to achieve the latter objectives might have created European and African unrest leading to delay in achieving independence— which KANU was not prepared to countenance. Opposition to *majimbo* gave KANU a cause, while its agreement to join the government in November following Kenyatta's release enabled it to avoid the criticism that it was oppositional. Kenyatta's views on land policy, described later, helped unify the party on a potentially divisive issue and to meet some European demands without selling out the interests of KANU's rank and file.

Through Mboya, KANU responded immediately and vigorously against the policy of *majimbo* announced by KADU. He observed that *majimbo* might leave Kenya open to the kind of disunity and weakness vis-à-vis other nations experienced by the Congo. He further argued that people should be educated to think in terms of the nation rather than exclusively in terms of their "tribe":

I submit that the best way to meet the tribal fear is by helping and working towards unity and national identification and by exposing those who preach tribalism to the ridicule that they deserve by talking honestly and openly and frankly against tribalists of all tribes and helping our youth to grow up with a national outlook as against a narrow tribal *cum* regional outlook.[55]

KANU spokesmen also argued that *majimbo* would involve a costly and uneconomic use of scarce manpower resources in duplication of governmental services at two levels of authority.

The insistence of the European community on comprehensive and immediate programs to secure the position of European farmers forced KANU to define its views on land policy. There had already been evidence that the party leadership was not united, and the KC and Convention of Associations' attack on the land problem simply increased the possibility that internal differences within KANU would lead to an open split. One group within the party, including Mboya and Gichuru, wished to postpone the issue of land until after independence, on the grounds that an African rather than a colonial government should deal with this subject so that African rather than European interests would predominate. This group also indicated that land titles would be protected and efficient expatriate farmers would be encouraged to stay, although such guarantees could not prejudice any needed reforms that a future government might consider essential. Another, more militant, group within KANU was less interested in providing European farmers with assurances and more concerned with finding relief for landless and unemployed Africans. They were less concerned about encouraging European settlers than about aiding and increasing the prosperity of Africans who already possessed land. Within this group, however, there were differences between men like Oginga Odinga and Bildad Kaggia, on the one hand, and leaders of the Kenya African Landless Union (KALU), on the other hand, who sought to replace KANU leaders as spokesman for the African landless and unemployed.

KALU was formed in 1961 by the KANU branch chairman in

---

55. *East African Standard,* October 18, 1961.

Kenyatta's own constituency of Fort Hall, where land shortage was extremely severe. It was dedicated to giving all landless persons plots to farm. Together with the Kenya Coalition, although for different reasons, KALU constituents were increased in number and made economically more depressed by the deterioration of the economy as independence approached. The numbers of unemployed and landless were swelled not only by population growth in excess of economic growth during the 1950s, by the return of detainees, and by the short-term effects of land consolidation, but also by the discharge of African employees from European farms as the Europeans scaled down their operations. The General Agricultural Workers Union in 1961 had successfully sought a minimum wage from the Kenya National Farmers Union, which represented the European farmers. Because of Europeans' uncertainties and the alleged low level of output by African employees, the increase in the price of labor affected European willingness to hire and retain employees. The growth of KALU's constituency of landless Africans was thus in part the direct result of the European crisis of confidence. During the interregnum following the election, KALU joined KANU in demanding the release of Kenyatta and urging the formation of a stable government that could attend to African land problems. Significantly, KALU was flexible on the means devised to employ the landless. "Our aim is that if it will be impossible for all landless to get pieces of land we shall try to see that they shall get a living." [56] At another time a KALU spokesman said: "This is to assure farmers and businessmen that there is going to be a stable and acceptable government soon so that they can start to expand their schemes and employ more people." [57] While KALU was flexible about employment, it criticized the World Bank/CDC settlement schemes as serving the interests only of the "more ambitious farmers." [58] Finally, KALU recognized the existence of land in the reserves that could and should be utilized, urging that a fund be created so that such

56. *Ibid.,* April 3, 1961.
57. *Ibid.,* April 6, 1961.
58. *Ibid.,* April 3, 1961.

land could be purchased for use as cooperative farms for an alleged 18,000-man force of unemployed in the Rift Valley and Central Provinces.[59] KALU wanted land for the landless but was flexible on whether land in the reserves or in the European areas was used and also on whether the landless were given their own plots or employed in businesses or other farms.

While KALU focused on solving the problem of landlessness and unemployment by whatever means were available, Odinga and Josef Mathenge, a founding member of KANU and future leader of government business in the Senate, concentrated more upon employing radical means to gain redistribution of land in favor of poor Africans. In May, 1961, they led a massive rally of perhaps 20,000 Africans at Ruringu (near Nairobi) at which, while condemning any recrudescence of Mau Mau, they got the crowd to agree that collectively they would never buy any land in the White Highlands and that land titles should never be given to Europeans. Said Mathenge: "We will not buy an inch of this White Highlands soil. . . . If there is going to be anyone settling the White Highlands he will live there free. It was our land and we want the landless to go there free." [60] On the eve of the 1962 Lancaster House Conference, and more or less in reply to a land-policy debate in the Legislative Council (of which he was not then a member), Kaggia said:

> All land hungry people must patiently wait until the government is in our own hands when we shall be able to formulate a suitable land policy. . . . It will be the prime duty of our independent state to see to the needs of thousands and thousands of poor and hungry landless people who are today roaming about in towns and settled areas without any hope for existence. The many evictions that took place to accommodate European settlers, especially the wholesale evictions of Masai and many others that took place in Kiambu, can remind anyone who is in doubt that the land now occupied by the European settlers was robbed from Africans. . . . In view of this it looks very absurd for Africans to buy land that was rightly theirs.[61]

59. *Ibid.*, March 18, 1961.
60. *Ibid.*, May 19, 1961.
61. *Ibid.*, January 27, 1962.

Finally, Paul Ngei, the acknowledged leader of the Kamba (Kenya's third-largest African community), told a large rally in Nairobi in September, 1961, that the Europeans were living on stolen land, that it would be taken over at independence, and that the Europeans would do well to pack their bags for imminent departure.[62] Ngei later modified his remarks slightly by saying he didn't mean land would be seized from the Europeans; rather, it would just be "taken back."[63] One can speculate how many African listeners were set right by this clarification and how many anxious European farmers were reassured.

The leadership of KANU was caught between making the European farmers secure in land tenure for the economy's sake and the historic position of African nationalism on land policy—that the colonial government and the European settlers had illegally and unjustly deprived Africans of their land. One of Kenyatta's major responsibilities following his release was to resolve this dilemma and at the same time to prevent the issue of land policy from widening existing divisions within the leadership of KANU. From the beginning of his reappearance on the political scene, Jomo Kenyatta made it clear that his primary objective was to put aside past conflicts and differences and to achieve a united Kenya. Increasingly, it became clear that he meant to include not only the members of his own party, but those of KADU, the Asian community, and at least some of the European community as well. His emphasis upon unity, however, tended to strengthen the position of the moderates such as Mboya and to isolate Kaggia, Odinga, and Ngei, although Kenyatta tried to prevent this isolation. In effect, Kenyatta put Kenya's unity ahead of its transformation according to some of the traditional objectives of African nationalism. That Kenyatta was able to maintain unity according to the formula of KANU moderates without finally isolating the militant wing until two and a half years after independence may be attributed to the man's stature in the eyes of most segments of the African population, to the fact that his isolation in detention

62. *Ibid.,* September 15, 1961.
63. *Ibid.,* September 16, 1961.

enabled all shades of African opinion to lionize him as the symbol of African nationalism, to the importance of maintaining a united front in gaining independence, and to the strategies Kenyatta employed upon his release. These strategies became most apparent in the area of land policy, where differences were perhaps the most sharply defined.

Through moderation in land policy, Kenyatta was prepared to accommodate not only the full spectrum of African political opinion but European views as well. He thus tried to obviate the minority coalition's interest in a *majimbo* constitution for independent Kenya. He appeared to recognize three distinct issues in formulating a common land policy: whether land titles would be honored following independence; whether regional governments or the national government would make land policy; and what measures had to be taken to deal with the landless and unemployed Africans. Their numbers had grown and their presence had become more sharply visible as Emergency restrictions on movement were lifted and Europeans scaled down their farming operations. Kenyatta sought to reassure Europeans by specifying that property titles should be secure, even when and if a future African government might undertake further land reforms after independence. He addressed himself to KADU in stating that, while he did not believe in *majimbo,* he did not propose to nationalize the economy at the expense of the rights of individuals or particular communities. Finally, he agreed with militants in KANU that measures were needed to help the landless and unemployed. Had KADU and the Europeans taken such assurances to heart, there might have been fewer African landless and unemployed, and consequently less basis for the KANU militants whom the minorities came to fear most, and less need for extensive land-resettlement schemes catering to European fears as much as to the Africans. On the other hand, settlement schemes diminished the politically anomalous but economically powerful European White Highlands, with which Kenyatta's government after independence would otherwise have been saddled. Settlement schemes and *majimbo* left advocacy of unity and economic development, which they jeopardized, to KANU moderates, who might otherwise have been driven to the position taken by Kaggia and Odinga. Had extensive settlement schemes and *majimbo* not been instituted, the post-independence African government would have been faced with a clearer choice between the concerns of African nationalism and defense of the colonial order symbolized by the existence of the White Highlands.

Kenyatta's attempts to create unity without *majimbo* through a moderate land policy were prejudged not only by the European community and some African leaders but by the British government as well. Europeans and some Africans apparently did not believe what Kenyatta said or in his ability to enforce his will, because neither the deterioration of the economy and the threats of the KC and the Convention of Associations nor the development of plans for a *majimbo* constitution were stayed by his pronouncements. After returning from a visit to Kenya, the new secretary of state for the colonies, Reginald Maudling, endorsed *majimbo* in a statement issued in London:

> The great danger I see is fear; fear of discrimination, fear of intimidation, fear of exploitation. I have seen enough to be convinced that there is truth underlying these fears. . . . From the discussions I have held, I am satisfied that there is more common ground between the main parties than might appear on the surface. There must clearly be a stable and competent central government, for without it there cannot be a Kenya nation. But more than this is clearly needed. If the rights of individuals are to be safeguarded, and if there is to be confidence that they will be, Kenya will need in addition other governing authorities with their own defined rights which do not derive from the central government but are entrenched and written into the constitution; and the constitution must be one that cannot be so changed that the purposes agreed at the constitutional conference are frustrated.[64]

Maudling believed that the creation of unity was possible, but only if the safeguards desired by the minorities and disliked by KANU

---

64. Great Britain, Colonial Office, *Report of the Kenya Constitutional Conference, 1962,* British Sessional Papers, 1962, Vol. XI (875), Cmnd. 1700 (London: H.M.S.O., 1962), pp. 7–8.

and Kenyatta were granted. The 1962 Constitutional Conference advanced Kenya's prograss toward independence and seemed thereby to reward KADU and the NKP for forming the government in defiance of Kenyatta and KANU. The terms of the new constitution rewarded Europeans and KADU and provided the institutional protection of the *majimbo* provisions they desired and the land-resettlement programs which European fears made necessary if the economy were to be preserved.

THE PRICE OF INDEPENDENCE

Given the support of the colonial secretary, it was predictable that the minority coalition government would succeed, at the 1962 Lancaster House Conference, in gaining a *majimbo* constitution for independent Kenya. The new constitutional arrangements included provisions guranteeing that the land, with certain exceptions, would be owned and controlled by the regions rather than by the central government. The regional and the central governments were to administer the land-resettlement schemes concurrently. The control of land transfers was vested in a Central Land Board independent of the regular central government and composed of members appointed primarily by the regions. Other important matters, such as control of health and educational facilities and the supervision of local governments, were left to the regions. The country was divided into six regions in a way that, on the whole, insured the political supremacy of the two African parties in three regions each. Further, the constitution established an upper house, called the Senate, which combined features of the American Senate and the British House of Lords. Finally, an elaborate Bill of Rights was written into the constitution which gave particular attention to the rights of those whose property might be expropriated by the government and which also provided a grace period during which those of expatriate origin could decide whether to become citizens of the new Kenya.[65]

65. *Ibid., passim.*

The Lancaster House Conference established a constitutional structure that it hoped would restore the confidence of those who feared the consequences of independence under an African government. The question of reestablishing confidence in the Kenya economy was, by early 1962, a matter not only of constitutional provisions but of the reorganization of the economy. Furthermore, not only did European confidence in the economy need to be restored, but also steps had to be taken to accommodate the vast numbers of unemployed and landless who by this time were putting considerable pressure on the African leaders. The Kenya Coalition and the Convention of Associations, representing a majority of the European farmers, threatened that their constituents would leave suddenly if measures were not taken promptly to underwrite the value of their properties. By January, 1962, the growing awareness of numbers of landless and unemployed for whom KANU felt responsibility increased (as did the articulateness of their leaders). Consequently, by early 1962 the parties representing the African majority and the European majority shared, for different reasons, an interest in land-reform measures to relieve the distress of many of their respective constituents. The immediate question was whether KANU would join a government that would function under the new *Majimbo* Constitution and whether the party would endorse the requirement that Africans must pay for the land they could acquire through resettlement schemes.

The problem facing KANU and the manner in which its leaders ordered the party's values are well illustrated by the decision of all KANU delegates to sign the conference report. Only the Masai members of the KADU delegation would not support the new arrangements. They alleged that inadequate recognition was given to the Masai's treaty relationship with the British government and the Masai people's claim to the White Highlands.[66] The constitution was obviously not in accord with the KANU delegation's preference for

---

66. *Ibid.*, pp. 29–30. These were the most notable nonsigners. Others included Sheikh A. Nassir and Mr. A. R. Khalif, who were concerned over the fate of the Coast Province's relationship with the Sultan of Zanzibar.

a strong national government; yet not to sign might have been to jeopardize progress toward independence, which KANU did not wish to do at any price. Kenyatta expressed his party's purposes in deciding to join the government: "Let us show them [the other parties and the colonial administration] that we do not want to dominate but wish to live happily together with others. Do not do anything to give them cause to fear the Kikuyu and the Luo." [67] Preserving unity and insuring deliberate progress toward independence suggested to Kenyatta and KANU the wisdom of participating in the post-Lancaster House coalition government notwithstanding the risk that KANU, and particularly its moderate leaders, might become identified with KADU and the outgoing colonial administration by the party rank and file. One price for maintaining political unity and insuring early independence was acceptance by KANU of a constitution embodying the philosophy of the rival KADU and the NKP, despite Kenyatta's own preferred strategy for gaining the same results.

The expansion of the land-settlement program to include large numbers of landless was, of course, in the interests of a significant number of KANU's constituents. The political costs to KANU lay in its being obliged to advocate expansion of an existing program created by the British government largely in response to pressure from European farmers rather than in the service of the African landless and unemployed. In addition, KANU had to ask its supporters to accept a program on terms and conditions specified by the colonial administration rather than by an African government in accordance with African ideas. Land resettlement, in addition to serving the interests of the European farmers, became a means of dissolving the threat to political stability posed by large numbers of landless and unemployed rather than a vehicle for the realization of the goals of African nationalism.

The emergence of this large, visible, and somewhat articulate class of landless and unemployed had become apparent rather suddenly after the 1960 Lancaster House Conference. KANU seized the

67. *East African Standard,* April 26, 1962.

initiative, urging the immediate expansion of programs to accommodate them. Representing KANU, James Gichuru introduced a motion in the Legislative Council on the eve of the 1962 Lancaster
House Conference, proposing that:

> This Council records that the settlement of the landless, unemployed
> and impoverished is a matter of the greatest urgency. It therefore
> supports as a general policy of land reform the principles of the
> settlement schemes and urges the government to examine all possi-
> ble methods by which such people may be provided with land and
> adequate finance in the quickest and most economical way possible.[68]

The debate on this program was noted with the greatest interest and
concern by all communities, since it marked Kenyatta's maiden
speech as a member of the Legislative Council. Kenyatta abandoned
the position, taken earlier by Mboya and Gichuru, and by himself,
that the colonial administration should leave major land reforms for
an independent government to undertake. He conceded that the
government should act immediately and resolutely on the problems
of African landlessness. Sensing why some feared the implications
of earlier KANU demands that land reforms be left to an independent African government, Kenyatta reasoned that there was no argument for delaying the implementation of such programs, since Africans would not get the land free either now or under a future KANU
administration.

> I did not say that Africans should sit idle and wait until Uhuru
> [independence] to get land for nothing. All I said was that the
> present government should get down to work and face realities and
> help landless, unemployed Africans, that if there was any land going
> it ought to be given to somebody who needs it and not the man with
> 500 or however much he may have.[69]

Kenyatta's argument was supported by Bruce McKenzie, the previous and future minister for agriculture. Although he was experienced
both as an agriculturalist and as an administrator of agricultural

68. Kenya, *Debates* (1962), LXXXVIII, 1405 ff.
69. *East African Standard,* January 26, 1962.

development programs, he stated that it was more important to get the people on the land than to plan the fine details of a comprehensive scheme prior to actual resettlement.[70]

In its subsequent paper on land use, KANU emphasized both its interest in providing the poor with land and its concern that resettlement not be at the cost of diminishing the productivity of the agricultural economy. On the one hand, the party leadership observed that "the overall scope of the present scheme is inadequate to meet the growing problem of landlessness and unemployment and the present rate of progress is dangerously slow." [71] This pronouncement reinforced the view expressed by Kenyatta in the Legislative Council debate that "the schemes we want to see functioning are those which will help the landless and unemployed and poor." [72] Gichuru had also observed that the poor were, after all, "citizens of this country and we feel they deserve as much attention from the government as any of the other people who have got plenty of money, who can buy bigger farms and so on." [73] On the other hand, the KANU land-use paper expressed concern about the economics of a program to assist the landless and unemployed. The paper specified three objectives: programs for the landless; increased over-all production; and economically viable schemes that would enable the new farmer to repay his loans. The explicit statement by both Kenyatta and the KANU land-policy paper that the new African settlers would have to pay for their land and other loans indicated clearly that KANU expected the African settlers to be responsible participants in the country's modern economy rather than wards of the government.

The KANU strategy of urging the expansion of a colonial administration's program to serve the needs of the landless for whom the party felt particularly responsible gained Kenyatta and KANU new respect from KADU and the European community and prompted protests from more militant nationalists. KADU and the

70. Kenya, *Debates* (1962), LXXXVIII, 1408 ff.
71. *East African Standard,* February 14, 1962.
72. Kenya, *Debates* (1962), LXXXVIII, 1417.
73. *Ibid.,* p. 1407.

European community shared KANU's desire to accommodate the landless without weakening the economy, and the European community in particular took comfort from Kenyatta's belief that the Africans should pay for land. Kenya National Farmers Union president Lord Delamere found Kenyatta's statement in the Legislative Council most encouraging.[74] Michael Blundell agreed and hoped that KANU and the African peoples would make their actions consistent with their leader's words by curbing the activities of the KANU Youth Wing and other local KANU organizations that were stirring the fears of European settlers and others by their extralegal activities.[75] However, the over-all impression of Kenyatta gained by European members of the Legislative Council was perhaps best expressed by one who later recalled having felt that "there is no evil in that man." Significantly, Ronald Ngala of KADU said his party shared KANU's concern for the landless and unemployed and agreed that undeveloped land should be used for settlement schemes to accommodate them. However, he said KADU did not wish such a program to be undertaken at the expense of other programs for encouraging economic development but only as a complement to them.[76] Bildad Kaggia and KALU were not pleased with the position of Kenyatta and Gichuru in the Legislative Council debate. Immediately after the debate, Kaggia told a large African rally that "landlordship in our country" must be ended and that Africans would refuse to buy one inch of the Highlands from Europeans.[77] A spokesman for KALU wondered out loud if Kenyatta had been betraying the African people throughout his forty-year struggle to have European land returned to Africans. "Does it mean that he has been deceiving Africans for forty years? If not, he should, like Mr. Ngei, say openly that no land should be sold to Africans by Europeans."[78] The price

74. *East African Standard,* January 31, 1962.
75. *Ibid.*
76. *Ibid.*
77. *Ibid.,* January 27, 1962.
78. *Ibid.,* January 31, 1962. KALU the next day denied that it had the previous day expressed shock. The union claimed it had not demanded free land, only settlement of the landless in some way; it supported the cooperative farming and the yeoman type of scheme; it still supported Kenyatta.

of Kenyatta's and KANU's acceptance of a colonial administration's program to solve a problem that would soon trouble an African government was the openly expressed displeasure of African leaders who claimed to be in the mainstream of Kenya African nationalism.

Beyond the cooperative stance adopted by KANU's senior leaders and the party's agreement to join a government that would implement a constitution it did not like, KANU was still called upon to demonstrate its specific support for the existing land-resettlement programs at a time when negotiations were under way for a second enlargement of the programs. Some early attempts to provide land for landless persons in Central Province revealed a reluctance upon the part of the intended settlers to join the scheme and pay what they could toward the cost of their resettlement.[79] Kenyatta was asked and agreed to send a telegram from London urging the would-be settlers to accept the plots and to pay what was required if they could.[80] KANU also demonstrated its willingness to cooperate with the administration by calling for an end to intimidation and extralegal behavior and for a general adherence to the requirements of law and order.[81]

In the months following the 1962 Lancaster House Conference, acceptance of Britain's and the colonial administration's land policy in Kenya was employed to distinguish those African leaders who were willing to cooperate with the colonial administration in the interests of preserving the economy, progressing toward independence, and relieving the problem of landlessness that would otherwise threaten an independent African government from those Africans who thought the price of cooperation too high. Odinga, for example, signed the Lancaster House Conference report but was refused a

79. *Ibid.,* March 15, 1962. The previous day F. R. Wilson, the Central Province provincial commissioner, expressed dismay that KANU branches were allegedly trying to upset the arrangements for the settlement schemes. Prior to that, a prominent Nyeri KANU leader had said that KANU leaders would not endorse the schemes until their leaders, in London for the constitutional talks, had been fully consulted. Even after Kenyatta's telegram the district commissioner for Kiambu reported considerable reluctance on the part of Africans to take up the plots at the Maguga location, although another at Tagwe was being taken up.
80. *Ibid.*
81. *Ibid.*

ministry in the coalition government on orders from the governor and the colonial office because of his opposition to the colonial administration's pre-independence program for landlessness. Four years later, Odinga was to identify this as the beginning of his alienation from KANU and Kenyatta.[82] Although Kenyatta was willing to sign the conference report, join a government with KADU to indicate his acquiescence in a constitution that did not reflect his party's views, and urge the expansion of a colonial administration's program to buy European farms in order to relieve African landlessness, he was unwilling to allow differences over land policy to divide KANU. Hence he went out of his way to indicate to an African rally the importance of having Odinga in the party and in the future government of the country. "My first choice was Jaramogi [Odinga] to look after the finance of the country properly, but the imperialists refused saying that he was not a good man. But they will not be able to stop him being in our own government and he will be the first man there." [83] In addition to the growing problem of landlessness and unemployment, the inadequacy of the existing land-resettlement program for the requirements of the European farming community and that community's uncertainty over whether the moderates or the militants were in control of KANU combined to maintain and increase the demand for a second enlargement of the resettlement program. In July, 1962, the British government responded with the announcement of a one-million-acre settlement program specifically for the African landless and unemployed, who would be settled on nearly one thousand farms subdivided to create plots for 25,000 to 30,000 African families.[84]

The basic objective behind the new massive land-resettlement program for indigent Africans and panic-stricken Europeans was identical with that for which earlier programs had been designed.

---

82. He indicated that his breach with Kenyatta began when the colonial administration would not countenance giving Odinga a ministry in the coalition government formed between KANU and KADU after the Lancaster House Conference. Interviews with Sir Patrick Renison and James Gichuru.

83. *East African Standard,* May 7, 1962.

84. Known as the Million Acre Scheme, a term which excludes the schemes already begun under the auspices of the CDC and the World Bank.

This purpose was to enable European and African communities to develop a political identification with the Kenya nation by persuading as many rural inhabitants of both races as possible to become responsible participants and beneficiaries in the modern agricultural economy. Prior to 1960, the objectives had been to use land consolidation and registration as a means of combating African identification with the leaders of Mau Mau by making them relatively prosperous participants in the modern economy, with the help of government loans and agricultural education. Europeans at the same time were urged to secure their future place in Kenya by making themselves economically indispensable through development of their farms. It was hoped that Europeans and Africans who responded favorably to these persuasions would all accept a multiracial society. The initial land-resettlement program sponsored by the Kenya government and financed by the World Bank and the CDC was designed to implement the political principles of multiracialism by financing the entry of qualified African farmers into the White Highlands. The expansion of the land-resettlement schemes, in November, 1961, and July, 1962, to include landless and unemployed, was designed initially to relieve those European farmers who were afraid of the new Kenya and to create a market in land for those who were willing to stay. As Blundell put it: "Once these schemes are completed I hope future Kenya governments will be able to see that good farmers whatever their colour are an asset to the country." [85] Finally, these same schemes were employed by the colonial administration with the cooperation of both African parties as a means of giving the African poor and landless, who might otherwise threaten the stability of an African government with limited resources, a political and economic stake in the new Kenya.

---

85. *East African Standard,* September 8, 1961.

4

THE POLITICS OF *HARAMBEE*

JOMO KENYATTA has made *harambee* the Kenya African word for
unity. From the time of his release in 1961 until the general election
of June, 1963, Kenyatta and his party accepted the terms and conditions for political unity as the European settlers, the colonial administration, and the smaller African communities represented in
KADU believed they needed to be defined. KANU's participation
in the coalition government between the 1962 Lancaster House Conference and its outright victory in the 1963 general elections gave the
party and Kenyatta their first chance to influence the conclusion of
the transfer of political power to their liking, subject to commitments
already made to the other parties in the coalition. These other parties, principally the moderate European-based New Kenya party and
the Kenya African Democratic Union, also were given an opportunity to identify KANU with policies undertaken in what they
conceived to be their own interests. KANU was obliged to steer
between the shoals of identifying itself too closely with policies advocated jointly by the colonial administration and the other parties
and of risking delays in independence or increased political and
economic instability by opposing such programs too vehemently.
The other partners in the coalition needed to beware of twin dangers:

(1) departing too far from what they conceived to be their own interests in order to accommodate KANU, and (2) insisting on the entrenchment of their interests to the point where KANU's own fragile unity might fall apart in determining how to respond to this entrenchment. In the latter circumstances the country might have no majority party, and a Congo-like situation, which the minorities feared, might emerge.

The million-acre program of land resettlement announced by the colonial secretary, Reginald Maudling, in August, 1962, critically affected the outcome of these negotiations among the partners to the coalition government, if for no other reason than because of the size of the program and the extent of human and financial resources tied up in its establishment and implementation. Under the new program, approximately one thousand European farms covering just over one million acres were to be purchased over a five-year period. Out of this acreage, smallholdings were to be created for 30,000 African families who, it was hoped, would average about £9 to £12 ($25 to $40) annual income over and above subsistence, farm expenses, and loan repayments. The total cost of the new program came to just under $60 million; one-third was an outright grant from the British government, while the remaining two-thirds was a loan which would be recovered by individual farmers from the earnings from their plots over a long-term period. Development loans were for ten-year periods, while land loans were repayable over a thirty-year period, each loan being issued at 6½ percent interest. This new program, plus existing resettlement programs and special programs added later, brought to nearly 1,500,000 acres the total land to be transferred from European to African hands, increased the number of African beneficiaries to nearly 35,000 families, and raised the total cost of the program to over $70 million.[1] The government estimated in 1966 that the land-resettlement program accounted for nearly half of the total agricultural development program for the period 1963 through 1965. The average farmer in the scheme, with no experience in cash-

1. Kenya, Department of Settlement, *The Million Acre Settlement Scheme* (Nairobi: Government Printer, 1966).

crop farming, was made responsible for earning sufficient funds to repay over one thousand dollars during a ten- to thirty-year period at 6½ percent interest. The magnitude of the responsibility which the total resettlement program placed on the Kenya government and on the new peasant farmers individually, and the opportunity costs involved in a program absorbing so much of the expenditure in Kenya's most important industry, could not have failed to have a decisive impact upon the subsequent development strategies and priorities of those parties associated with the government of Kenya.

The new resettlement program had three important political consequences. First, it did a great deal to relieve the pressures created by African landlessness and unemployment, of which leaders of all political shades of opinion had become increasingly aware. Land resettlement realized the ambitions of thousands of Africans, even though the program was instituted largely at European insistence and Africans had to pay for the land. The program therefore removed one obstacle to KANU's closer association with the other parties in the coalition, since it relieved a problem for which the party took primary responsibility. The price of KANU's acceptance of this program, however, was the further alienation of Odinga, Bildad Kaggia, and other militants within its ranks who believed that payment for the land by Africans was contrary to that tenet of African nationalism which argued that the White Highlands had been stolen from Africans. Second, the announcement of a program of such magnitude contributed to a clarification and redefinition of future policies vis-à-vis the land by all parties. All the members of the coalition began to argue that such resettlement, dictated by the urgings of landless Africans and anxious European farmers, was sufficient to meet the needs of these groups. They believed policies stressing better land use and development by Africans already in possession of land and Europeans intending to stay should be emphasized in the future in order to build the economy. On the other hand, the Kenya Coalition, which was outside the coalition, thought the whole resettlement program too little, too late, and too stingy in reimbursing departing European farmers for their farms. KANU radicals were to argue later that too few landless, unemployed Africans had been cared for by the KANU government. Third, such land policies, in moving KANU closer to the views of KADU and in accommodating the land needs of the Kikuyu, helped to prepare the ground for ending *majimbo*. Apart from the *majimbo* and Kenyatta questions, KANU and KADU had demonstrated few basic disagreements since their first contest in the 1961 elections. The eventual merger of KANU and KADU would be achieved at the price of losing Odinga and the other KANU militants, who would form the opposition Kenya People's Union in 1966. The land-resettlement program, in combination with reassuring gestures by the independent government, were to encourage those European farmers remaining in the country to farm efficiently and in full security, thereby contributing to the country's economic growth. Land resettlement also diminished the European farmers' ability to harm the economy not only by enabling many of the most conservative of them to leave but also by halving their numbers.

Despite the size and cost of the resettlement program, the right-wing European groups remained dissatisfied. After it became known in mid-July that the Million Acre Scheme was under consideration, Cavendish-Bentinck, leader of the Kenya Coalition, told the press: "My first reaction is that Mr. Maudling's bare statement [about the Million Acre Scheme] is more likely to increase the feeling of instability in the colony than to decrease it." [2] He observed (erroneously) that the program amounted to "only" an additional 700,000 acres of land to be resettled with Africans. Another member of the Kenya Coalition observed that the program was too little and too late, and that it should be completed within three years rather than five.[3] On the latter point, the KC largely got its way, as the program was greatly telescoped so that most of the new settlers were on the land within three years of the program's inception. The Association of Settlement Board Farmers, those who came to Kenya after World War II and had not in most cases yet become full owners of their

---

2. *East African Standard,* July 13, 1962.
3. *Ibid.* Comment by L. R. M. Welwood, sometime minister in the government and leading figure in the Kenya Coalition.

farms, advised members to leave Kenya immediately.[4] The Convention of Associations and the Kenya Coalition both urged that the program be accelerated so that it could be completed before an African government had time to attack European interests in the country.[5] The Kenya coalition government supported this view and successfully urged acceleration on the British government. The Kenya government's impatience must be attributed to the interaction of the pressure of African landless and unemployed and European fears about their future in Kenya.

In contrast with right-wing European dissatisfaction over the pace and scope of the resettlement program, the two major African parties and the NKP members of the governing coalition seemed to put very little emphasis upon the resettlement program. This was evident from policy statements, speeches, responses to advice from the international financial community, and definition of spheres of influence for African peoples. The views of KADU and the NKP were both represented in KADU's statement that the solution to land hunger lay in raising productivity rather than in simply giving land to the landless.[6] For these two parties, land resettlement was a political necessity to remove a possible threat to political stability during the transfer of power and after independence. But they were not enamored of such land redistribution as a basic nation-building strategy in the future, because they did not believe it resulted in maximum assistance to the economic development of Kenya. Their position was much easier after large-scale resettlement programs were in progress. The danger that land hunger and unemployment among the Kikuyu might result in Kikuyu assaults on the territorial integrity of the minorities they represented was substantially diminished by the settlement program. Landlessness and unemployment were not prominent difficulties for the minorities. Programs similar to those initiated in Kikuyuland in the 1950s, on the other hand, might increase the economic health and prosperity of the smaller

4. *Ibid.*, July 16, 1962.
5. *Ibid.*, July 18, 1962.
6. *Ibid.*, July 6, 1962.

African communities as they had for the Kikuyu. Such programs would also be consistent with renewed European contributions to economic development as they were seen to be in the 1950s. KADU and the NKP thus emphasized the importance of security of tenure so that most of the good land, which was to be found in areas never colonized by European settlers, could be developed by Africans.[7]

One of the assumptions behind the enlarged settlement schemes was that relief of landlessness and unemployment and removal of the anomaly of a European farming enclave in the Highlands would result in a new climate of economic confidence in the country. Leaders of all parties hoped and anticipated that such confidence would be expressed in the restoration of land values and a strong market in agricultural land and in a climate favorable to economic growth. A "climate favorable to economic growth" came to mean one in which processes of economic development could occur without the alleged disruptive effects of political activities and pressures.[8] Economic development, and particularly agricultural development, eventually was considered of such importance that the leaders came to believe it should be insulated from and stand above politics. Only then could investors, both domestically and externally, gain the confidence to invest their needed capital in Kenya. Those policies which implied reversals of social status or transfer of economic power for their own sake and as logical corollaries of the transfer of political power were to be given lower priority than those which resulted in an increase in Kenya's economic strength. This change of policy became apparent in KANU's strategies, especially after the inauguration of the enlarged settlement program.

KANU's policy statement on the eve of the new million-acre

---

7. The report of the World Bank mission to Kenya indicated that "approximately four-fifths of the total acreage of high-potential land is in the non-scheduled areas. . . . At the time of the mission's visit, only about one-sixth of the high-potential land in the non-scheduled areas had been consolidated or enclosed or both." See *The Economic Development of Kenya* (published for the International Bank for Reconstruction and Development; Baltimore: The Johns Hopkins Press, 1963). Daniel arap Moi, KADU'S chairman, held similar views.

8. This was the theory behind the establishment of the Central Land Board at the 1962 Lancaster House Conference, in the view of KADU and its European supporters and the Kenya Coalition. Subsequently, this view was implicitly adopted by the independent government in its Sessional Paper on African Socialism and its 1966 Development Plan.

resettlement scheme contained two strategic elements. First, KANU attacked the regionalist ideas of KADU and accused KADU of giving *majimbo* more weight than *uhuru* itself.[9] KANU disliked the Lancaster House Conference, which had written in a number of regionalist features. KANU took the line, however, that its presence at the conference had prevented regionalism from going still further. It also indicated that its purpose in joining the government was to watch over the African national interest and to make sure that no unnecessary delays interrupted the country's progress toward independence. Second, KANU addressed itself to the task of improving the status and economic position of ordinary Africans—without implying that such improvements had to be at the expense of both Europeans and Africans who had already achieved those desiderata.

> In fact the motive behind our nationalist struggle is the deep desire to improve the lot of our people. We are confronted with the grimness of the boy who grows to be an adult and dies without ever having owned a pair of shoes; the man or woman or child who cannot be sure of eating even one square meal a day; the pregnant woman who dies in childbirth because she cannot go to a maternity hospital; the worker who is discarded in old age without care; the chronic indebtedness of most workers in urban areas. . . . The challenge before us can only be met through our resolve to wage war against poverty.[10]

This position did not imply transfer of existing resources from Europeans to Africans but rather increases in the number of resources by augmenting the contributions of those who had not in the past added measurably to the economic growth of the country. The KANU statement said:

> But clearly Kenya cannot continue with development based on such weak foundations as in the past. We must move away from dependence on European farming and economic enterprise. We must vigorously exploit the Africans' own potential as a producer, worker, and

9. *East African Standard,* July 30, 1962.
10. *Ibid.*

consumer. This has been tragically neglected in the past. We must encourage self help projects and cooperatives. We must supplement the scarcity of capital with maximum use of the abundant labor available in the country.[11]

Instead of pressing Europeans and the colonial administration to accommodate the existence and objectives of African nationalism, KANU, after it joined the government, began to speak in terms of policies that would assimilate the purposes and policies of the nationalist movement with those designed to maintain the economy of Kenya. It prepared to do this by interfering with the existing economic structure as little as possible. The government hoped to guide the objectives of ordinary Africans so that their objectives would not threaten the position of more fortunate Europeans and Africans. It hoped that by measures such as the massive land-resettlement scheme those of low status and in poor economic situations would be persuaded to accept the new objectives. During the terminal year of colonial rule and the regime of the broad-based coalition government, this policy became apparent in a number of significant developments.

One of the earliest indications came in a speech by Tom Mboya to settlers in Eldoret in late July, 1962. In that talk he stressed that the key to security lay in emphasizing the positive side of nation-building. For Europeans, he said, this meant identifying themselves with Kenya and its nation-building objectives or leaving the country. For Mboya, the key indicator of whether a European was willing to identify was whether he would agree to take out Kenya citizenship.

> You cannot take up any compromise position now. Either you are going to play your part wholeheartedly or you are going to run away from it all. . . . So often we talk of fears about personal security. The only way to absolve such fears is to remove their cause. . . . We are all involved in the business of building a nation. Your security fears will disappear when the people can see that you are

11. *Ibid.*

pulling on the same rope as everybody else, towards a goal that everybody wants to reach, for rewards that we all can share.[12]

The ways to indicate this identification with the common struggle were to accept Kenya citizenship and to continue developing farms and businesses as Europeans had done in the past. The government was prepared to welcome and encourage to stay those who were willing to take these steps. The government advised those who were unwilling to do so to leave. Mboya wanted a European sector fully assimilated to the political realities of an independent Kenya and the economic objectives it would pursue.

Before the enlarged settlement program, it would have been difficult for KANU leaders to talk in these terms. Without extensive measures to accommodate the African landless and unemployed, KANU could have dealt with building the economy without reference to providing land for them only at the risk of precipitating the open opposition of the KANU militants. Providing land for which such Africans would be required to pay produced expressions of dismay within KANU's ranks. To have ignored the landless completely would have risked even greater divisions. Given the enlarged settlement program, KANU could begin to outline a policy under which remaining European farmers who took out citizenship and contributed to the growth of the agricultural economy could combine with Africans, on whom greater reliance would be placed, in building Kenya's economic strength.

The European farming community responded to Mboya's attempt to divide its own numbers by pointing to division in KANU. The settlers acknowledged that Mboya spoke as a moderate but wondered if he really spoke for all sections of his party. L. R. Maconochie-Welwood, a European minister in the coalition government, noted that Mboya was a moderate and speculated about what might happen if the less moderate Odinga and his caucus gained control of KANU. He believed that only a government that spoke for all Kenya's African communities could really reassure the Euro-

12. *Ibid.*, July 23, 1962.

pean settlers. He was especially concerned at what he believed to be deep divisions between the communities represented in KANU.[13] The Convention of Associations, another European caucus, attacked the idea that European settlers might have to take out citizenship in order to retain the security of their property: "Convention has always maintained that anyone who changes his citizenship should do so from a sense of conviction and from a desire to identify himself with the new State and not merely to retain certain rights and privileges." [14] These responses by the European community indicated the vulnerability of KANU's own strategy. As long as the European farming community remained on their land they could undermine the unity and the economy KANU wished to build by continuing to cease developing their farms and by increasing unemployment, thereby building the constituency of the landless and unemployed Africans with which Odinga and his group were especially concerned. However, the Europeans' power to do so would shortly be lessened, since half of them would be replaced by Africans under the settlement program. Once the settlement program had been undertaken, the settlers' real interests would lie in helping rather than in undermining KANU leaders like Mboya, for if Odinga really did gain control of the party or dominant influence with Kenyatta, that program which they had sought might be scrapped. Odinga had, after all, hinted that Africans should not pay for the land.

A second indication of the change in KANU's strategy came in its response to the economic survey missions sent out from Washington and London. The World Bank began its work in mid-September, 1961, and presented its report, *The Economic Development of Kenya,* in the closing weeks of 1962.[15] At about the same time, KANU in particular had the benefit of a report by Arthur Gaitskill, a member of the board of the Commonwealth Development Corporation. The report of the World Bank was published, and the government in turn published a sessional paper outlining its essentially favorable re-

---

13. *Ibid.,* July 24, 1962.
14. *Ibid.,* July 26, 1962.
15. *Economic Development of Kenya.*

sponse to the analysis and recommendations made. Gaitskill's report, by the government's own admission, had a substantial influence on the thinking of KANU leaders and on leading civil servants in the government. However, it has never been circulated or published, and its findings are not common knowledge outside a restricted circle in government.[16]

The essence of the recommendations of both reports seems to have been that existing programs of economic development, particularly with respect to agricultural progress, should be the basis for post-independence policies. Policies such as the Swynnerton plan and land consolidation and registration, although adopted under the colonial regime, were considered to be in independent Kenya's best interests. In the agricultural sphere, the reports supported the view that most of the best land in Kenya lay in areas already in African possession, that land consolidation and Swynnerton plan programs (with certain minor modifications) were proven vehicles to rapid agricultural development, and that the settlement schemes, while necessary to relieve political pressures posed by landlessness and unemployment, endangered the economy. Among the dangers were a possible loss of production, no significant net addition to the numbers of people employed, loss of foreign exchange, less efficient production, and the low net income per farmer that made the difference between economic survival and failure very small.[17] The government acknowledged the dangers in the schemes, noted efforts to raise the budgeted net income per farmer, and stressed that it understood the importance of making both the African areas and the settlement program economic successes.[18]

The government also accepted the commission's view that sub-

16. N. S. Carey Jones, former permanent secretary in the Ministry of Lands and Settlement, says of this privately and confidentially circulated report: "Fundamentally, and stating its recommendations in the simplest terms, it recommended the continuation and intensification of colonial policies." See N. S. Carey Jones, *The Anatomy of Uhuru* (Manchester: Manchester University Press, 1966), p. 142.

17. *Economic Development of Kenya*, p. 60.

18. Kenya, *Observations on the Report of an Economic Survey Mission from the International Bank for Reconstruction and Development,* Sessional Paper No. 1 of 1963 (Nairobi: Government Printer, 1963), p. 5. See also Kenya, *Report of the Fiscal Commission* (Nairobi: Government Printer, 1963).

stantial reliance would need to be placed on the private sector of the economy and that economic growth would have to take precedence over welfare programs. "The government endorses the view that the main emphasis should be placed on measures to improve production rather than on welfare projects." [19] This view, adopted during the regime of the coalition government, has become the official position of the KANU government since independence. The chief consequence of this policy has been the deferral of programs designed to realize the social and economic aspirations of Kenyans, associated with the development of nationalism and intensified during the transfer of power, to some unspecified future date when the economy will presumably be stronger.

KANU's new strategy of emphasizing economic production and development rather than the transfer of economic resources between the races was a crucial step in effecting a transition between pre-independence nationalism and post-independence nation-building policies. Recovery of the "stolen lands" was nearly as important as the achievement of political independence in the development of African nationalism. It appealed particularly to the thousands of Africans, notably the Kikuyu, who had been tenants hoping to achieve ownership of land and who had been confirmed as landless during the process of consolidation. It appealed to tenants on European farms who had been expelled either during Mau Mau or during the transfer of power. All Africans, especially the Kikuyu, whether or not they possessed individual title to land, wished to be relieved of the implied threat to secure land tenure represented by European colonization and alleged theft of African land. The new policy of the Kenya government was consistent with previous African nationalism insofar as it included measures to defend private property and assist farmers to facilitate their contributions to economic development in Kenya. Such security of tenure and economic encouragement favored those who had gained private ownership of land under consolidation. KANU's new strategy kept faith with pre-independence African nationalism by emphasizing the development of areas

19. Kenya, *Observations,* p. 2. See *Economic Development of Kenya,* p. 34.

that had always been under African control. Colonial policy, especially in the early years, had tended to favor development of areas under European control.

But KANU's new strategy, while keeping faith with African nationalism in these ways, broke faith with it in other ways in what it believed to be the interests of post-independence nation-building. Logically, emphasis on security of tenure and assistance in development of the land should have included the Africans who realized their hopes for land through the process of resettlement, especially since their hopes had been encouraged by African nationalism. The government has chosen to desert African nationalism by excluding the resettled Africans from those upon whom it relies for nation-building, because the program was initiated and designed to serve European interests. The government thereby fails to identify with the new Kenya nation those who have realized one of the chief aspirations of Kenya nationalism. Such a policy represents a choice between two horns of a dilemma: for the government to identify with the resettled Africans would have been to identify with the 2 percent who realized their ambitions while serving European interests. However, the government has not simply identified nation-building with the majority who have not gained their aspirations for land at the expense of those who have. It has identified with those who have gained individual title to land through consolidation of other means at the expense not only of those who participated in resettlement but also of those in the African rural and urban areas who remain unemployed and seek land as a means of earning a livelihood. The new policy thereby seems to reinstate European multiracial policies under new African management, at the expense of both the landless and those who gained land while serving the departing European farmers. As long as land remains of great importance to Africans, and as long as the memory of colonial-European land policies remains alive in African minds, colonial experience in Kenya will continue to frustrate nation-building policies about the land, because the colonists made the land aspirations of African nationalists serve their own purposes. Most land policies, therefore, that the government might adopt endanger the government's legitimacy because they appear to maintain continuity with previous colonial policies. Even the furtherance of economic development, the basis on which the government has chosen its land policies, can appear suspect in the eyes of Africans who remember that colonial European leaders used this goal as a means of combating African nationalism.

A third and final indication that KANU had begun to adopt a new strategy was recorded in the party's position on provincial boundaries and spheres of influence for particular African communities. In October, 1962, the Council of Ministers of the coalition government issued a statement affirming that each African community need have no fear for the integrity of its existing sphere of influence. All communities were promised that their land would remain in their possession. A motion to this effect was tabled in the Legislative Council and supported by Kenyatta and Ngala, the leaders of the two main African parties.[20] This policy was of particular interest to the African communities in the Rift Valley and Coast Provinces. Coming from the leaders of parties representing the larger as well as the smaller African communities, this promise appeared to be meaningful. In addition, while still minister for agriculture, Michael Blundell had laid down that each major African community should have its sphere of influence extended by being given at least one settlement area on formerly European soil.

Two weeks after the October statement, the Regional Boundaries Commission further ratified African spheres of influence.[21] The commission was appointed by the secretary of state, pursuant to the report of the second Lancaster House Conference, for the purpose of dividing Kenya into six regions plus the Nairobi area. It was charged with taking into account the wishes of the constituents of any given area respecting the boundaries of the regions. Over 200 separate delegates representing each party, tribal elders, and other

20. *East African Standard,* October 25, 1962.
21. Great Britain, Colonial Office, *Kenya: Report of the Regional Boundaries Commission,* British Sessional Papers, 1962, Vol. X (543), Cmnd. 1899 (London: H.M.S.O., 1962). See statement of KANU land use policy (*East African Standard,* February 14, 1962): "It would be necessary to differentiate between the scheduled and the non-scheduled areas over land compulsorily acquired—all transfers of non-scheduled land would be subject to the control of the local authority."

local dignitaries appeared before the commission to present their views. The significance of the commission's report is twofold. First, KANU, whose supporters came from the communities most in need of more land, argued that the boundaries should be retained in their present form. This argument could legitimately have been advanced in order not to arouse local community apprehensions and anxieties at a critical period in Kenya's political development. On the other hand, its effect was to serve notice that KANU did not wish to expand the frontiers of Kikuyuland in particular by advancing the boundaries of Central Province in which the Kikuyu predominated.

The other significant point about the report was that the commission chose to ignore the representations of delegations speaking for local KANU organizations and in fact changed the boundaries of Central Province to the west in such a way that all the settlement schemes involving the Kikuyu would be placed in Central Province. This had two important effects. First, an area of difficult formerly European farming land which had been excluded from the settlement-scheme purchase was surrounded by Million Acre Scheme land. The European farmers in that area were able to persuade the British government on security grounds to make an additional expenditure to buy out this land, the Ol Kalou Salient. The land, of doubtful suitability for small-scale farming, is now being farmed on a cooperative basis, and its viability is still a matter of controversy and uncertainty. Second, including all Kikuyu settlement schemes in the Central Province by pushing the province boundaries westward meant that the neighboring Rift Valley region remained an enclave of European farming in a region in which African communities supporting KADU were dominant. This development was not lost on Mboya, who commented adversely on the Regional Boundaries Commission recommendations: "We also regret to see that the new Rift Valley Region will be to a large extent a region of European influence and possible European control. This is something which must be watched very carefully and guarded against by a future government." [22]

22. *East African Standard,* December 21, 1962.

In attempting to accommodate the wishes of the various ethnic communities, the commission created regions that could with one exception be clearly identified with one or the other of the two major African political parties. Although KANU had objected to the creation of a European sphere, it did not publicly object to KADU spheres. In addition to the Rift Valley, the commission created a Western Region for the Luhya and the Teso out of what had been part of the Nyanza. The Luhya especially did not wish to share a region with the Luo, and this antagonism led them to seek a separate region of their own.[23] On the whole, the Luhya thus supported KADU, whose wishes the Regional Boundaries Commission recognized in this particular instance. The Coast Region was enlarged to include people who had previously been part of the Northern Frontier Province (NFD), but this extension did not change the Region's basic association with KADU. Central and Nyanza Provinces became the main bastions of KANU support, since the Kikuyu and Luo numerically dominated these regions. In the case of Nyanza Province, the Kisii, whose relationships with the Luo had been notoriously unharmonious and who supported KADU, were left in the same region with the Luo. Eastern Province, like the Coast Province, was extended to include part of the old NFD. This move was largely intended to bring the NFD under local administrations less inclined to separatist activity.[24] In effect, a region whose peoples might have been expected to support KADU was divided between the Coast and Eastern Regions. In the Coast Region, this only created a larger KADU-oriented region. In the Eastern Region, potential KADU support was linked with the much larger Kamba community, which on the whole supported KANU.

23. Great Britain, *Kenya: Report,* pp. 15–16.

24. The commission's terms of reference included a specification that Kenya be divided into only six regions, exclusive of the Nairobi area. The commission argued that this consideration, plus the expressed wishes of the inhabitants involved, dictated the decision to divide the Northern Frontier District between the new Eastern and Coastal Regions. The commission specifically stated, of course, that its terms of reference did not include deciding the issue of secession. The logic of dividing this outlying region of Kenya between two regions without any separatist inclinations is clear, and many government officials at the time considered that the commission was sensitive to these considerations.

Land resettlement alone did not necessarily enable KANU to support the retention of existing regional boundaries or to tolerate boundaries that made political control of three of the six regions by KADU a probability. KANU might have done so in any event. But land resettlement, in combination with the decisions of the Regional Boundaries Commission, helped to reassure the smaller communities represented in KADU that they would not be invaded by Kikuyu looking for land or employment, and also solved a potential difficulty between two KADU communities. If the settlement schemes on the Kinangop Plateau had been placed in the Rift Valley Province they could have substantially diminished KADU as well as European influence there. Without those settlement schemes, no placement of the boundary between the Rift Valley and Central Province could have reassured the Rift Valley peoples that landless and unemployed Kikuyu would not spill over and invade their region in great numbers. Controlled Kikuyu westward expansion onto the Kinangop and the plateau's inclusion in Central Province preserved the Rift Valley as a solid KADU bastion containing smaller African communities. Land-resettlement schemes in Western Province controlled eastward expansion of the Baluhya into land formerly within the Rift Valley. The Baluhya were given their own region, separate from the Luo whom they distrusted, while their settlement schemes in Western Province prevented them from haphazardly invading the Rift Valley, which might have caused antagonism between KADU peoples.

Thus KANU's policy came to resemble KADU's, although at the price of alienating some within its own ranks who did not believe that Africans should pay for the land on which they were settled or that enough land had been provided for the landless. The new emphasis on economic development by consolidation, registration, and cash crops rather than by further land resettlement was confirmed by the parties' response to the Gaitskill and World Bank missions. The declaration by the Council of Ministers about preserving African spheres of influence and the actions of the Regional Boundaries Commission to respect KADU's political control of the smaller African communities combined with resettlement to reassure KADU-supporting communities that KANU-supporting communities would not invade their spheres. The fears which had led KADU to advocate *majimbo* were thus considerably diminished.

KANU's emerging strategy differed from that of the colonial administration and the parties represented in the previous minority coalition government. It did not give priority to European interests over African interests but allowed European cooperation in a common quest for economic development in which primary reliance would be placed on African contributions. KANU was willing to respect the integrity particularly of African minorities in ways that did not involve expensive outlays of funds (like resettlement) or diminish national unity (like *majimbo*). It distinguished between constitutional unity and political unity under a one-party state in opposing *majimbo* but tolerating the Boundaries Commission decisions that helped KADU consolidate its strength. Finally, KANU took the view that the economic and social well-being of the African people lay in long-term economic growth which would provide employment and security, if not land, for all, rather than in short-term solutions like immediate land resettlement to provide for the African landless. But, unlike similar policies in the 1950s, the policy put much more emphasis upon contributions by African than by European producers.

CONSTITUTIONAL AND POLITICAL INTEGRATION

The constitutional and political reorganization of Kenya has been directed in large measure toward removing the institutional safeguards devised by, and on behalf of, those minorities that sought to protect themselves against the possibility of an arbitrary and irresponsible independent government. Most of these safeguards were enshrined in the *Majimbo* Constitution: the reservation of substantial powers to semi-autonomous regional governments, the upper house or Senate, and the Central Land Board. The peaceful constitutional removal of these safeguards, together with the consensus on policy that had begun to emerge between KANU and KADU, left KADU little basis for continued opposition to the KANU government, and the way was prepared for KADU's voluntary merger with the government party.

The *Majimbo* Constitution was an extremely long and detailed document that emerged from negotiations at the London Constitutional Conference at Lancaster House in 1962 and 1963. It made provisions designed to guarantee to every citizen, especially in the Asian and European minorities, a comprehensive set of political and economic rights. Constitutions are notorious for their observance in the breach in some countries, but it is worthwhile to point out these rights, as well as the other central provisions of the constitution, because the KANU government has on the whole been very scrupulous in observing the letter and spirit of these provisions. This observance arises in part from the convictions of Kenya's leaders and in part from the idea of convincing those inside and outside the country with capital to invest that Kenya is a politically safe country for their investment. Observance of constitutional protections serves the political end of creating economic development, in the view of Kenya's leadership.

An essential feature of the *Majimbo* Constitution was the broad range of powers given exclusively or concurrently to the regional governments at the expense of the national government. In particular, the regions gained a large measure of control over land and land policy. Apart from certain trust lands, including settlement-scheme lands and land whose title was vested in the county councils, and with the exception of the Nairobi area, all land was vested in the regions. This was never fully defined, since the regional constitution lasted only a little over two years. However, the intention in leaving the disposal of land to the regions was to prevent the national government from interfering with existing land-tenure patterns, or encouraging or condoning any large-scale migration of persons between ethnic spheres of influence to the disadvantage of smaller groups in less densely populated areas. In short, the measure vesting land in the regions, more than any other provision, indicated the government's determination to protect the integrity of ethnic communities against possible domination by other communities that might possess a popular majority and command the central government. In addition, the regions were given exclusive control over agricultural services outside the land-resettlement schemes and concurrent authority with the central government on matters concerning land resettlement. On land resettlement, the regions were to be responsible for selection of the settlers to go onto the settlements, while the central government would be responsible for administering the schemes and purchasing the land. The effect of this provision was to prevent the central government from using the settlement schemes as a means of breaking down existing tribal spheres of influence by moving "alien" tribes into a region via the settlement schemes.

Finally, the *Majimbo* Constitution attempted to divide governmental authority at the central level. The introduction of the Senate as a second chamber of Parliament reflected KADU's strategy of attempting to create constitutional protections for the smaller tribes whose support it commanded against the larger tribes which KANU represented.[25] The Senate was created to insure a substantial voice for smaller tribes, which would be outnumbered in the lower house by the large ethnic communities. Said Ronald Ngala, "We believe that a two-chamber Parliament with a Senate especially charged with preserving the rights of the regions is the only way to ensure the continuing liberty of the individual."[26] The European and Asian groups stood to gain, too, from any measure designed to protect minority African communities.

In common with other features of the constitution drawn up at the Lancaster House Conference of 1962, the Central Land Board reflected the interests of the smaller African communities and the European settlers who hoped to protect themselves against an independent African government elected by universal suffrage.[27] The eight-member CLB was to be led by a chairman and a deputy chairman appointed by the governor, who, it was generally expected, would come from outside the country. In addition, the governor was

25. See also J. H. Proctor, "The Role of the Senate in the Kenya Political System," *Parliamentary Affairs,* Vol. XVIII, no. 4 (Autumn, 1965).

26. *East African Standard,* February 12, 1962.

27. Subsequent discussion of changes in the CLB reflected these views on the part of the KC. See *ibid.,* March 30, 1962.

to appoint one member to represent each region, acting in accordance with the advice of the presidents of the respective regional assemblies. There would also be a representative of the Kenya government, appointed by the governor on the advice of the prime minister, plus a representative, appointed by the governor on the advice of the CLB chairman, for the European settlers who wanted to sell their land. The European community understood and expected that the chairman would also protect the interests of the settlers. The Central Land Board was given comprehensive and complete control over the settlement program by the 1962 Lancaster House Conference, a grant that subsequently proved embarrassing to the Kenya government. The constitution, as it read after the 1962 conference, gave the CLB "sole responsibility for the formulation and implementation of settlement schemes in the Scheduled Areas (the European farming areas)." The European community sought the CLB's independence of the central government in order to prevent an elected African government from denying them the full value of the land they wished so badly to sell. KADU wished the board to be composed of representatives of the regions as a further safeguard, to prevent the central government from introducing into settlement schemes settlers of ethnic groups different from those that inhabited the remainder of the region. KADU was able to reinforce this safeguard by writing into the constitution a provision that the regional authorities would be consulted on the ethnic composition of the various settlement schemes, with a right of appeal to the Supreme Court in case the CLB and a regional government could not agree.

Within each region there would be a regional assembly which would be substantially a replica of the lower house of the national Parliament. The assemblies were to elect presidents who would be the principal spokesmen for the regions. The central government and the regional assemblies were each to exercise executive authority in the regions and to administer the responsibilities entrusted to them by the constitution.

Immediately after the Lancaster House conferees signed the document outlining the framework of Kenya's future constitution,

KANU began to campaign for its revision and promised that, given the necessary electoral support, KANU would remove those features of the document that established fragmented decision-making by providing for semiregional autonomy and separate administration of the land program as well as two chambers of Parliament.

KANU's first step in strengthening the central government was to modify the powers allocated to the Central Land Board. The creation of a Ministry of Land Settlement and Water Development after the 1962 Constitutional Conference should in itself have been seen as an indication of KANU's intentions regarding the Central Land Board. If the CLB was to have sole responsibility for the formulation and implementation of the settlement schemes, there would scarcely have been any need for a separate ministry. The understanding seems to have been that the Ministry of Land Resettlement would be created to last during the period prior to self-government for the purpose of assisting the Land Development and Settlement Board, which had been administering the schemes up to that point.[28] A number of officials in positions of responsibility for the schemes seem to have thought that the Ministry of Land Resettlement would eventually be reabsorbed into the Ministry of Agriculture. On the other hand, many officials in the new ministry came from the middle ranks of the Department of Agriculture and were told that they would have no possibility of advancing in the Agriculture Department because of the approach of independence and should consider settlement as an alternative path of upward mobility or continued employment.[29] They were not, it appears, given any

28. The settlement schemes were to have a period of two and a half years of special administration by the Department of Settlement, after which they were to be incorporated in the normal rural development administration by the other ministries. Consequently, many in authority considered that the Department of Settlement would eventually be reincorporated in the Department of Agriculture.

29. Leslie Brown, "The Settlement Schemes," pt. 8, *Kenya Weekly News,* no. 2070, October 15, 1965. Brown was former chief agriculturalist in the Kenya government's Department of Agriculture. He said: "In order to staff the Settlement Department effectively many of the most experienced officers were taken from the Agriculture Department so that the Department was seriously weakened. There was nothing else to be done. Most of the men who were coming toward the senior posts were told that there were no prospects of promotion for them and they had the choice between staying in a dead end job which they liked or doing something less attractive but better paid. In almost all cases filthy lucre won, as it usually does, and it was well for the Settlement Department that it did" (p. 22).

indication that the Settlement Ministry would be a long-term proposition.

With the creation of the Million Acre Scheme program in August, 1962, it became apparent to Bruce McKenzie, the minister, and to his senior civil servants that the constitutional provisions regarding the Central Land Board were administratively unacceptable as well as politically undesirable from the standpoint of KANU. KANU's political objections have already been described. And neither the Central Land Board nor the existing LDSB, with which it shared many structural similarities, was suitable for the kind of planning and administrative demands the Million Acre Scheme presented. In 1961, the Land Development and Settlement Board replaced the European Agricultural Settlement Board (EASB).[30] The differences among the boards were very few. The CLB had appointed African representatives to represent the regions; this distinguished it from its predecessors, which had included European settlers and civil servants from the Ministry of Agriculture. The LDSB differed from the EASB only in that it was intended to be multiracial in its concerns. Each of these boards was contemplated as a sort of board of directors with a very limited staff that would see to the formulation and implementation of the settlement schemes and the needs of the settlers. But the requirements of the Million Acre Scheme were vastly different from those of the post–World War II European settlement schemes. The EASB had been created to serve the needs of two thousand Europeans who emigrated from Britain to take up farming in Kenya. The EASB was perfectly appropriate for a limited number of settlers who were well-educated by African standards, who had a certain amount of capital of their own, and who were accustomed to working within a cash economy even if they lacked particular farming skills. The board was established and administered by European settler farmers with their tenants' interests at heart. In each of these particulars, the EASB was therefore inappropriate for a program which purported to serve the interests of Africans, who as a group lacked education, farming skills, the experience of previous employment, thorough acquaintance with a modern cash

---

30. This was incorporated in the Agriculture (Amendment) Bill passed November 18, 1960.

economy, and capital resources of their own. There were, further-more, 35,000 African families rather than 2,000 to accommo-date.

Since the EASB structure was so inappropriate for the Million Acre Scheme, why was it used at all? The reason most frequently given has been that use of existing machinery was necessary if the programs were to be administered with the requisite speed. By itself, however, this is not sufficient, because the government could have decided to utilize the machinery of the African Development Board. This board and its successors had, since the end of World War II, been engaged in a comprehensive effort to assist Africans in develop-ing their land and had even overseen some resettlement of Africans within spheres of influence reserved to their particular communi-ties.[31] Unlike the CLB and the LDSB, it did not purchase land, but this disadvantage might have been more than compensated for by its experience in dealing with agricultural development by African farmers. At the very least, more effort might have been made to apply the lessons of these development programs, whether negative or positive, to the new settlement schemes.[32] One major reason that the EASB was used initially and then replaced by the LDSB was that Europeans wished to have an administrative apparatus over which they could exert some control. The LDSB, by general admission, was dominated by Europeans and civil servants sympathetic to them. The chairman of the LDSB, Mr. Lipscomb, was also the chairman of the Board of Agriculture (Scheduled Areas), which advised the minister on agricultural development in the European areas. He was also a European farmer in his own right and had written a book extolling the contribution of the European farmer settlers to the economic progress of Kenya.[33] The African Development Board, though it included European membership, was less settler-oriented, at least in

31. See Kenya, Ministry of Agriculture, Animal Husbandry and Water Resources, *African Land Development in Kenya* (Nairobi: Government Printer, 1962).
32. The government actually proposed in 1966 that the process work the other way, i.e., that the lessons of the recent schemes be applied to the problems of the old ones. Kenya, *Development Plan 1966–1970* (Nairobi: Government Printer, 1966), p. 147.
33. J. W. Lipscomb, *We Built a Country* (London: Faber & Faber, 1956). See also his *White Africans* (London: Faber & Faber, 1955).

part because its duties were focused exclusively on Africans. Its last chairman, R. O. Hennings, was more liberal in his views than most Europeans in or out of the civil service.

The remarkable feature about the LDSB is the fact that McKenzie, who sought its creation to get away from racialism, permitted its membership to have what he himself later considered undue European sympathies.[34] This apparent inconsistency may be explained in the following ways: that McKenzie recognized that the Europeans would have to have confidence in the settlement apparatus if they were to be prevented from leaving the country before they could be replaced by African settlers; that McKenzie paid a political price for having administrators of proven ability and knowledge of farming; that McKenzie's own view may have changed considerably and rapidly from the time when he first joined the government; and/or that McKenzie himself did not expect the massive Million Acre Scheme, which forced reorganization of the administration simply because of its size and comprehensive demands upon government services. A further possibility is that McKenzie and KANU saw from the start that a European-oriented settlement administration would help to retain the European settlers' confidence initially and at the same time provide an excuse for disassociating the government from the settlement program at a future date. Each

34. McKenzie argued during the debate on the opening of the White Highlands to African farmers that the EASB would need to be changed to get away from the biases of a board oriented toward European settlement. Subsequently McKenzie reportedly grew dissatisfied with the operations of the board and especially its chairman, and exercised frequently his power to give the board directions in order to get it moving on the settlement problem. There was a considerable problem in the board's operations because the price of the land as it was used by a single European farmer was, in some cases, more than its value collectively to a group of African smallholders. One of the board's difficulties was in getting the Europeans to accept something approaching the smallholding price of their land. In theory, all European settlers were to be free to sell or not to sell their land. The government in most cases wound up getting substantial blocks of land to form settlement schemes, especially in the area to the west of Central Province, known as the Kinangop (subsequently Nyandarua District). Many farmers and even some former civil servants argue that considerable pressure was eventually put on the farmers to sell their land at the "smallholding price." This conflicts with the panic of European farmers to sell as reported by the Kenya Coalition and the Convention of Associations, but is consistent with the view that many European farmers wanted a land-stabilization fund that would allow them to go when and if they chose. The land-resettlement schemes required them to make a choice at a given time once and for all.

of these reasons appears to have had at least some bearing on KANU's and McKenzie's actions.

The creation of the Central Land Board caused two further complications for the Kenya government. First, the new board could not constitutionally come into existence until June, 1963, so that for nearly a year it would be necessary to work with the old LDSB and all its inadequacies in dealing with the new and politically very important settlement program. For all parties, there was the danger that the LDSB would be unable to administer the program with sufficient dispatch to remove the worst of the political pressures that had made the Million Acre Scheme necessary before independence. One may even speculate that the necessity, three short weeks before independence, for a "crash program" to relieve pressures that independence would release among the African peoples arose from the organizational confusion and consequent delays during the early months of the Million Acre Scheme program.[35]

Second, even the new CLB was unsatisfactory from the administration's standpoint, and particularly from the standpoint of KANU, because of the composition of its membership and because of its apparent administrative inadequacy for such a comprehensive program. The real difficulty was that of political control, for the British government, the CDC, and the World Bank liked the idea of an independent body such as the CLB because they could fix upon it complete responsibility for the use of their funds. If settlement were to be administered in the normal way, several departments would be involved and responsibility would be hard to pin on any one minister or organization. From a financial standpoint, the independent board was also desirable because of the need to maintain separate accounting procedures for an organization that was to operate on semicommercial lines in contrast to other government ministries.[36] McKenzie and KANU, for somewhat similar reasons, could not

35. On the instructions of the president, a crash program was undertaken to settle several thousand Africans, mainly Kikuyu, in the Kinangop during the three weeks prior to independence. This will be discussed at greater length in chapter 5.

36. According to officials in the Ministry of Lands and Settlement, particularly N. S. Carey Jones, its permanent secretary and the officer administering the Settlement Fund, 1962–64.

accept that the proposed CLB be independent from any ministerial direction, because the Kenya government and not the CLB bore ultimate responsibility for any failure of the scheme to achieve economic success or refusal of settlers to repay land and development loans.[37] With KANU's growing concern for economic development, the government could not merely watch from the sidelines while a program operated which used such a heavy proportion of Kenya's development funds and upon which the growth of the economy was therefore dependent. Even the old LDSB was more desirable than the new board, for the Agricultural Act that established the LDSB included a provision that the Minister of Agriculture could give general or specific directions to the board, and the new constitution lacked any provision for ministerial guidance of the CLB.[38]

The Commonwealth Development Corporation was skeptical from the start about the appointment of Lipscomb as chairman and about the generally strong European influence on the LDSB.[39] The Colonial Office, on the other hand, thought that a single board rather than separate boards for European and African farming areas (as had existed previously) with strong European influence was completely consistent with multiracial principles but feared nonetheless the CDC might decide to pull out of its agreement to finance the development of Kenya's low-density settlement schemes over the issue.[40] The Colonial Office therefore tried to pacify the CDC by suggesting that its membership could be expected to include increasing numbers of Africans as time went on.[41] The CDC had more basic

---

37. Tom Mboya told the CDC and IBRD officials at meetings in London, on August 8, 1962, that they would have to trust the Kenya government on the matter of scheme administration, particularly of the loans. Consequently, he said, they would have to accept the Kenya government's ideas on the structure. He rejected the views of the CDC general manager that the CDC might try to shield the Kenya government from this somewhat onerous responsibility.

38. Compare the Agriculture (Amendment) Bill passed by the Legislative Council on November 18, 1960, with the Kenya Independence Order in Council of 1963.

39. The views in particular of the CDC's chairman, Lord Howick of Glendale (formerly Sir Evelyn Baring).

40. Gorell Barnes (Colonial Office) to (Sir) Patrick Renison, EAF 54/5/04, February 13, 1961.

41. *Ibid.*, and Renison EAF/S/04 (5/04) Cypher Telegram, February 13, 1961.

objections, however, for its officers felt that the interests of the European settlers selling the land and those of the settlers who would take their place were antithetical. They were the first to suggest the separation of land purchase from settlement and proposed that there be one board for each purpose. The CDC sought to protect the new Kenya government from what might prove an onerous and unpopular burden of collecting loan repayments from the settlers. However, KANU and KADU were united in thinking that this responsibility should be assumed directly by the Kenya government, whether or not it proved unpopular, since the government was in any event ultimately answerable for the economic success of the program.[42] The lenders were also worried about the relationship of their program to that of the new Million Acre Scheme, which involved less qualified farmers aiming at less ambitious economic targets. They hoped to have some form of independent administration to insure the integrity of their more ambitious schemes.[43] McKenzie's thinking seems to have paralleled that of the lending banks on the desirability of separate organizations for purchasing the land and implementing the programs.

Despite agreeing to the creation of an autonomous CLB when Kenya achieved self-government, McKenzie went ahead with a makeshift division of responsibility between the LDSB and the Department of Settlement, which was under his direct administration. The LDSB retained nominal responsibility for effecting government policy on settlement schemes. Its real task was only to arrange for the purchase of the land. The LDSB submitted proposed subprojects to the lending banks, but only after the government had reviewed them. The executive officer of the LDSB was also made director of settlement and in that capacity became responsible for maintaining liaison with other departments involved in the implementation of the settlement program and arranging for necessary administrative personnel. The director of settlement also gained the power to take the

42. Meeting at CDC Hedd Office; for pertinent comments, see *East African Standard,* May 16, 1963.
43. CDC, EMB 257/62 Amended, B 64/62 November 10, 1962.

initiative in proposing settlement plans to the LDSB for its approval rather than having to wait till the board proposed projects.[44] Consequently, the LDSB began to move into more of an advisory position than it had held and more of an advisory role than the future CLB would play. In these ways McKenzie took a step in the interim period toward integrating the settlement program with the administrative structure of the central government. In so doing he removed some of the safeguards that the lending banks and the European settlers relied upon, and he also made it possible to administer the program with more dispatch. He took this step with the apparent support of KADU.

The future Central Land Board members were to be chosen to represent the new regions created by the Regional Boundaries Commission. They were not necessarily required to be people with agricultural or administrative skills and knowledge—an additional reason for moving the new board into more of an advisory role. Their chief skill would be to determine which ethnic groups could be safely settled in any given area of the country. Until the CLB came into existence, there would be no specialized group within the government that could give reliable advice on this all-important question. Since McKenzie was dissatisfied with the officers of the LDSB and wanted specialized advice on the location of settlement programs and placement of settlers, he sought approval for an Interim Central Land Board with membership more closely resembling that of the future CLB. It was to include three members of KANU and three of KADU, on the assumption that there would be three KADU-oriented regions and three regional KANU strongholds. Thus McKenzie sought to bring the administration of land resettlement into line with the political contours of the existing KANU and KADU coalition government.

These changes in the structure of the settlement administration, although designed by a KANU minister and reflecting administrative and political realities as KANU perceived them, were worked

---

44. Agricultural (Amendment) Bill, passed in the Kenya Legislative Council November 18, 1960.

out within the framework of the coalition government and accepted by the KADU ministers. The World Bank and the CDC also accepted them, although most reluctantly, in the latter part of 1962. The reorganization became public knowledge only when the chairmanship of the new CLB became a public issue. The Colonial Office took a great deal of time to find a new chairman, partly because the nature of the appointment would be affected by the negotiations over what responsibilities the CLB was to assume, and partly because the Colonial Office could not find anyone suitable to accept the post. Early in 1963, the Colonial Office was able to announce that Major General Sir Geoffrey Bourne, a retired officer of some distinction in the British army, had accepted the position at a salary of £15,000 per annum.[45] On the same day the Kenya government announced that the CLB would have only the limited function of land purchase, while the regional and central governments would share the administration of the program.[46]

The appointment, the salary, and the change in the CLB's responsibilities caused political furor in Kenya. The Kenya government was appalled at the salary Bourne was to be paid and apparently had not been consulted before it had been established.[47] However, both KADU and KANU stood behind the proposed change in the responsibilities of the Central Land Board.[48] KADU accepted the Department of Settlement's proposed role in administering the program, on the assumption that the CLB would protect the interests of the various regions in purchasing land. Both parties opposed paying the chairman a higher salary than the Prime Minister of an independent Kenya would receive.[49] Neither KANU nor KADU looked favorably upon the appointment of a general to the CLB chairmanship. The Kenya Coalition complained that the changes in the responsibilities of the CLB constituted a breach of the 1962

45. *East African Standard,* March 1, 1963.
46. *Ibid.*
47. *Ibid.,* March 8, 1963.
48. Minutes of meetings held between officials of the Kenya government and the lenders at the Ministry of Lands and Settlement, September 11–14, 1962. See also *East African Standard,* March 8, 1963.
49. *East African Standard,* March 4, 8, 1963.

Lancaster House agreement and a further demonstration to them of the British government's untrustworthiness.[50] The KC thought the changes would put the settlement program back into the arena of party politics, where they alleged that the interests of the European settlers would suffer. General Bourne apparently did not realize in accepting the appointment that the role of the CLB had been at issue or that its responsibilities had been diminished. He was also apparently unaware that the European settlers looked to him as their special guardian. When he was told what the Euroepan settlers expected of him, he is reported to have asked, "Can't they read?" In March he resigned. In May the Colonial Office announced that Sir Richard Turnbull had accepted the chairmanship.[51] Turnbull had been instrumental in facilitating Tanzania's progress toward independence and was thus popular and acceptable among the African leaders. Turnbull had been chief secretary in the Kenya colonial administration in the early postwar years and was therefore also known and respected by the European settlers.

The importance of these pre-independence constitutional changes affecting the organization and operation of the land-resettlement program lay in the cooperation evident between KANU and KADU as partners in the coalition government. Despite the diminishing of the CLB's powers, which in turn meant lessened influence for the regional assemblies in the execution of the land-transfer program, KADU and its moderate European NKP allies supported the changes. Only the Kenya Coalition and the Convention of Associations were openly opposed to giving the central government more direct authority over land resettlement. This indication that the post–1962 Lancaster House Conference coalition between the two major African parties had led to the beginnings of a genuine *modus vivendi* for them came at the opening of the 1963 election campaign.[52] The victorious party in this election would lead Kenya to independence six months later. The major issue in this campaign

50. *Ibid.*, March 4, 5, 8, 1963.
51. *Ibid.*, May 16, 1963.
52. Agreement on this issue had actually preceded the public furor by about six months, and was worked out a few weeks after the announcement of the Million Acre Scheme.

was the desirability of *majimbo*. While the two African parties fought the election on this issue, they were compromising on one important aspect of the *Majimbo* Constitution—the question of who would control land policy.

In the 1963 campaign, KANU and KADU did not differ on the desirability of maintaining the constitutional provisions for individual rights, although these were designed with the fears of the European community as much in mind as the needs of Africans.[53] The main issue between the two parties was whether the *majimbo* structure of the constitution was necessary or desirable to further secure such rights. KANU argued that the ending of *majimbo* and the creation of a strong central government were essential if the political integrity of Kenya was to be insured and if the economic development of Kenya was to be effected successfully and efficiently. KADU leaders were not unmindful of the need for national integrity and economic development, but they considered that the diversity of ethnic groups within Kenya, and the possibility of misuse of governmental power by a government that did not represent all such groups, made *majimbo* necessary and desirable.

The contrast between the stances of leaders of both parties during the election and the evidence of an incipient *modus vivendi* between them in the coalition government over land policy revealed the nature of the task of building grass-roots political rapport for the government after independence. In the short term, KADU fought the 1963 election on the issue of maintaining the *majimbo* features of the constitution. In the longer term, expansion of the *modus vivendi* of KADU and KANU would require the KADU leaders to convince the rank and file and the grass-roots leadership of their party that the fears which inspired *majimbo* no longer justified such elaborate institutional precautions. Similarly, KANU fought the election on a platform of abolishing *majimbo* as a necessary step in the task of encouraging economic development and protecting national integrity. The task of KANU's future government would be

53. Clyde Sanger and John Nottingham, "The Kenya General Election of 1963," *Journal of Modern African Studies*, II, no. 1 (1964), 1–40.

to persuade its rank-and-file supporters and their spokesmen that wholesale attacks upon law and order, free land, free education, and free health facilities would not follow immediately after independence.

KANU won the 1963 election and became the government that would lead Kenya through internal self-government from June to December and into independence. Although KANU won nearly 70 percent of the popular vote, it did not gain enough seats in the new Senate and the House of Representatives to fulfill its election pledge to end *majimbo* by constitutional means.[54] In the House of Representatives, approximately two-thirds of the seats went to KANU, but in the Senate the party received a majority of only two seats over KADU. The actual requirements and procedure for amending the Kenya constitution had, somewhat strangely, been left out of the Kenya Order-in-Council promulgating the new constitution. The draft of the constitution that appeared after the 1962 Lancaster House Conference had suggested that 75 percent majorities in both houses of the Kenya Parliament be required to amend the "ordinary" provisions of the constitution.[55] To amend so-called entrenched provisions affecting the Senate, regional autonomy, and the rights of individuals, the 1962 Lancaster Conference report had suggested that a 90 percent majority of the Senate be required in addition to 75 percent of the House.[56]

KANU claimed that its substantial election victory had been a mandate to change the constitution according to its own preferences. KADU insisted that KANU had been given a mandate only to govern the country. KANU argued, further, that in addition to creating a costly and inefficient duplication of governmental services, the *Majimbo* Constitution did not serve the interests of constitutional government by making the amending procedure so difficult. The new colonial secretary, Sandys, agreed to reopen the issue at a further

54. *East African Standard,* January 23, 1963; also, see Sanger and Nottingham, "General Election."
55. *Kenya Independence Order in Council of 1963,* December 10, 1963.
56. Great Britain, Colonial Office, *Report of the Kenya Constitutional Conference, 1962,* British Sessional Papers, 1962, Vol. XI (875), Cmnd. 1700 (London: H.M.S.O., 1962).

conference in London in September following the election.[57] There KADU argued that the existing amending requirements should be left as they were, while KANU wanted 65 percent majorities of both houses to be sufficient to amend any provision of the constitution.[58] Sandys accepted two-thirds approval of a proposed amendment to the "ordinary" provisions in a referendum as a suitable alternative to gaining 75 percent majorities in both houses, which was maintained as one means of passing an amendment. In effect, an amendment to the constitution proposed by KANU could be passed if it were approved by the same percentage of voters as had favored KANU in the most recent election.[59]

During the next two years, KANU succeeded in making the constitutional changes that it desired without serious danger of opposition in the House and without undertaking a popular referendum. The explanations for the peaceful constitutional transition are to be found in the flexibility of the Colonial Office, in KANU's determination after taking power to pursue moderate policies calculated to enhance economic development without offending the sensitivities of Kenya's racial and ethnic minorities, and in the KADU leadership's shrewd recognition that its best course lay in supporting and underwriting KANU's policies rather than in risking further disunity in the country by defending *majimbo* until it was effectively demolished by constitutional means. Sandys' willingness to renegotiate the amendment provisions of Kenya's constitution following the elections, and, perhaps, his tactic of not writing the amendment provisions into the final draft of the constitution until after the election, suggested that the Colonial Office was not prepared to permit the defense of minorities as a possible threat to political unity.[60] The indications of possible cooperation between KADU and KANU over the Central Land Board issue and KANU's general moderate stance on the land issue could only have strengthened the Colonial Office's willingness to be flexible on the amending procedure.

KANU's moderation and KADU's unwillingness to force

57. Proctor, "Role of the Senate," pp. 395–96.
58. *Ibid.*
59. *Ibid.*
60. *Ibid.*, p. 395.

KANU into a militant position became apparent in the six months prior to the June, 1963, election and in the year following. In January, 1963, the Kenya African Freedom Fighters Union was created and its president, J. K. Maina, announced that 25,000 people were expected to join.[61] The reason for its creation was expressly that KANU had not carried out the promises made during the elections in 1961. Shortly after independence, the general secretary of the Kenya Plantation and Agricultural Workers Union said that the African Nationalists had made promises to the masses that, once the British were gone, the African government would control all land, work toward equality in land distribution, and insure that landless Africans received their share of the land. These pronouncements did not alleviate the fears of remaining European farmers and other expatriates, and they bothered the new African government, which was beginning to develop programs furthering general economic development at the price of immediate relief of landlessness and unemployment. KANU replied by preaching unity both to dissatisfied Africans and to worried Europeans. To the Africans, Kenyatta said that Mau Mau was a disease and all Africans should work together as one nation. "We were stupid," he said, "to be divided allowing the Europeans to keep divisions among us. Whether you were in detention or in the forests, a chief, a headman or an *askari* [guard, soldier], all Africans are brothers." [62] At the same time, KANU showed solicitude for the European farmers in Nyandarua, where the bulk of the Kikuyu settlements were to go, for the leadership blocked the formation of KANU branches there after the 1963 election.[63] Activities associated with the local party branches had increased European settlers' fears for the maintenance of law and order. Similarly, McKenzie quietly established a policy of allowing Europeans in the areas around Kitale and Nakuru to continue to farm and encouraged them to stay.[64] In each instance, the govern-

61. *East African Standard,* January 10, 1963.
62. *Kenya Weekly News,* February 28, 1964, p. 11.
63. *Ibid.,* August 31, 1963.
64. *Ibid.,* March 16, 27, and July 5, 1963, shows that farmers were concerned about their future in the Nyandarua area, that some were buying land in the Rift after selling land elsewhere, and that some KANU politicians were unhappy at this prospect. Also, in Land Development and Settlement Paper 35 the government said, in connection with the new

ment's posture reflected not only a sincere desire on the part of Kenyatta and many of his senior ministers for unity but also respect for the European contribution to the economy. Finally, Kenyatta, accompanied by several of his cabinet members, told a large audience of primarily European farmers shortly after independence:

> Kenya is large enough and its potential is great. We can all work together to make this country great and show other countries that different racial groups can live and work together. Some European farmers are worried about their future. . . . I say to you today that we want you to stay and to farm and to farm well in this country. Let's join hands and work together for the betterment of the land. I beg you to believe that this is the policy of the Government—we must work together and try to trust one another.[65]

KADU's weakness after the 1963 elections contributed to a series of defections to KANU. One KADU member crossed the floor immediately in the Senate. In September, six African Peoples party members of the House and two in the Senate joined the government benches. Motion for a KADU-KANU merger in October failed, but immediately after independence three prominent members of KADU crossed to KANU in the House of Representatives, to be followed a few days later by KADU's chief whip in the House, who argued: "It is best to line up together as brothers and build our nation." [66] KANU, in early 1964, had the requisite three-fourths

---

scheme: "The Kenya Coalition Government attach the greatest importance to arrangements being made to enable the Land Bank to finance land transactions outside the proposed areas of settlement. It is an essential feature of their economic policy that the areas around Kitale and Nakuru should be kept free of settlement over the next five years and retained in their existing state of large economic holdings to feed the country and to provide the dairy products, cereals, etc., required to maintain local industries and Kenya's share of the general East African market. African ministers are anxious that European farmers in these areas who are determined to leave should be enabled to do so since they are unlikely to maintain the productivity of their farms, even, in the absence of the possibility of sale, abandon. . . . At the same time there will be European farmers in the settled areas who wish to stay in Kenya but on farms out of the settled areas. African ministers are anxious that such of these as need assistance to take up other farms should be enabled to do so and help sustain the economy."

65. *Ibid.,* February 28, 1964, p. 6, quoted in the editorial.
66. *East African Standard,* December 2, 1963. Comments by Mr. Khasakhala.

majority it needed in the lower house but still lacked this majority in the Senate. Rather than rely upon the Senate to block the constitutional amendment, Ngala announced that KADU would join the government and vote for the constitutional amendment that would make Kenya a republic and end *majimbo*. His reasons for doing so amounted to an endorsement of KANU's position on the need for unity. He said that a united front to the world and a common cause on the problems facing Kenya and East Africa must take precedence over personal dignity, tribal or racial jealousies, or differences on economic and social policies. KADU might have been able to force a referendum by blocking the constitutional changes in the Senate, but at the cost of deepening divisions in Kenya rather than healing them. Later statements suggested that the difference in policy between KANU and KADU and the threat to KADU-supporting communities from those supporting KANU were less than the dangers of creating the fragmentation that might have resulted if KADU had fought to the last to preserve *majimbo*. It appears therefore that a *modus vivendi* on policy questions, if not an absolute consensus, had emerged between KANU and KADU during the year and a half that they had governed together in the coalition. This *modus vivendi* overrode the divisive effects of the election and the approach to independence, in turn making possible a peaceful constitutional change in the directions KANU desired. Indication of the growing policy consensus came in the fact that between 1964 and 1966 former KADU leaders achieved very high places in the government at the expense of the left wing of KANU, which had been supporting the government despite moves in the direction of moderation by Kenyatta, Gichuru, Kiano, and Mboya. Ngala, the leader of KADU, is now a senior minister in the government and a vice president of KANU. Moi, the chairman of KADU, is now vice president of Kenya, replacing Joseph Murimbi, who had in turn replaced Odinga, and is a vice president of KANU. Ngala replaced Odinga as chairman of the KANU parliamentary party in July, 1964.

The consequence of the pre-independence growth of a *modus vivendi* between the major parties, and of the constitutional unification which resulted, has been the decline of political activity per se as an integral part of the process of nation-building. Nation-building includes developing the economy, expanding training facilities to produce manpower to run the developing economy, and encouraging such social amenities as full attention to economic development will permit. Nation-building has not included creating increased political awareness among the people as a whole or modernizing the institutions of political expression. The institutions of political activity—the parties, the assembly, etc.—have remained, but their function is more to lend legitimacy to decisions already taken by the government than to initiate policies and engage in allocating social values. They exist more to create the impression of formal constitutionalism for international consumption than actually to undertake the process of articulating and aggregating political opinions and creating legislation. If policies and political roles have any place in the process of nation-building in Kenya, it is in an alliance with economic activities, roles, and institutions. The alliance is such that political activity is empirically indistinguishable from economic activity, and the two are fused in policy-making, administration, and grass-roots responses. If modernization is described as the process of increasing specialization and the manifestation of separate roles, modernization in theory is something quite distinct from Kenya's policy of modernization.

AFRICAN SOCIALISM AND LAND POLICY

The KANU government attempted to give ideological expression to the new manifestations of unity between the two major parties in the publication of a Kenya version of African socialism.[67] The African socialism manifesto set forth the outlines of a political and economic system within which efforts were to be made to achieve social objectives believed to be universal: political equality; social justice; "human dignity including freedom of conscience"; freedom

---

67. Kenya, *African Socialism and Its Application to Planning in Kenya* (Nairobi: Government Printer, 1965).

from want, disease, and exploitation; equal opportunities; and "high and growing per capita incomes, equitably distributed." Basic principles of African socialism, Kenya style, were applied to critical nation-building issues.

The basic message of the manifesto was that Kenya proposed to establish a political and economic system fully reflecting its political independence. To establish this independence, Kenya was to draw upon the best of African traditions, remain ready to adapt to changing circumstances, and avoid a satellite relationship with other countries either individually or in groups. Two traditions were given particular emphasis: political democracy and mutual social responsibility. Political democracy in contemporary Kenya was to mean, as it was supposed to have meant in pre-colonial times, political equality undiminished by economic inequalities and unqualified by the rule of political elites regarding themselves as superior or as a vanguard. Political democracy in Kenya would, therefore, be distinguished from communism because there would be no elite vanguard, and from capitalism because economic inequality would not be permitted to dilute political equality. Mutual social responsibility meant in the pre-colonial past, and was to mean in the future, that all would participate in society's prosperity, because all would cooperate in the building of such prosperity. It implied "an extension of the African family spirit to the nation as a whole, with the hope that ultimately the same spirit can be extended to ever larger areas.[68] As a corollary, socially productive behavior as defined by the state would have to prevail over individual unregulated pursuit of self-interest.

> The idea of mutual social responsibility presupposes a relation between society, its members and the State. It suggests that the State is a means by which people collectively impose on individual members behaviour that is more socially constructive than that which each would impose on himself. The State, therefore, has a continuing function to perform, not in subordinating the individual in society but in enhancing the role of the individual in society. Individuals

68. *Ibid.*, p. 4.

derive satisfaction not only from the goods they consume but also from those they accumulate.[69]

Mutual social responsibility, rather than political democracy, became the more important tradition with respect to nation-building in Kenya. The former was assigned a direct relationship to the processes of economic development, whereas the latter was to remain independent of economic relationships. Since political democracy was to be maintained without regard to any economic equality that might exist, the converse was that political democracy might not be employed to remove existing inequalities. Mutual social responsibility, in the government's view, meant that "all citizens must contribute to the degree they are able, to the rapid development of the economy and society." For those who did not contribute actively, mutual social responsibility had meant in the past that "African society had the power and duty to impose sanctions on those who refused to contribute their fair share of hard work to the common endeavor.[70]

Land policy was to be one of the prime illustrations of African socialism in operation. The land-resettlement program was a negative example of African socialism because it offended two fundamental principles of the new ideology. The program "was inherited from the British and was designed more to aid those Europeans who wanted to leave than the Africans who received the land. . . . Land problems," the manifesto continued, "should not be settled on terms decided in the United Kingdom." [71] Land resettlement was also deemed inappropriate because it allegedly made uneconomic use of scarce resources. Consequently, the purposes of African socialism could best be served by returning to an emphasis on land consolidation and registration. "Consolidation and registration will make farm credit and modern methods of agriculture possible and should expand employment much more rapidly than settlement can, by

69. *Ibid.*, pp. 11–12.
70. *Ibid.*
71. *Ibid.*, pp. 28–29.

bringing more land into productive use." [72] In addition, African socialism would be furthered by measures to insure the efficient use of resources: proper use of loans, prompt collection of due payments, insistence that the minority who refuse consolidation be forced to undertake it and that the recalcitrant Africans be made to join cooperatives. Idle and mismanaged land would not be permitted. The manifesto suggested the possibility of taking measures to "establish ceilings on individual ownership of property." This has never been implemented.

Kenya's new version of African socialism did not include an answer to a basic political problem that began to plague KANU's emerging nation-building strategy. The inherited experience of colonialism and European political and economic influence made it very difficult for the new African government to adopt any policy of agricultural development whose legitimacy would not be undermined in the eyes of those Africans who remembered pre-independence political and economic developments. The African manifesto did not specify what was to be done with the existing land-resettlement program. The program went against present objectives by using resources to serve European more than African interests, but the government still retained a very large investment in the program. The legitimacy of government agricultural programs designed to further African socialism is susceptible to political attack not only because such programs have expenses as well as benefits; also, the costs are magnified when associated with deprivations during colonial times, and the benefits are discounted when associated with programs established previously by the colonial administration and Europeans in their own interests. Only a totally new economic program, such as industrialization of the country, or a novel reorganization of its social and economic infrastructure, could avoid being associated with colonial and European influences. But the government has chosen to concentrate on building a sound economy capable of resisting political attacks by those who seek to perpetuate

72. *Ibid.*

Kenya nationalism. Conversely, it has argued against sacrificing the economy in the short run while implementing thoroughly African innovations.

THE POLITICS OF RESOURCE ALLOCATION

The processes of allocating economic resources and stimulating productive efforts by the citizens of Kenya have reflected the principles of mutual social responsibility and political democracy in two important ways. First, the government has attempted to stimulate individuals to use economic resources effectively in the interests of economic development at the expense of private economic interests whenever the two conflict. However, as the quotation from the government's policy statement indicates, private accumulation of economic assets may be seen as compatible with the nation's general objective of building the economy. Second, and more fundamental, the allocation of resources and their efficient use occur without much reference to the sphere of formal politics. Political democracy in Kenya does not appear to suffer any less or any more from the influence of economic inequality than in other countries seeking to maintain democracy. The important point, however, is that the converse is quite clearly realized: the practice of political democracy may not be employed to restructure economic relationships. Since the formal political process is largely external to the processes of allocating and developing economic resources, those who seek to influence the allocation of economic values must do so through the economic process itself. The authoritative allocation of social values and the authoritative allocation of economic resources tend to become synonymous with one another. Citizens indicate their political demands by the way they respond to the government's ideas on how economic resources can be used most efficiently. Political support for exisitng allocations is indicated by citizens' following the government's advice. This fusion of economic and political behavior is not necessarily a conscious strategy. In the case of decision-makers, it is the natural consequence of their belief that there is little need for formal political debate and discussion on the wisdom of economic development. Discussions on economic policy occur in Parliament, for example, but usually after the decisions have already been made by the government. In the case of the citizens themselves, the fusion of economic and political behavior results from the unprofitability of political dissent. Dissent may be tolerated, but the basic allocation of resources is not changed as a result. The remainder of this chapter will trace the operation of this phenomenon at the level of national political decision-making. Chapter 6 will illustrate this theory at the grass-roots level in the settlement schemes.

The parliamentary system contributes to the isolation of formal institutions of political decision-making, because it tends to result in centralized policy-making by members of the cabinet who are, in addition to being party leaders, also heads of the bureaucracy. In Kenya the isolation may be more advanced in that ministers who on the whole achieve power based on their influence in the party are dependent upon the technical expertise of their subordinate civil servants in proportion as economic development is assigned preeminent political importance by the ministers themselves.

The importance of administrative initiative in the planning process and the relatively small place of political debate over alternatives in the implementation of economic development policies are indicated by the structure of Kenya's planning process.[73] There are six essential planning and development functions: to develop knowledge of existing resources available for use in achieving given economic objectives; to devise specific targets for development which will contribute toward eventual realization of the broad goals; to devise a strategy for mobilizing existing public resources and guiding the use of private resources; to coordinate and communicate plans to insure "reciprocal flow of information and analysis" between planning authorities, ministries, local authorities, and public and private enterprise; to implement plans by assigning tasks for authorities in ministries and in local areas and evaluating results upon the basis of reports from these authorities; and to revise and adapt plans on the

73. Kenya, *Development Plan.*

basis of these reports where targets prove unrealistic. There are development committees consisting of heads of departments or the senior representatives of the various ministries in a given district. The development advisory committees for each district consist of these same people plus members of the county council, the local chairman of the KANU branch, members of the Parliament from the district, and two or three leading citizens selected by the district or provincial commissioner from the district and provincial committees respectively on the advice of their respective development committees.

Despite the existence of these advisory committees, there is no evidence in the operation of these planning processes to suggest that the local representatives have enough influence in the allocation and implementation of resources in their districts to overrule the appointed administrative officers. The emphasis is on explaining the projects to local authorities and representatives of private enterprise and coordinating their activities with those of the government hierarchy; it is not on a dialogue between the government hierarchy and the private enterprise which is supposed to do the implementing. Consequently, the planning process and implementation of plans are a two-step process: (1) decision-making; and (2) the response, which may be either positive or negative. There is little opportunity to modify policies according to a continuing discussion and evaluation of the programs in question. The first step in this decision-response model comes between the ministry charged with economic planning and the other ministries in the central government. The other ministries find themselves in a position of having to accept or reject initiatives from the planning agency based on its integrated blueprints. At the local level, the decision-response model operates between the administrative officers and the ordinary citizens in the economy, who are supposed to respond favorably. The citizen's option is not one of modifying the policy or selecting alternatives, but of accepting or not accepting it. Among ordinary farmers on a settlement, for instance, this takes the form of performing the activity required or not performing it, rather than of helping to decide on the merits of the program or effecting its revision. The directives of administrative officers vary from suggestions to demands, but, even in the case of demands—e.g., loan repayment—there is safety in numbers and in the inability of a government officer to counteract widespread noncooperation on the part of the people. Hence, even when demands are made on the people, there are limits within which they can safely indicate their displeasure by simply not performing the required act.

There may be no alternative to this decision-response political model in the form of a real dialogue on broad policy and specific aspects of its implementation. Even where, as in cooperative societes, local people are elected to serve in responsible positions, the record does not always bear out their faith in democracy. If the measure in question is not popular, the mere fact that it is implemented by locally elected officials who presumably have agreed voluntarily to the measure does not guarantee a positive response.[74]

Elected politicians representing the people in local bodies and in Parliament can do very little to restore the policy-making initiative to the party or to the legislative branch of the government. Fundamentally, the only constructive role they can fulfill is to identify themselves with the administration in their districts and try to help sell the development projects or procedures recommended or insisted upon by the administration. If they do so, they must accept the shortcomings of existing development programs that appear when the programs are judged according to the expectations politicians have led their people to have of the African government in the times before independence. Politicians then gain favor with the administration, but at the price of alienating their own constituents. If they oppose administration projects or insist on their modification, they may oppose whatever benefits the administration is able to convey to the people of a given district and may be pictured by the administration as mere troublemakers. The basic point is that many of the politicians, through lack of knowledge of the technical requirements of development, do not find themselves in a position to do anything but provide trusting support or opposition. They are not

74. See chapter 6.

ordinarily able to suggest constructive alternatives in a language that the technicians or the administrators understand and appreciate. The problem for the M.P.'s is that they have no way of demonstrating meaningfully to their constituents that they have done or can do anything to deserve support. They are not, and do not appear to be, closely associated with the decision-making process, unless they appear as tools of the administration. Ordinary citizens can quietly refuse to support government policy by just not doing what is requested, but if the politicians advocate this kind of noncompliance they are immediately shown to be troublemakers working against the people's best interests. Even those who otherwise disapprove of the government and may wish to support politicians who oppose the regime will not support them when the chips are down, since power is seen to lie with the administration and not with the politicians as representatives of the party.

A major principle of Kenya's African socialism is that state supervision of the process of economic development should be undertaken by a flexible and wide range of controls rather than through any fixed, universally applicable set of control mechanisms.[75] These controls vary from ownership to minimal regulation by the state or private enterprise. However, this flexibility in regulation is not primarily a response to popular wishes. It is rather a response to the probable changing nature of the economic problems of the country and the requirements of those who can provide capital, resources, and personnel to assist the development process. "Variety is an important means of attraction whether it is customers, savings, capital or management that is wanted."[76] Thus the relationship between the state and the participants in development may be influenced by factors external to this relationship. A specific example is the system chosen to administer the settlement schemes when, before independence, the lending banks preferred a body somewhat independent of the government but one which would maintain very close supervision over the settlers. On the one hand, the intention to create certain

75. Kenya, *African Socialism*, p. 12.
76. *Ibid.*

changes in the social and economic environment of the country may cause the administration initiatives to operate more or less independently of the formal political processes. On the other hand, the institutions and mechanisms by which the government deals with participants in the development process may be affected by the need to create control mechanisms reflecting requirements other than those of the rank-and-file participants.

This account of the allocation of economic resources resembles in some ways the style of government that existed prior to 1960, when development occurred largely on administrative initiative and in the absence of any very substantial reliance on formal political processes for the allocation of social values. There is, however, a vital difference. Before 1960, development occurred, notably in land consolidation, on the initiative of the colonial administration, which bypassed African leaders in detention and sought to create a social class that could act as a buffer against these leaders and their militant nationalism. In the present situation, development policies are established and administered very largely by elected Africans and designated expatriates in whom the people are presumed to have confidence. Their task is almost certainly not undertaken with the idea of building a social class hostile to political activity. Rather, they must try to convert the popular orientation away from economic and social behavior or expectations created by nationalist mobilization prior to independence and toward behavior which indicates acceptance of nation-building projects proposed by the government. The government's aim is not to oppose the nationalist movement but to build economic and social progress upon the foundations of its political achievements. The consequence of this policy is that the relevance of political aspects of nation-building, in the sense of distinct political activity per se, seems to have ended with the achievement of independence as a direct result of the government's insistence upon economic development as the prime objective of nation-building. The Kenya government did not choose its policies because of hostility to formal political activity, but the deemphasis of channels of formal political activity is one consequence of the emphasis upon economic development as the government's first objective.

The deemphasis on the specialized political input functions of interest articulation and aggregation has affected the manner in which social values are allocated and in which outputs are created. The process of value allocation is no longer activated so much by demands communicated to decision-makers through party and legislative spokesmen as by "perceived demands," demands by decision-makers themselves based on their perception of the kind of society they believe Kenya should try to create. Furthermore, having accepted funds from international agencies and foreign governments for the purpose of developing the Kenya nation, the Kenya decision-makers are apt to be activated by the demands of these external lenders rather than by their own people, whose desires cannot be met immediately because of the development objectives of the decision-makers. Once decisions have been made on the allocation of social values, a strategy must be devised to create support for them.

Since the allocation of resources is not directly in response to demands made upon the system by ordinary citizens, special efforts may need to be exerted to gain their support for such allocations if they are to be translated into increased development. Decision-making according to external or perceived rather than internally communicated demands means in practice that decision-makers adopt measures calculated to further the growth of the economy rather than to meet immediately popular demands for land, health, or educational facilities. Acting to create the necessary popular support for economic growth means attempting to induce popular participation in the process of enhancing economic development. This amounts to getting people to "ask not what your country can do for you, but what you can do for your country." In short, the political leaders of Kenya are concerned primarily with enhancing the development of the economy and with gaining appropriate popular participation in the process.

The Kenya government had decided by 1966 that popular participation in the economic development of the country is an appropriate substitute for rapid Africanization of the economy and immediate granting of free education, free health facilities, and free land. The government has tried to shift its constituents from support of Africanization and immediate welfare measures to support for a different set of programs. The heart of the strategy of economic development as outlined in the *Development Plan 1966–1970* is what the government calls a "social" approach, by which it means that it seeks "to involve the people of Kenya at every step and to an increasing extent in the economic development of the nation." [77] The government thus intends to rely as far as possible upon citizens of Kenya to develop the economy rather than upon noncitizen residents and/or expatriates. This popular participation is to be guided toward activities that will benefit the country in strictly economic terms, because the life of Kenya's citizens cannot be improved by following any other course of action. "If projects do not offer benefits in excess of their costs, they cannot contribute to economic development and it is unlikely that they would make a substantial contribution to social change and improvement." [78] The social approach is also to be distinguished from simple Africanization of the economy. The government is concerned not so much to Africanize the existing economy as to involve Africans in its further development. Africanization of the existing economy is deemphasized in the *Plan,* because it does not contribute to economic development:

> Involvement of the people should not be taken to mean mere transfer of existing assets to Kenya citizens—although such transfer may be necessary in some cases and is already being done. Involvement means that new development projects, the expansion of existing economic activity, and the generation of new economic opportunities have been designed to achieve the fullest possible participation by the people of Kenya.[79]

The citizens' demands for government programs to improve living standards and welfare are not discarded but deferred. Their realization is to be the product of increased and improved popular participation in the development of an economy which will in turn support such improvements in the standard of living. Foreign capital and

77. Kenya, *Development Plan,* p. 56.
78. *Ibid.,* p. 57.
79. *Ibid.*

manpower are to be utilized where appropriate in the process of building an economy for the benefit of Kenya's citizens.

The social approach to economic development raises three major questions which have a bearing upon both the political and the economic systems of Kenya. First, where greater economic development can be achieved with less widespread participation in the process, will the government choose to emphasize participation or economic growth? Effective and widespread participation may be necessary on political grounds, economic development on economic grounds. Second, what is to be done with and for those Africans for whom there is not yet any place in the modern economy? From an economic standpoint, they may constitute a labor surplus. From a political standpoint, failure to care for their needs may be risky where participation in the modern economy is synonymous with participation in the new Kenya nation. Third, how can popular participation be achieved with reasonable speed and without undue hardship? A satisfactory answer to this question may be necessary if enough participants are to be attracted to meet planned growth rates. Participation must be speedy and reasonably satisfying to the participants if it is to be a viable substitute for immediate government steps to raise the standard of living.

The Kenya government has elected to give agricultural development priority over industrialization. Its reasons for making this choice reflect an attempt to make the allocation of scarce resources serve the requirements and further the objectives of both the economic and the political systems. The economic reasons advanced in the *Plan* were hypotheses that industrialization might take place at the cost of a corresponding decrease in agricultural output, that agricultural development might lead to a higher gross national product than industrialization, and that on the basis of past experience the employment opportunities created by industrialization may be overestimated by its advocates. Perhaps the most important reason for awarding higher priority to agricultural development was the hypothesis that industrialization, in the absence of a supporting agricultural expansion, might create a dual economy with a small wealthy sector enjoying high living standards and employing a disproportionate share of the country's investment capital and skilled manpower, and another and much larger sector with the opposite characteristics. The creation of such a dual economy would, in the government's view, perpetuate and probably magnify the pattern of Kenya's pre-independence dual rural economy, with its small modern European sector and its vast, much less modern African sector. The government's dislike of a dual economy reflects two political choices: (1) elimination of the dual economy is a necessary step to widespread involvement of the people in the process of nation-building, which in turn is essential to national unity; and (2) urban unemployment is less tolerable than rural unemployment or underemployment, perhaps because it is more visible and more susceptible to being organized in opposition against the government.

In the government's view, agricultural development is desirable because it is believed to encourage participation in the modern economy more than would industrialization. Fundamental to the government's decision to emphasize agricultural development is the assumption that the traditional sector of the economy can and will continue to cushion the transition by African subsistence farmers to participation in the modern cash economy. Where industrialization, in the government's view, implies a complete divorce from the traditional economy for those who are to participate in it, agricultural development does not impose such requirements:

> An alternative approach [to industrialization] favored by the Kenya Government is to start with people in the circumstances in which they now live and with the traditions and knowledge to which they are already accustomed and build on this knowledge an increasingly more modern economy. It is for this reason that the principal emphasis in planning development in Kenya is placed on the development and modernization of agriculture on which most of the people depend for their livelihood.[80]

The government thus believes that the barriers between the traditional and modern rural economies can be broken by creating oppor-

80. *Ibid.,* pp. 66–67.

tunities for individuals to move gradually from subsistence to cash-crop farming.

The decision and the rationale for emphasizing agricultural development over industrialization provide tentative answers to the problems of making acceptable the transition from traditional to modern economic practices and of providing for those for whom no place yet exists in the developing cash economy. By relying upon the traditional sector of the economy to perform these functions, the government finds itself able to emphasize agricultural productivity more and agricultural employment in the modern sector less.

The government's strategy for implementing this policy of gradual and selective participation by Africans in the modern economy calls for reliance upon the benefits of the modern economy itself to stimulate effective African participation.

> Development of the monetary economy will itself generate opportunities that were not available in the traditional subsistence economy. These opportunities will induce changes in behavior patterns and incentives by making available to people a range of consumer goods that were not available to them before and by opening up markets in which they can sell their increased production.[81]

This strategy rests upon assumptions regarding the behavior of ordinary African citizens. First, it assumes that Africans will find the modern economy more attractive than the traditional sector. Second, it assumes that attempts by the administration to channel the productive efforts of Africans will not still their desire to participate in the modern economy. Third, it assumes that Africans who desire to participate in the modern economy will substitute participation along lines desired by the administration for participation in an immediate rise in the standard of living. Fourth, it assumes not only that the modern economy will generate participation but that it will regulate increases in participation in such a way that adequate manpower will be attracted. In addition, it is assumed that the presence of the modern economy will not provoke an unacceptable frustration

81. *Ibid.*, p. 60.

in those who are attracted by its benefits but are unable to participate fully in their creation or enjoyment. The presence of the traditional society provides a possible mechanism for absorbing those who cannot participate in the modern economy or cannot participate completely in it, but little is done to enhance the possibility that such arrangements will be acceptable to the Africans. Fifth, the government's strategy assumes that the traditional economy and the modern economy can compete side by side in such a manner that those Africans who have a stake in both will not find themselves torn by incompatible requirements of the two systems. These assumptions will be examined in chapter 6, where the responses of Africans in the settlement program are surveyed.

The government's strategy of regulating Africanization to enhance rather than detract from or fail to assist the development of the economy has been employed to reinforce the economic arguments against the land-resettlement schemes. The economic argument against the resettlement schemes was first made by the new government in the African manifesto in early 1965. It was reinforced by the need to take decisions in that year on future land-resettlement programs.

The British and Kenya governments anticipated that the actual transfer of the more than one million acres of European farmland to African smallholders would be completed in 1965 or early 1966. As the Million Acre Scheme was announced, the then colonial secretary, Reginald Maudling, indicated that the British government would consider an additional program when the initial program had been completed, if circumstances warranted and British government finances permitted. Both governments wished to review the accomplishments and the impact of proposals made by the Kenya government to the British government for an additional settlement program in April, 1964, and the new Labour government decided to appoint a commission to study the impact of the Million Acre Scheme before reaching a decision on financing further resettlement programs.[82] The chairman of the commission was to be Maxwell Stamp, an

---

82. *The Times* (London), December 15, 1964.

economic consultant in private practice in London. Also on the commission were Dr. Alistair McFarquhar, an agricultural economist at Cambridge University, and Roger Swynnerton, who had become agricultural advisor to the Commonwealth Development Corporation. The Stamp Mission toured Kenya to look at the settlement schemes and take testimony from those involved directly or indirectly with the land-transfer process as well as with consolidation and registration. The commission's report in late 1965 was to be confidential, but the British minister of overseas development released a summary of its findings along with the decision on further financing of land development and transfer in Kenya.[83]

The Stamp Mission concluded that land transfer in and of itself does not contribute to any increase in economic development and that, given Kenya's rapidly expanding population, low standard of living for most Africans, and other pressing economic difficulties, allocation of scarce resources for programs that did not contribute to increased agricultural development was unjustified.[84] It observed that broadened African participation in the development and benefits of the economy could be facilitated only by measures calculated to achieve expansion. Finally, the commission expressed the belief that success in expanding the economy would permit Europeans to continue to participate in it and that many European fears were without foundation. The leader of the commission leaked this last conclusion at the Nairobi airport before returning to London and provoked an outburst from the European community. The *East African Standard* remarked editorially that those who had risked maintaining their farms during the uncertain days of the transfer of power in the belief that they would be rewarded by a further land-resettlement program had been forgotten.[85] The commission recommended that some additional funds be allocated for land purchase but that far greater emphasis be placed on consolidation and registration of land in the former African areas. It believed that land-resettlement funds should

83. *Ibid.,* November 19, 1965.

84. Report of the commission's findings in "For the Record" (Nairobi: British Information Services, November 19, 1965).

85. *East African Standard,* November 19, 1965.

be part of the development assistance budget rather than something over and above. In effect, the commission said that land resettlement must stand or fall on its contribution to economic expansion.

The British government claimed to offer more funds for resettlement than the Stamp Mission recommended but less than the Kenya government requested. It offered Kenya £18 million in interest-free loans over the years 1966 to 1970 for new development projects. This aid would permit 100,000 acres of land to be transferred during each of the following years, amounting to one-third of the total aid program. The remainder was to be allocated to land consolidation and registration—which both governments reportedly agreed was of great economic importance—and technical assistance.

The Kenya government's reported demand for substantial new funds for resettlement was somewhat inconsistent with the views it expressed in the African socialism manifesto which appeared while the mission was in Kenya, and with the thoughts expressed in the *Development Plan 1966–1970* that appeared six months after the British government made its offer. In both, the government made it clear that land-resettlement programs were in neither the economic nor the political interest of the new Kenya. The inconsistency could have been removed if the Kenya government had argued that the British government had a responsibility to prevent panicky European farmers from disrupting the economy and should supply resettlement funds for this, so that Kenya's development capital could be directed to more appropriate projects.[86] However, British funds employed in resettlement were nevertheless British funds foregone for other Kenya development programs.

Africanization for its own sake is objectionable to the African government not only because Africans are not involved in net increases in the economic growth of the country but because relatively few Africans benefit in the process: "Africanization of the modern sector alone is not an answer to this problem [dual economy]. It only means that a minority of Africans would become privileged members

---

86. Proposal in private circulation for a further takeover of European land in the Kenya Highlands. This was prepared by the deputy director of agriculture, A. W. Peers, in early 1965.

of the modern sector in the dual economy." [87] It is assumed that Africanization for its own sake would result in the maintenance of the dual economy of pre-independence days, minus only the color contrast, rather than in its destruction. Implicit in the government's opposition to Africanization is a further indication that the government is prepared to accept the presence of productive European farmers. The government wants the remaining European farmers, it would seem, to continue to support the existing economy, while more Africans are brought into the process of expanding the development of the economy.

The government's second economic objection to land resettlement is that it costs too much and yields too little, in addition to involving too few Africans in the process of expanding the economy. "All told, it is clear that for the same expenditure, development of the former African areas [by consolidation, registration, and farm planning] will provide employment for, and increase the living standards of a much larger number of people than settlement." [88] The Kenya government planners are prepared to admit that the relative cost of a given level of productivity under the two land programs cannot be tested accurately on the basis of existing quantitative evidence. [89] However, the government has been ready to assert that more employment can be created by consolidation and registration than by resettlement, despite the reported findings of a 1966 study group on this particular subject. The Stamp Mission is reported to have argued that there were fewer farmers outside the former White Highlands as progressive as the new African settlers than had been assumed. Among those progressive farmers on whom the government is prepared to concentrate its development funds, the settlement farmers may represent a rather high percentage. However, if this is the case, settlement farmers may still require more financial assistance per unit of productivity than those involved in land consolidation and registration.

87. Kenya, *African Socialism,* pp. 28–29.
88. Kenya, *Development Plan,* pp. 126–27.
89. Clive S. Gray, "Agricultural Sector Planning in Kenya: Planning without Facts." Paper presented at Conference on Agricultural Planning, Dar es Salaam, April, 1967.

In addition, the largest proportion of Kenya's high-potential agricultural land lies outside the areas settled by European farmers and, therefore, steps such as consolidation and registration should be taken to insure that maximum productivity is achieved in these areas. The missions of the CDC and the World Bank that appraised Kenya's agricultural prospects in the years just before independence recommended that development funds be concentrated in such areas, if for no other reason than because the banks themselves demanded such land be used where their development funds were involved. The prevailing estimates are that approximately 80 percent of Kenya's best agricultural land lies in areas that were never settled by Europeans. Furthermore, not all the land used for settlement schemes, particularly those high-density schemes financed by the Britsh government, was especially suitable for intensive farming by smallholders. For example, the Kinangop plateau was best for wheat-farming and sheep-raising on a large-scale basis by farmers with enough experience and capital to risk these relatively difficult kinds of agriculture. Most of the Kikuyu settlers are now farming on the Kinangop. In the area around Nyeri, also resettled by Kikuyu farmers, many have experienced difficulties with soil that is alternately waterlogged and bone-dry.

Fundamentally, the government's opposition to resettlement as a means of nation-building reflects continuity with the political and economic strategies of rural development established during the 1950s. The government continues to support in practice the idea of multiracial cooperation in the expansion of a modern economy. The statements of Kenyatta and some of his cabinet ministers, the views of the CDC and World Bank missions, the Stamp Mission, and the policies articulated in the *Development Plan 1966–1970* established the policy of expanding African participation in the development of the economy through creating new employment opportunities rather than simply placing Africans in positions held by Europeans. This strategy is justified, as was pre-1960 multiracialism, on the economic grounds that more resources are utilized and more Africans benefit than would be the case if Africanization were the guiding policy. Where multiracialism was conceived by moderate Europeans in the

1950s in their own interests as well as out of conviction, multiracialism in independent Kenya has been restored by an African government trying to act in the interests of the African majority as well as out of the conviction that racial discrimination in any form is unacceptable. The government has no program to increase the number of European citizens, but those who remain are encouraged to play an active part in the process of nation-building free of any kind of racial discrimination.

The land-resettlement program, while not fully consistent with the political and economic philosophy of the post-independence government, nevertheless is admitted by that government to have constituted an essential precondition for the establishment of programs to develop the economy. The land-transfer program permitted those Europeans who did not believe that an African government would adopt such tolerant policies to liquidate their assets and leave the country. It immediately introduced to the modern economy a substantial number of disinherited African families and in the process thoroughly breached the former racial exclusiveness of the White Highlands. The land-resettlement program prevented political instability from causing further economic decline, while it also facilitated the present strategy of more gradual and perhaps more widespread introduction of Africans to participation in the expanding modern economy. In post-independence Kenya, the land-resettlement program must continue to establish preconditions for the successful practice of the government's present policies by insuring that Africans are able to repay their loans from the British government, the World Bank, and the CDC. By so doing, the new settlers enable the government to liquidate its financial responsibility and establish the country's international credit, thereby encouraging further international investment in Kenya's economy.

The fundamental difficulty in the implementation of the settlement program and in its relationship to post-independence nation-building is that it is caught between conflicting policies and institutions. On the one hand, the land-resettlement program is supposed to effect the final transfer of political and economic power, which it was created to facilitate, by liquidating the debt used to finance it. On the other hand, as subsequent examination of the implementation of the settlement program will demonstrate, policies and institutions designed primarily to secure loan repayment seem to conflict with those designed primarily to stimulate increases in productivity. As long as the two policy objectives are unresolved, the implementation of the scheme may satisfy neither. To the extent that loan repayment is given priority over economic development, the former European and African areas will not be fully integrated, because differences in political and economic strategies will re-create the barriers between the two areas maintained before independence by racial policies. As long as the two areas remain unintegrated, the post-independence objective of a Kenya politically united in the pursuit of economic development will be frustrated.

5

ESTABLISHMENT OF THE SETTLEMENT SCHEMES: OBJECTIVES, NEGOTIATIONS, IMPLEMENTATION

THE LAND-RESETTLEMENT SCHEMES are collectively the Achilles' heel on Kenya's post-independence agricultural development program and of the country's development program as a whole.* There are three major reasons why the settlement schemes remain at least partially alienated from other aspects of rural development in post-independence Kenya. First, the Kenya government continues to consider the settlement schemes as an unpleasant reminder of the heavy price Africans have had to pay to gain independence and to eliminate the political and economic power positions of the European settlers. The Kenya government takes pride in the fact that 35,000 African families have been given land in the former White Highlands, and it certainly does not mourn the departure of the European settlers. Yet the government continues to believe that the British government

---

* These remarks preceding the sections on low- and high-density schemes refer to both kinds. The low-density schemes were initiated in 1960, the high-density schemes in late 1961 and 1962. The former are for Africans with some capital and farming experience; the latter, for landless and unemployed Africans with or without real farming experience. The schemes are usually lumped together in policy discussions, though they are quite different, as this chapter will show.

initiated the schemes in European rather than African interests and that the Africans have had to pay too high a price to serve the interests of non-Africans. The economic independence of Kenya, in its government's view, has been undermined by its own and the new settlers' responsibilities to a foreign government for a program conceived in European interests. In the government's scale of political values, economic independence takes priority over immediate realization of partial solutions for the land hunger which has always been a major concern of Kenya's African nationalists.

Further, the government does not place much responsibility upon untrained and impoverished Africans to contribute directly and immediately to the principal post-independence political objective of economic development.[1] Most of the settlers, who were supposed to be landless and unemployed prior to joining the Million Acre Scheme, lack the education, experience, and capital to make effective contributions to economic development. However, the settlers are fortunate in that they have drawn a higher per capita outlay of scarce development funds than those upon whom the government does, and would prefer to, depend. KANU leaders have frequently spoken of their intention to assist the poor and destitute Africans, but they do not wish to do so at the expense of over-all economic development. Because of the dual pressure from the European settlers and from the African unemployed and landless in the months before independence, KANU was obliged to agree to a program that would expend more scarce development capital upon these Africans than the government now believes they deserve on the basis of their ability to contribute to economic growth.

Third, the administration of land-resettlement schemes has been somewhat independent of the rest of the administrative apparatus of the central government. The old LDSB and the more recent CLB were both constitutionally independent of the central government administration. Today, even the Ministry of Lands and Settlement retains a certain independence because of the comprehensive nature

1. Kenya, *Development Plan, 1966–1970* (Nairobi: Government Printer, 1966).

of the program for which it is responsible. Rather than involve half a dozen or more government ministries directly in the settlement-program administration, the Ministry of Lands and Settlement has enjoyed the services of numerous employees seconded from other government ministries. The Ministry of Lands and Settlement thus has total responsibility for one geographical area of the country, while in all other areas the various ministries of the government share responsibility. The reasons for this lie in the preferences of the British government and the lenders for a single organization upon which they can fix responsibility, and in the ministry's different accounting system required by its semicommercial character and activities. Those in positions of responsibility in other ministries are ambiguous in appraising this arrangement. Many are glad not to have any responsibility for a program that is both difficult and politically somewhat tainted. On the other hand, they resent being deprived of experienced and valuable personnel who might have been put to better use had they not been seconded to the Ministry of Lands and Settlement.[2] However, particularly in the Ministry of Agriculture, some of those seconded to settlement were willing to go because they were Europeans or colonial civil servants who would not otherwise have been promoted or even retained very long after independence.[3] Most of those whom the Ministry of Agriculture has subsequently recalled from the Ministry of Lands and Settlement are Africans, although some of the few Europeans who continue to be essential and are identified with the new Kenya have also been recalled.

Thus the government has been unable to integrate and reconcile settlement with the nation's over-all development plans. The government has had to divert personnel and scarce resources to the settle-

2. Information derived from interviews with senior officials in the Ministry of Lands and Settlement: A. Storrar, former director; G. R. Henderson, former deputy director; V. E. M. Burke, former deputy director.

3. Senior officials in the Department of Agriculture: Geoffrey Karithi, former permanent secretary; R. D. A. Bennison, provincial agriculture director; R. J. M. Swynnerton, former director of agriculture; N. S. Carey Jones, former permanent secretary, Ministry of Lands and Settlement.

ment program. In short, the government feels a responsibility for the settlement schemes which it resents, because this responsibility interferes with the main task of achieving greater economic growth.

THE OBJECTIVES OF LAND RESETTLEMENT

Because of the unresolved ambiguities in the relationship of land resettlement to other aspects of the Kenya government's nation-building program, the objectives of land resettlement in post-independence Kenya are difficult both to establish and to legitimize. This problem is magnified by the fact that the program has given the government some very long-term responsibilities, even though the original objectives of land resettlement were primarily short-term: to facilitate the transfer of power and to increase the chances of political stability after independence. Furthermore, the program was necessarily begun and the settlers placed in great haste, so that there was little time in the course of implementing the program to reformulate its objectives. Such reformulation must take place now, after the basic structure of the program has been established. Finally, the British government, and even some of the Europeans who stood to benefit from the opportunity to sell their farms, now decry the impact of the program on the country's economic, and to some extent its political, health.[4] Consequently, it is difficult to find staunch defenders of the settlement program's contribution to post-independence development outside the present and former personnel of the Ministry of Lands and Settlement itself. The ministry personnel, some of whom regretted the necessity of the program, subsequently developed a belief in its comprehensive approach to rural development as a sound strategy for building an independent nation, notwithstanding admitted mistakes in implementation. The settlement program has thus become a sort of ideological battleground

---

4. Interviews with Sir Ferdinand Cavendish-Bentinck and Sir Michael Blundell, both former settlers and ministers for agriculture; Humphrey Slade, speaker of the Kenya National Assembly; and others.

between the apologists for the program within the Ministry of Lands and Settlement and those critics outside the ministry (including some of the seconded personnel) who have in varying degrees sought to integrate the program with the objectives and strategies of the government for rural development as a whole.

The basic social philosophy of those (largely expatriate) who worked within the Ministry of Lands and Settlement at the outset can be reduced to a series of articles of faith.[5] First, there are a belief in the importance of involving the ordinary African smallholder in the process of development, and a conviction that settlement contributes to development by increasing the numbers of efficient smallholder farmers. As the first African director of the Department of Settlement put it: "Our task as a Department has been to allay these fears [concerning the success of the program] by committing ourselves to success based on the fundamental confidence in our organization and the conviction that smallholders, whether in Settlement or not, will be the mainstay of this agricultural country." [6] Then, proponents of land resettlement argue that the economic development of the country will be best served by thinking in terms of increases in production per acre rather than in terms of increases in production per man. Since labor is plentiful and land is scarce, and since unemployment remains a serious problem, economic development and political stability are best sought by devising ways to maximize the production per acre and the carrying capacity of the land through heavy use of manpower rather than by trying to channel scarce resources into the hands of the most productive farmers. Third, many of the most senior officials who saw the land-resettlement program through its early and most difficult stages left with a belief that it, for all its mistakes, provided a model for rural development that could be applied elsewhere. They retained a certain faith in the idea of combining specialists in all phases of rural life under one ministry whose task would be to transform given areas and given

5. Based on discussions with V. E. M. Burke, A. Storrar, G. R. Henderson, N. S. Carey Jones, L. R. Lawrence Brown, settlement officer, and others.

6. James Maina, director, Department of Settlement, *Annual Report* (Nairobi: English Press, Ltd., 1965–66), p. 1.

sets of rural Africans into prosperous, healthy, and happy rural communities. Fourth, along with the belief in comprehensive rural development programs went a belief in the transformational approach to rural development. Rather than relying simply on the expansion of the whole economy to effect a largely voluntary and gradual evolution of Kenya into a modern society participating in a modern economy, they believed in transforming the economy and society by planned, coordinated, comprehensive programs designed to accomplish the process in a relatively short time. Greater emphasis is placed on providing the assistance necessary to facilitate the transition and less is placed on relying upon individual effort and achievement. Evidence in support of these articles of faith is sought in indications that smallholder farmers become efficient when given assistance, that production levels achieved by the departed European farmers are at least matched if not surpassed, that the ministry functions as an efficient organization now that early mistakes have been rectified, and that settlers respond favorably to efforts to provide schools, markets, health facilities, and the like.

In the minds of those who are influential in shaping and financing the country's development program, both outside of the settlement schemes within Kenya and in the international financial community, these arguments have been more than counterbalanced by arguments that are reflected in and derive from the country's current development plan. A most influential series of articles analyzing the economics of the settlement program, written by former Kenya Chief Agriculturalist Leslie Brown, appeared in the *Kenya Weekly News* in the latter half of 1965.[7] They were read and generally accepted by numbers of policy-makers in the Kenya government, in the international financial community, and in the Ministry of Overseas Development in London. These articles reflected a general pessimism about the economic future of the program and suggested that its economic failure would vitiate even the political purpose it was intended to serve. It is probable that the ideas and evidence recorded

7. *Kenya Weekly News,* July to November, 1965. These appeared just on the eve of the British-Kenya government negotiations over future land-resettlement programs.

in these articles had a significant bearing on the decision, in November, 1965, not to encourage further high-density settlement, and they may also have influenced the thinking of the Stamp Mission.[8] They reflect the views of people who were influential in formulating the present development plan. They should be examined briefly because they show the difficulty of relating the present program to the Kenya government's post-independence strategy of maximizing productivity and making optimum use of scarce resources.

Brown argued that as of late 1965 the population pressures and resultant land hunger among Africans were growing rather than diminishing, and that the settlement schemes had thus failed in their essential political purpose of relieving some of the unemployment and landlessness. "Of one thing I feel certain in advance and that is that the steam is still in the kettle because the basic source of heat, the 3% per annum increase in population, is still beneath it." [9] Furthermore, in Brown's judgment, the settlement schemes had been undertaken in defiance of any consideration of the opportunity costs involved. Consequently, he argued that "it is my opinion . . . that if this amount had been spent on extending and developing irrigation schemes and land consolidation in existing African areas, a comparable number of landless families could have been settled at at least equivalent standards and there would have been a greater upsurge in the over-all production and standard of living." [10] Kenya's basic problem of providing employment for a growing potential labor force could not, in his view, be relieved simply by the expedient of land transfer. Land transfer, unlike land consolidation, he found to be motivated by political rather than economic ends, because it had been deemed essential to the successful transfer of political power (see chapters 3 and 4).

If the achievement of increased production and economic growth becomes a prime objective of government, as indeed it has in Kenya, then the distinction between political and economic ends becomes

8. Described in chapter 4.
9. L. H. Brown, "The Settlement Schemes," *Kenya Weekly News,* July 16, 1965, p. 11.
10. *Ibid.*

more difficult to draw. To the extent that those who have been influential in Kenya politics have argued for making the country's economy the prime concern of government, they have in effect made the allocation of scarce resources and the authoritative allocation of social values one and the same process. It follows that those who argue, as Brown does, for a rational allocation of economic resources independently of "political" considerations are in effect replacing one set of political considerations with another. What, then, are some of the political parameters underlying Leslie Brown's economic analysis of the settlement schemes?

He postulated three essential requirements for the achievement of optimum agricultural production. These were, first, a sound system of farming that would take into account ecological factors and the experiences of other farmers in dealing with them. Second, farmers of proven ability, skill, and capacity for hard work would be required, even under otherwise favorable farming conditions. Third, capital to carry out necessary farm development would have to be available. The settlement schemes, in his view, were formulated without adequate attention to the first and second requisites. Consequently, the money spent on the settlement schemes could have been used better elsewhere.

The settlement schemes were indeed established in defiance of the first principle, since the Rift Valley and the Kinangop plateau, where most of them were located, were better suited to extensive, large-scale farming than to intensive, smallholder farming. Brown observed that "the attempt to force an intensive farming system on land which is suited only to farming in large units is, in the long run, certain to fail, and to lead to disappointment, frustration, misery and poverty, rather than to progress and increased production. It is this which makes one fear for the success of many settlement schemes in the erstwhile White Highlands." [11] The alternatives, it appears, would have been either to leave the existing large-scale farms in European hands or to transfer them, with little or no subdivision, to qualified Africans wanting to purchase farms. The corollary, pre-

11. *Ibid.*

sumably, would have been that most of those in the overcrowded areas of Western, Nyanza, and Central Provinces in search of land or employment could have found either or both by developing underutilized land in their own provinces, or by seeking employment as farm laborers at home or in the Rift Valley.

Similarly, the settlement schemes did not fully reflect Brown's second principle. "It is essential," he argued, "not only to farm it on the right system but with the right people. Land should belong to the people who can farm it best, whatever their race, color, and creed." [12] His particular application of the principle was to groups rather than to individuals, for he claimed that Kenya's various ethnic groups were not equally capable of sound farming. "There are those," he admitted, "who would say that there are no real differences between individuals or tribes and that given an adequate chance and devoted teaching anyone will make a success of it. But there are comparatively few practical agriculturalists who would agree with this view." [13] Elsewhere he said, "Individuals or groups unwilling to work will cause to founder the most soundly designed scheme in the world on the best possible land. This may even be said to apply to different tribes; some are known to be better farmers and harder workers than others." [14] The settlement schemes were allocated to all major African ethnic groups roughly in proportion to the dimensions of land hunger and population density in their respective home areas. Presumably, application of Brown's second principle would have entailed more strict screening and perhaps lower priority for applicants from ethnic groups thought to be less able and conscientious. According to Brown's first principle, the Highlands would have remained an area of large-scale farming, and careful screening of applicants wanting to purchase these larger enterprises would have been warranted by the greater skill and experience required on these by comparison to smallholdings. Two applications of Brown's second principle would be possible. If it were applied to

12. *Ibid.,* August 6, 1965, p. 21.
13. *Ibid.,* p. 20.
14. *Ibid.,* July 16, 1965, p. 10.

all rural landholdings or all rural larger-scale landholdings, then all ownership of farmland would become a privilege earned through demonstrated farming ability. If it were applied only to the Highlands, this area, because of the large-scale holdings, would then be given a higher priority in the allocation of good farmers than other areas where smallholdings predominate. In the former case, the implicit political decision that must first be accepted is the wisdom of creating an elite class of farmers. In the latter, the political decision involved is continued special consideration for the area once known as the White Highlands despite the fact that greater amounts of high-potential land are by general admission located elsewhere.

Brown's third principle is the requirement that money be supplied to qualified farmers on decent land in sufficient quantity. Applied to Kenya and to the settlement schemes, the corollary is that those who are less qualified and/or who farm less favored land require more money than they deserve, since good farmers who may also be working better land are deprived of adequate capital by the demands of their opposites. In Brown's view, the European farmers who preceded the present settlers and the farmers engaged in land consolidation in the former African reserves could both have used the money more effectively than the settlers. The settlers may become good farmers, but only through an expenditure that could bring quicker and more substantial results applied elsewhere. The Kenya government has essentially adopted this view, perhaps in part because international lending agencies require that agricultural assistance be channeled to competent farmers working high-potential land. The settlement schemes are in general an exception to this principle, since the Million Acre Scheme farmers have no particular qualifications and are not necessarily farming land that is high potential for smallholders.

There are two fundamental difficulties with Brown's line of argument. Because of the government's general acceptance of the ideal that economic development should receive priority and that politics as such should be deemphasized, political participation in the new Kenya is undertaken primarily through involvement in programs to expand the economy. Given this situation, the acceptance of Brown's principle of restricting significant participation in the development of the economy to an elite corps of farmers means that the majority of rural inhabitants would have no significant opportunity to participate in nation-building and thereby to develop a commitment to the nation. Distribution of the amenities of a higher standard of living is postponed and emphasis on participation in politics is deferred pending the achievement of a prerequisite level of economic development. If the majority of farmers are deprived of both participation and the fruits of development, how are the mass of rural Kenyans to build an identification with the new Kenya? Vicarious identification with the country's individual leaders, reliance upon the traditional subsistence sector to absorb the energies and attention of most rural Kenyans, or a major program to condition rural Kenyans to accept the prospect of being landless employees of commercial entrepreneurs or elite farmers suggest themselves as possible solutions. The last presumes transformation of the social structure and attitudes of rural Kenyans to fit the realities of a developing rural economy. The first two presuppose building the modern rural economy without transforming the behavior and attitudes of most rural Kenyans and without involving them in the development process; it is this strategy which the government seems to have adopted by relying upon the traditional sector to absorb those for whom the modern economy is not yet prepared.[15] The new African settlers are faced with a difficult choice. They are supposed to be removed from the traditional sector of the economy and society by virtue of their responsibility for loan repayment, their obligation to maintain production at pre-settlement levels, and their compulsory participation in cooperative societies to the exclusion of competing economic institutions outside the settlement schemes. But they are not a part of the elite corps of qualified participants in the development of a modern rural economy because of their lack of financial and educational qualifications, the relatively low agricultural potential of their land when divided into smallholdings, and the circumstances that led to the creation of the settlement schemes.

15. See chapter 4.

The second difficulty of Brown's line of argument, and of the view of the many people in responsible circles in Kenya who share his perspective, is that it does not come to terms with the fact that 35,000 African families are now actually on the land. All of Brown's principles seem to reflect a certain nostalgia for the *status quo ante*. He would argue on economic grounds that it would be better if, today, the Highlands were still farmed by competent large-scale farmers. Without settlement schemes, these large-scale farmers, if they could have been persuaded to stay at all, would have been Europeans. If it is accepted that scarce capital resources should be allocated in such a way that maximum productivity results, a sounder approach would be to estimate how far the settlement schemes saved the economy of the Highlands from the condition that would have resulted had there been no Million Acre Scheme. Furthermore, attention should be given to means whereby the contribution of the settlement schemes to economic development can be maximized without depriving other sectors of the rural economy. Now that the schemes are in progress, what is the soundest policy for encouraging them further?

The heart of the matter is that the settlement schemes, the new African settlers, and the thinking and policy-making concerning them, are a significant part of a general transition in which the country as a whole is engaged. This is a transition from a pre-independence Kenya, divided geographically as well as socially along racial lines, to a post-independence Kenya where these divisions will eventually be eliminated and the country, particularly the rural sector, will be fully integrated. The problem is that, although the previous racial division of rural Kenya between Europeans and Africans has been substantially eliminated, the rural economy is still compartmentalized. The peculiar economic and social circumstances of the settlement schemes and their inhabitants derive directly from the fact that the schemes were largely forced upon the British government and the colonial administration by the European farmers. There are three special circumstances which differentiate the new settlers from Africans in the former African areas: a heavier burden of debt; more difficult farming circumstances; and fewer educational and financial qualifications for successful farming than are possessed by many of those in the former African areas upon whom the government relies for the bulk of post-independence agricultural development. As long as these peculiar circumstances remain and as long as they are emphasized by policy-makers as a justification for isolating the settlement schemes from the rest of the modernizing economy, the transition from the racial and economic compartmentalization of pre-independence Kenya to a socially and economically integrated post-independence Kenya will be incomplete. Policy-makers, then, must find means of preventing the peculiar circumstances of the settlers and the schemes from constituting an insuperable barrier to integration with the rest of the modernizing sector of the rural economy. Success in this task may enable the settlement schemes to avoid the dire fate Brown forecast for them and the country.

THE PROCESS OF IMPLEMENTATION

Low-Density Schemes. [16] There are two kinds of settlement schemes: low-density schemes for financially and educationally qualified Africans, financed in part by the Commonwealth Development Corporation (CDC) and the World Bank (IBRD); and high-density schemes for landless and unemployed Africans, financed almost entirely by grants and loans from the British government. The implementation of the two parts of the settlement-scheme program reveals an important interrelationship between two processes. One involves changing the system of authoritatively allocating social values through giving Africans the responsibilities formerly exercised by Europeans and the colonial administration. The other process involves maximizing the particular social value of economic productivity by effectively allocating scarce material resources.

The low-density schemes resulted from a commitment given by

16. Much of the material in this section is based on research done with the assistance of the Commonwealth Development Corporation and the World Bank. I am particularly grateful for extensive conversations with members of the Africa Department, International Bank for Reconstruction and Development in Washington; A. Storrar and G. R. Henderson, now of the IBRD (World Bank) office in Nairobi; and Peter Wise, G. Bacs, and R. Kemoli of the CDC office in Nairobi.

the British government as part of the 1960 Lancaster House Constitutional Conference. After the conference had ended, the British government recommended that Kenya seek financial assistance from the CDC and IBRD. The British reasons for suggesting this course of action were political as well as economic. In addition to Britain's own difficult financial circumstances, there was also some concern that a future African government might be reluctant to maintain its responsibility to the British government for the repayment of a development loan. It was thought that a new African government might be less inclined to default on the repayment of a loan from independent or semi-independent international financial houses than on one from the former colonial power. This reasoning could also have explained the British government's and the CDC's desire to launch the settlement program jointly with the World Bank. It might well have been thought less likely that a new Kenya government would default on a loan from a source closely associated with the United States, since the United States had a reputation in Britain and Kenya for being in favor of decolonization.

The Kenya government's period of negotiations with the CDC and the IBRD lasted from shortly after the 1960 Lancaster House Conference until a few months following Kenya's independence in December, 1963. During this time, none of the money for the low-density schemes was disbursed by the lenders (IBRD and CDC). The terms of the initial agreement, concluded in 1961, provided that before any funds could be released the lenders had to certify that the schemes for which they were sought met their standards. None of the low-density schemes was approved for IBRD and CDC funding until after independence, largely because of difficulties arising from constitutional changes and from the establishment of the Million Acre Scheme in connection with the transfer of political power. During the transfer of power, the Kenya government went ahead with implementing the schemes and subsequently attempted to raise them to IBRD and CDC standards by temporarily drawing on its own financial resources. The British government undertook to finance these low-density schemes in the event that the lenders should terminate the agreement because of insuperable difficulties in bringing the schemes' organization up to the lenders' standards. Consequently, while Kenya was engaged in an internal struggle over the constitutional and economic structure of the new nation, the leaders of its government were absorbed simultaneously in an external dialogue with two major international financial houses over political, institutional, and economic requirements for an independent Kenya to qualify for international economic assistance.

The CDC and IBRD project standards for financing agricultural development programs were similar to those which some influential members of the Kenya government had tried to establish before 1960 and which the Kenya government has tried to establish since independence. The essential requirement upon which the lenders insisted was that their economic assistance must contribute to the economic development of the country. The CDC insisted that its loans assure the creation of economic assets that did not exist before. The IBRD criterion of an increase in "net benefit" or increased national product was perhaps somewhat more flexible, but both banks agreed that the loan must be used to further Kenya's economy. The mere transfer of economic assets or the establishment of programs whose purpose was purely political could not be financed if they did not also lead to some net addition to the Kenya economy. During the transfer of power, the banks sought without success the establishment or preservation of governmental institutions for administering their funds that would insure the priority of economic development above, and without the influence of, political considerations. The Kenya government was obliged to structure political institutions according to the political values of individuals, communities, and parties in Kenya, and to channel economic assistance through institutions embodying such values.[17] Since independence the Kenya government's position has moved closer to that of the banks, though not necessarily because of their influence.

The strategy behind the CDC's and IBRD's participation in the financing of the low-density schemes and the institutional structure through which they initially expected the program to be imple-

17. See discussion in chapters 3 and 4.

mented reflected the political ideology and institutions of pre-1960 Kenya. As the lenders understood it, the low-density schemes (where settlers were expected to have educational and financial qualifications and to make £100 per annum net) would be a vehicle for integrating the formerly racially exclusive White Highlands. The settlements were to be "currants in the cake," in the words of some of the lenders' officers. This political purpose was incidental to the over-all economic objective of contributing to the development of Kenya's economy and stimulating the re-creation of a land market in Kenya. The economic argument for the settlement schemes was based on the success of smallholders under the Swynnerton program of agricultural assistance for farmers on consolidated holdings in the former African areas and on the idea that African smallholders in the White Highlands would be placed on farms not fully developed by the departing European settlers. Initially, the agreement between the lenders and the Kenya government provided two kinds of low-density schemes: a Yeoman Scheme for farmers with £500 to £1000 of capital to contribute toward the objective of wresting a £250 net income per annum from a Highlands smallholding; and a Peasant Scheme that would require farmers to contribute £50 plus working capital toward making a smallholding produce an annual net income of £100. Both schemes were intended for the relatively prosperous rural Africans rather than for the landless and destitute. Finally, the programs were to be administered through a partially reconstituted Land Development and Settlement Board (LDSB) under a European chairman and a European chief executive officer and with largely European civil service personnel. The multiracial objective, the kind of settlers to be chosen, the reliance upon Swynnerton plan experience, and the use of the traditional institutional structure of settlement suggested the program's over-all continuity with the politics of the 1950s in Kenya and initial disregard for the changes initiated by the 1960 Lancaster House Conference.

The negotiations leading to the signing, in April, 1961, of the initial agreement between the Kenya government and the banks revealed important differences between them despite the general similarity of their approaches at the time. The basic difficulty lay in the attempts made by Europeans and the colonial administration to bend the mutually held objectives to their own purposes. The lenders agreed that the settlement program had economic merit but did not believe that it could be accomplished before Kenya's independence three years later. The colonial administration wanted the program implemented quickly out of concern for the fate of such an agreement under an independent government whose proclivities could not yet be divined. The CDC's chairman, Lord Howick (formerly Kenya governor Sir Evelyn Baring), and the rest of the head office objected to what they considered excessive European representation on the LDSB. The CDC anticipated that the interests of the European settlers selling the land and the interests of the Africans and the lenders who were to cooperate in purchasing and developing the land would be antithetical. Hence the CDC wondered not only about the European representation on the board but also about the wisdom of combining on the same board the function of land purchase with the functions of land transfer and development. The lenders also had doubts about the appointment of J. W. Lipscomb as chairman of the LDSB. Lipscomb had long been involved in European settlement operations, was himself a respected Highlands farmer, and had written extensively to extol the contribution of European farmers to Kenya's development as a colony. In 1959 he had said publicly that the Europeans would and should have a strong position in Kenya and had supported future European settlement, despite a growing feeling that political change was imminent. The banks questioned whether these were appropriate qualifications for the chairmanship of a board that would deal with the relatively poor rather than the relatively affluent, with Africans as purchasers as well as with Europeans as vendors, and with the decolonization rather than the colonization of the Highlands. Lord Howick himself, in a letter to his successor, Sir Patrick Renison, said "I do realize your difficulties but we have to look a little ahead and think in what position we will be when the country becomes independent."

Renison argued that European good will and experience were required, that the Lipscomb appointment had already been announced and its withdrawal would prompt the resignation of all the

European members of the Legislative Council, and that Lipscomb's experience as a farmer and his knowledge of settlement problems were indispensable. Renison did not accept or give credence to the CDC's views on the advisability of separating land purchase from land transfer and development. He argued that the IBRD agreed with him that the organization must have "closely linked stages of a single operation in which costs both of purchase and development are assessed against the potential of the land," and that division of the board would not be in the lenders' interests. Clearly the lenders suspected that the European predominance on the board would lead to unwise and unjustified inflation of land prices that might render the new schemes uneconomic propositions. Renison, on the other hand, thought this result could be avoided only if land purchase were not separated from land development and transfer, and he discounted the possibility that the European representatives would be unduly influenced by those members of their own community who wished to sell their farms. Finally, the governor argued that the Africans had voiced no objections to the amendment to the Agriculture Ordinance that had written the new LDSB structure into law. This claim was somewhat inaccurate, since the African members of the Legislative Council had objected to the settlement program itself in terms which would bear on this issue. They questioned whether the settlement program was conceived in African or European interests and protested that it seemed to take responsibilities away from the future African government. Thus, they objected to the program if not to the particular institutional structure for its implementation.

The Colonial Office lent its support to the colonial administration in Kenya and undertook to persuade the CDC of the wisdom of the governor's position. The Colonial Office believed that a single board with strong European membership and increasing African participation was preferable to two boards. It believed this to be in line with Kenya's developing agricultural policy. Even after the 1960 Lancaster House Conference, the Colonial Office thought in terms of the multiracialism of the 1950s with its selective and gradual accommodation of Africans to positions of political and economic responsibility rather than in terms of the more rapid changes envisaged by the

1960 Lancaster House Agreement. On the other hand, for institutions concerned with economic development to the exclusion of politics, the banks did not hesitate to strike at the heart of Kenya's post–Lancaster House political situation, in which European power continued to be very substantial despite impending independence. The banks' essential position appeared to be that, as a prerequisite for the award of development funds, political arrangements should be appropriate for the achievement of economic development. Their point of view was clearly indicated by an IBRD official who reasoned that "if the hazards, all rooted in political uncertainties are adjudged to be risks worth taking, the project would on technical grounds be suitable for a Bank loan." The banks were not unconcerned with politics; they were concerned that political institutions adopted by the independent Kenya be suitable for those who might want to concentrate on the objective of maximizing economic development.

In addition to political conditions, the banks imposed comprehensive and detailed reporting requirements on the Kenya government, to insure that subprojects were designed in such a way that economic development would be maximized and that, once established, such subprojects continued to meet the banks' specifications. The procedure established was that the CDC would have primary responsibility for investigating subprojects. Subproject proposals were to be sent to the headquarters of both banks and to the CDC Regional Office in Nairobi. The Regional Office would investigate and report to the headquarters of the CDC in London, which would in turn convey its views to the IBRD in Washington. The banks reserved the right to demand more information and investigate the sites further, as well as to approve or disapprove the subprojects. The banks were concerned with the location, acreages for individual plots, soils, water, communications, marketing facilities, population densities, and present land use. They required the submission of a typical farm budget including the proposed development outlays, proposed sources of income, and net income projected. The banks wanted to know the background of the settlers, including their "tribe," the number of working-age members of the families, previous farming experience, and cash and capital resources possessed.

They wanted a timetable for the achievement of the required £100 annual net income by the typical settler, and the sources and extent of proposed staffing of the schemes' advisory teams. The banks insisted that high-potential land be used, that qualified staff be provided, that settlers have the required financial resources and previous farming experience, and that the subprojects be consistent with the program as a whole in terms of costs and timetables.

The Loan Agreement between the lenders and the Kenya government was concluded on April 14, 1961, and signed in Washington and Nairobi the following month. In addition to the political and economic conditions mentioned above, the Loan Agreement rested on three fundamental assumptions: (1) that requisite funds were available to carry out the program over and above those provided by the lenders; (2) that the Agricultural Ordinance passed in 1955 and subsequently amended continue to remain in force; and (3) that the program would be administered through the Land Development and Settlement Board subject to existing legal provisions granting the minister of agriculture the right to issue directives to the board. On these conditions and subject to the requirement that subprojects qualify according to bank standards for development assistance, the banks agreed to provide £4,500,000 (£3.0 million by IBRD and £1.5 million by the CDC) to be repaid in twenty-one equal yearly installments following a four-year moratorium. The funds were not to be taxed and the interest rate was to be 1¼ percent above the rate at which the British government lent money as determined by the Overseas Resources Act of 1959.

A noteworthy feature of the Loan Agreement was the absence of any very specific provisions for constitutional and other institutional changes in Kenya in connection with the transfer of political and economic power. The agreement contained an understanding that the LDSB would retain "principal responsibility" for coordinating and executing the program. It was also understood that the Kenya minister for agriculture would inform the CDC and the IBRD of any changes in the structure or functions or principal personnel of the LDSB and afford the banks an opportunity for "discussion" on the proposed changes. This was the provision that was to cause the greatest difficulty after the agreement was signed. The agreement was premised on the maintenance of an efficient and expanding agricultural economy (the purpose of the 1955 Agricultural Ordinance and its later amendments) at a time when that very economic structure was threatened by large numbers of Africans who had no opportunity to participate in it. It was based on the continued existence of the administrative structure developed to meet the requirements of European colonization of the White Highlands at a time when the colonization process was in full retreat. The provision for "discussion" implied a mutual recognition that the political institutions of Kenya might change in connection with the transfer of power but did not include any guidelines indicating what would be acceptable lines of change from the point of view of the parties to the agreement. Indeed, no such guidelines could have been established without Kenya's in effect compromising the independence it was bent upon achieving.

The transfer of political power in Kenya very nearly coincided with the period of conflict and adjustment in the relationship between the Kenya government and the lenders—a period which was concluded by the signing in mid-1964 of a new and revised agreement. The problem was not primarily one of disagreements on specific policies or on institutional arrangements, although such disagreements existed and were important. However, they were derivative rather than fundamental. They arose because of a basic initial misunderstanding between the lenders and members of the Kenya government over the nature of the political process in Kenya and its relationship to economic development. The question was twofold: whether or not the political process was only coextensive with the process of allocating scarce material resources; and whether the achievement of maximum productivity from such resources was subordinate or superior to other political values.

There were three main problems in the relationship of the Kenya government to the lenders in implementing the settlement-scheme program, and these problems reflected the more fundamental questions concerning the nature of the political process in an independent Kenya. They were created by the expansion of the settlement program, by the rather stringent technical conditions the banks required, and by the replacement of the LDSB by the new Central Land Board.

The banks became concerned about the expansion of the settlement-scheme program almost as soon as it was proposed. This expansion included the "New" Scheme in late 1961 and the Million Acre Scheme in mid-1962. One official of one of the banks argued that the proposed expansion was problematical because it was unlikely that the original and the expansion programs could coexist without undermining the integrity of the banks' schemes. He believed that the two branches of the total settlement program (low- and high-density schemes) were very different and should not therefore be administered by the same board or agency. The lenders wanted the IBRD/CDC schemes to be kept distinct and their more ambitious programs and requirements to be maintained. They also worried that the classification of the two kinds of schemes could be impervious to political and administrative pressures. Underlying the lenders' concern was an unspoken assumption that the more ambitious schemes would be unpopular because they were designed to give the smallholders involved larger incomes and more prosperous farming enterprises than the other settlers and most other rural Kenyans would enjoy.[18] The difference between the two schemes, as a CDC head official expressed it, was that "one scheme is aimed at raising the standard of living of the settlers, the other is designed to start up subsistence farming in areas where the viability of more ambitious projects would be doubtful."

The banks' suspicions were increased because the Kenya government indicated very soon after the agreement was signed that it wanted to reduce the scale of the yeoman farmer section of the IBRD/CDC scheme and also the Assisted Owner Scheme. The future prime minister of Kenya, Jomo Kenyatta, was reported to have felt that the Assisted Owner Scheme was serving only the interests

18. These were views expressed by Swynnerton, Lord Howick, and Regional Comptroller Peter Wise, based on Kenyatta's talks with Arthur Gaitskill, then and still a member of the CDC board. They were also voiced in public by prominent members of KANU such as Gikonyo Kiano, then minister for labor in the government.

of the rich Africans at a time when the main concern should be to help the unemployed and landless Africans. Arthur Gaitskill, whose report influenced much of the present Kenya government's thinking, is said to have been sympathetic to this viewpoint.[19] In addition, the British government in late 1961 agreed to meet by grant the cost of pre-settlement and one-third of the cost of the land to the new smallholders. Consequently, the financial requirements for African settlers were significantly reduced. The British decision to take a more active part in the settlement program through the provision of a part of the land costs and the very substantial addition of the Million Acre Scheme was significant, also, because the British government did not believe that the two kinds of settlement schemes should be compartmentalized and isolated from one another. "We have nonetheless recognized the impracticability of running in harness the IBRD and CDC schemes on the present basis and the new peasant settlement schemes that are necessary. There must be no major difference between the two types of schemes if both are to be made to work. We have therefore accepted that modifications of the IBRD and CDC schemes are necessary for that reason and also because there are certain financial features of the existing scheme which Kenya maintains make it difficult to work." The Colonial Office was aware of the need to be circumspect in any modification of the IBRD/CDC project because of the possible objection and withdrawal of the IBRD.

After discussions between the Colonial Office and the Kenya government, the Kenya government proposed that the settlement program be modified by reducing the acreage and number of families in the IBRD/CDC Yeoman Scheme from 90,000 to 60,000 and 1,800 to 1,200 respectively, and that the IBRD/CDC Peasant Scheme be brought into line with the "New" Scheme for settling 12,000 landless and unemployed African families. This would differ from the existing requirements of the IBRD/CDC Peasant Scheme in that under the "New" Scheme settlers were not required to have previous farming experience or capital, land did not need to be underdeveloped and

19. Interviews with Lord Howick, R. J. M. Swynnerton, and N. S. Carey Jones.

of high potential, and the size of the development loan issued each settler was to be £100 rather than £400. It was even proposed—but rejected by the Kenya Council of Ministers—that the IBRD and CDC funds be transferred to some other phase of agricultural development and out of the settlement program altogether. This significant rejection implied that the Kenya government wished to give great emphasis and at least temporary high priority to the needs of the disinherited but did not wish to abandon settlement programs for the wealthier and more experienced African farmer. The British government also moderated the change in priorities by initially rejecting the settlement of 25,000 families under the "New" Scheme in favor of a 15,000-family program. Subsequently, however, the Million Acre Scheme increased the number of landless and unemployed families to 30,000. The British government held back the full Million Acre Settlement Scheme at least partly because it felt there might not be sufficient qualified manpower to implement it. The economic requirements of the settlement program were lowered in order to increase the numbers that could be settled, and the provisions for social services were also kept minimal. A major reason was the need to implement the schemes as fast as possible. A directive to all permanent secretaries concerning the implementation of the settlement schemes stated that:

> Some ministries already referred to the desirability of these settlement schemes being developed as model schemes so far as social services are concerned. However desirable this may be, it is not practicable if the target is to be achieved. It must therefore be accepted that, for the time being, such services will be below the normal standard set. The first object is to get settlers on the ground. Social services must be brought up to standard after this primary objective has been achieved.[20]

The settlement schemes for the most part could not be made models of economic development and rural living because of the need for

20. Issued on August 16, 1961.

haste. If anything, they would initially be less happy places in which to live than other rural areas. In relation to the total Kenya development budget for the years encompassing the transfer of power, a disproportionate amount of money was spent in a very short time on relatively few people. Hence the settlers were in one sense the favored elite of the rural areas. However, in relation to what was required to increase the productivity of the settlers and the Highlands and to create model rural communities on the settlements, too little money was available. Too much was required for too many in too short a time. In another sense, therefore, the inhabitants of the settlements were to remain among the less fortunate rural Africans. The expansion of the settlement program reflected the fact that too few Africans were being introduced to the modern economy via the IBRD/CDC schemes and that the high standards of those schemes made it difficult to implement them quickly. To achieve a viable post-independence political system it was essential that large numbers of Africans be given a stake quickly in the new Kenya. Creating viable economic farming units in the Highlands, which was the concern of the CDC and the IBRD, did not necessitate such speed and such numbers, nor were they desirable. The clash of these contradictory requirements of Kenya's economic and political systems in the establishment of the settlement program was temporarily resolved by an understanding between the parties that the IBRD and CDC yeoman and peasant farmers would remain the core of the land-settlement proposals in Kenya. This understanding, emerging out of talks between the parties in mid-1961, was short-lived. In mid-1962 it became clear that the British government contemplated a further expansion of the settlement program along the lines of the "New" Scheme, i.e., for landless, unemployed Africans not necessarily experienced in farming. The lenders immediately suspected that their program did not have the support of Kenya's African political leaders. One official of the CDC wrote a counterpart at the World Bank that he anticipated the possibility that the Kenya government would decide to give up their program in order to concentrate on the new high-density scheme. He pressed these misgivings despite the assurances given him by senior civil servants in the Kenya government that, in spite of the reduced acreage of the lenders' program, there was room for both kinds of schemes.[21]

The response of the IBRD and the CDC to the expansion of the settlement program demonstrated that the lenders believed its insulation from politics to be essential if the economic objectives were to be realized. They observed that the support given the program's objectives by the politicians was merely lip service, since politicians found it impossible to defend the standards of the IBRD/CDC scheme before their followers. The banks also observed that while the European and African communities for their differing reasons supported, even enthusiastically, the idea of the settlement program, they did not support the means whereby it might realize its purpose according to the lenders, i.e., economic development.

The IBRD and the CDC groped for a means of restructuring their investment in Kenya's land reform in such a way that their objective could be realized within a general program of land reform which, for political reasons, was not designed with economic development as its primary goal. One idea was to drop altogether the distinction between the IBRD/CDC schemes and the British "New" Scheme. The IBRD and the CDC would then channel their funds into those parts of the total land-resettlement program that showed economic potential. The requirements for land of a certain quality and for settlers with capital and previous farming experience would be dropped and funds would be channeled to those schemes and those settlers that had demonstrable economic potential. Underlying this proposal was an assumption that it would be possible and desirable to isolate the IBRD/CDC investment from political influence by redirecting it in this fashion. A CDC official explained that "there is just a possibility that by channelling our financial aid through a loan bank or something similar we could achieve a non-political

---

21. The Colonial Office assured CDC of continued support for the scheme, as did N. S. Carey Jones, permanent secretary in the Ministry of Lands and Settlement, and Bruce McKenzie, the minister. The leaders had no direct indication, however, of the views of African leaders and were perhaps not clear at the time on the major role McKenzie was to play in the independent government.

institutionalization of the loan department whilst leaving the selection, purchase, division, and allocation of land to the tribal, regional, and central politicians." The lenders believed that rapidly increasing the numbers of participants in the modern economy and diminishing the qualifications necessary for such participation in terms of land quality, farming experience, and working capital were "political" objectives not conducive to economic development. They proposed, therefore, to let these political movements take their course and to focus on those particular aspects of the total program that happened to possess economic potential.

The second difficulty between the banks and the Kenya government arose from the failure of the government to meet the standards for approval of subprojects established in the 1961 agreement between the lenders and the government. The inability of the Kenya government to meet the agreed subproject standards to the satisfaction of the lenders resulted in part because the standards themselves may have been impractical on technical grounds. In large measure, however, they were unworkable because of the political environment in which the program was to be implemented.

The Kenya government's initial subproject proposal allegedly contained six fundamental flaws sufficiently important to the lenders to make them reconsider the whole program. These shortcomings were: *(a)* too heavy a commitment of capital to the purchase of land and farm buildings and equipment; *(b)* too much low-grade land on the schemes recommended for CDC and IBRD financing; *(c)* a loan policy unsatisfactory for both the lenders and the borrowers; *(d)* the low level of the "true development element" on the proposed schemes; *(e)* the unsatisfactory budgeted net income for settlers on the schemes; and *(f)* the insufficiency of staff and training facilities vis-à-vis the settlers. Of the six, only the third was purely a technical problem. The development loans for cattle and for cash-crop development were for different periods of time. From the lenders' standpoint, the loan periods, extending up to fifteen years, were too long. From the settlers' perspective, the different loan periods were a cause of confusion and uncertainty. It was eventually agreed that all individual development loans would be for a period of ten years.

One of the first deviations from the Kenya government's initial plans that attracted the lenders' attention was the high prices being paid for farmland, buildings, and equipment. At first the high prices were attributed to a larger average plot acreage and greater need for farm machinery and equipment than had originally been believed necessary. The lenders noted that the higher capitalization resulted in the creation of a wealthier class of farmers, and correspondingly fewer farmers, than anticipated. The lenders considered that this constituted a fundamental change in the structure of the settlement scheme. The CDC's regional controller observed that, by approving maximum capitalization at such a level, they would be agreeing to a substantial modification of the scheme by allocating a large amount of capital for settling middle-class farmers instead of peasants and yeomen. The lenders expressed a willingness to be flexible on many of the subproject flaws as long as economic viability and net income accruing to the settlers were maintained. On the other hand, the relatively high capitalization lay in the higher land prices. If the settlement schemes, particularly the British government's high-density Million Acre Scheme, were intended in part to restore a market in land, it is noteworthy that the program apparently achieved this objective almost before it was implemented. Consequently the departing European settlers obtained a better price than the Kenya government must have anticipated, and fewer African settlers were placed on the land and at a greater expense to each individual settler. High officials in the Ministry of Lands and Settlement expressed the view, in late 1962, that the cost of land might be lowered if it were more carefully selected.[22] They justified the higher land and equipment investment on the grounds that such expenditures were necessary if the settlement schemes were to flourish, and that the schemes were essential if political foundations for Kenya's post-independence economic growth were to be established. As a high ministry official commented: "This was basically a political matter rather than a

---

22. Estimated 1959 values were the bases for calculating a fair value. The theory was that 1959 represented the last year when values would not have been abnormally affected by political uncertainty. There is some counterargument, though not a strong one, that prices were already in a decline that year.

purely economic scheme. The available money could be better spent in the African areas. If, however, it was not spent on settlement schemes it would render useless any expenditure in African areas or elsewhere." Some people in the Kenya government had already come to consider the scheme investment as a kind of political ransom forced upon it jointly by departing settlers and the large numbers of landless Africans. It was also, however, forced upon the government by the increase in landless and unemployed resulting from the program of land consolidation and registration which was the foundation of the Swynnerton plan.[23]

The higher-than-anticipated prices for land are even more remarkable given the lenders' objection that much of the land purchased was of less than high-potential quality. The IBRD and the CDC were evidently under a partial misapprehension concerning the character of the land in the European farming areas. One of the lenders' officials observed that the best land for settlement would be land of "reasonably even quality and level on gently undulating geographical features," suitable for a valuable cash crop. "In practice," he noted, "there is very little land like that in the highlands of Kenya and practically all the land on offer for settlement schemes can be classified as 'mixed farms' and it stands to reason that the original owners developed them as such because mixed farming was the only suitable form of utilization for their holdings. When the agriculturists are faced with the problem of subdividing such farms for settlement, purely technical considerations would result in AO units [the Yeoman-Assisted Owner part of the IBRD/CDC project] of several hundred acres being side by side with . . . smallholders on 15 acres, yeoman farms of 50 acres and . . . plots of 100 acres on the steep grazing slopes." The lenders' opposition to mixed farming suggests that they had assumed the existence of more high-quality land in the Highlands than was actually there. But it is surprising that the lenders should have been unaware of the Highlands' agricultural potential, since the CDC's chairman was a former Kenya governor with a deep personal interest in farming, and the

23. Interview with R. J. M. Swynnerton.

corporation's agricultural advisor was none other than R. J. M. Swynnerton. The Kenya government took the initiative in suggesting that the yeoman and peasant sections of the IBRD/CDC scheme be merged because of the difficulty of fitting subprojects into predetermined categories. The lenders agreed, and eventually the Peasant and Yeoman Schemes were renamed the Low-Density Scheme wherein farmers were budgeted to achieve a net income of £100 per year rather than the £250 for which the Yeoman Scheme farmers were budgeted. The lenders accepted the merger on condition that all the units meet the CDC's and the IBRD's terms and be economically viable. However, the banks retained their objections both to mixed farming and to the excessive amounts of less than high-potential land they believed were included in the first subproject. The technical problem in the selection of land may have been enlarged by political considerations. The minister of agriculture, Sir Michael Blundell, directed that the LDSB purchase land for one IBRD and CDC scheme and one British government scheme for each major African ethnic group as soon as possible.[24]

The IBRD and CDC found that the "development element" in the budgets proposed for the individual farmers was too low for their approval and financing, because of the unanticipated high capitalization and the lower agricultural potential of the land selected. These two problems, combined with an observed tendency on the part of the settlers to resort to staple crops rather than high-value cash crops, produced a lower budgeted net income for the farmers than the original proposals for the IBRD/CDC schemes indicated.[25] One estimate of the change in the "development element" was produced by one of the lenders' local officials, as shown on the next page.

The lenders took the view that the schemes, as they were beginning to appear, were far closer to the British government's high-density

24. Interview with Sir Michael Blundell.
25. None of the schemes as of 1966 attained the intended average income of £100 per settler. Some have come close, but only with the assistance of nonfarm income. See Farm Economics Survey Unit surveys of the settlement schemes, 1964 and 1965, unpublished. Interviews with Isaiah Mutuki, director of the FESU study; C. S. Gray, planning advisor to the Ministry of Economic Planning and Development; and A. T. Brough, chief statistician.

	Original Estimate		Existing Budgets	
Land/Buildings	30%		29%	
Permanent Improvements	0%	[30%]	11%	[40%]
Government Services	12%		28%	
Development Loans	58%		31%	

schemes than to the original proposals of the Kenya government to the CDC and the IBRD. They were thus fortified in their conviction that their schemes were outside the mainstream of Kenya's economic development program during the transfer of power and that Kenya for political reasons preferred to settle more farmers in more modest circumstances than the IBRD/CDC agreement envisaged. The banks did not wish to be outside the mainstream of Kenya's development. Thus they first considered restructuring their investment in the scheme, as described above, and they agreed to lower the budgeted net income figures for the settlers to £100, the minimum figure under the original proposals for the IBRD/CDC project.

Another major difficulty in the negotiations between the lenders and the Kenya government arose because the institutional framework for the settlement program began to change as a result of the impending transfer of political power. The original arrangements were for the Land Development and Settlement Board to operate in conjuction with the Department of Settlement. The LDSB was to be primarily in charge of implementing the government's policies vis-à-vis land resettlement. It was to be solely responsible for choosing properties to be bought for settlement and for negotiating their purchase. The board was to approve both the issue of development loans to the new settlers and the subdivision of the newly purchased farms for resettlement. The LDSB was to be the body principally responsible for preparing low-density settlement schemes and subprojects for submission to the IBRD and the CDC. On a day-to-day basis most of these responsibilities devolved on the board's executive officer, including the classification of land according to its suitability for IBRD/CDC schemes or for British-financed high-density schemes. The Department of Settlement, and particularly its director, were originally established for liaison. "The purpose of creating this post is to ensure the maximum cooperation and cohesion on the part of the various government departments and ministries in the execution of the schemes." In addition, once the subproject and scheme proposals and the land had been prepared, the director of settlement was to supervise getting the settlers on the land and established on their plots.

The difficulty between the lenders and the Kenya government concerned the structure and functions of the LDSB and in particular the officials who were to be in charge of loan administration. Very soon after the agreement was signed, the Kenya government proposed to modify the Land Development and Settlement Board in such a way as to strengthen the Department of Settlement.[26] They also sought to create a Central Land Board, as agreed at the 1962 Lancaster House Conference. This involved changes in the relationship of the settlement apparatus to the other departments of the government and a closer integration of loan administration and other board activities with the Department of Settlement. Since this was in part an internal change, as both the LDSB and the emerging Department of Settlement were under the control of the same minister and permanent secretary, the lenders initially tried to take an accommodating view of these administrative changes. However, they were concerned that the appointment of a principal financial officer responsible to the permanent secretary would not insure that adequate attention would be paid to the IBRD and CDC loan, because of his other duties. They were also doubtful whether such an officer would be as well insulated from politics as a corresponding officer of the LDSB might be. They also felt that the proposed creation of a Central Land Board would amount to a basic change in the structure and functions of the board as set forth in the agreement between the lenders and the Kenya government.

26. See chapter 3.

The proposed constitutional and administrative changes were the subject of discussions in mid-1962 in which the lenders, the Kenya government, and the major political parties were all concerned. These discussions were particularly important because the representatives of Kenya's future independent government responded to the lenders' concern for the maintenance of a satisfactory institutional structure, and especially to their concern that the settlement schemes remain insulated from politics. The Ministry of Agriculture representative emphasized the Kenya government's intention of excluding the large-scale farming areas around Kitale and Nakuru from settlement-scheme planning. For these areas he wanted the CDC, in particular, to lend £400,000 to the Land and Agricultural Bank to enable farmers, both European and African, to purchase farms. The European farmers in the settlement-scheme areas would thus be able to sell their farms to the LDSB (later the CLB) and to buy in one of these areas reserved for large-scale farming. The agriculture officials suggested that, although the Million Acre Scheme necessarily commanded first priority at the time, the proposal to secure aid for Land Bank financing of large-scale farm purchases by farmers of all races was a portent of the Kenya government's intention to emphasize economic production rather than simply to transfer farm assets between the races. In the new environment, the IBRD/CDC scheme would gain higher priority because it was designed with economic as well as political objectives in mind. KADU ministers expressed a fear of economic bankruptcy resulting from the fragmentation of large farms. The evident purpose of these arguments was to persuade the lenders that the future Kenya government would create an environment favorable to economic development. Since there was apparent conflict between the maintenance of rigorous economic requirements and the political responsibility of elected leaders to their constituents, it appears that the Kenya government was proposing in effect the creation of an economic system independent of formal political processes. Political processes would be molded to fit the requirements of the developing economic system rather than vice versa.

A great deal of the discussion in mid-1962 focused on the

proposed Central Land Board (CLB). The CDC in particular insisted that it was a fundamental premise of their commitment to the Kenya resettlement program that their loan be administered by a body that was independent of political influence. They feared that loans might be issued on the basis of political influences rather than economic criteria, because civil servants would not be able to remain aloof from politics. The representatives of the Kenya government insisted that, since they were ultimately responsible for the repayment of the loans from the IBRD, the CDC, and the British government, they must control the loan machinery. Oddly, the CLB that had emerged out of the 1962 Lancaster House Conference with the approval of nearly all the representatives of both major African parties had given the Kenya government rather less control over the day-to-day implementation of the settlement program than its predecessor, the LDSB.[27] The enabling statute of the LDSB gave the minister specific powers to direct the activities of the board, while the provision for the CLB clearly excluded any ministerial direction of its operations. Agriculture officials complained that their minister had found that the LDSB required frequent directives from him and was not able to function efficiently on its own. The lenders were prepared to permit the CLB to handle the purchase of the land but wanted a separate official to administer the CDC and IBRD funds. They did not consider that the director of settlement and the proposed principal financial officer were sufficiently independent of political influence. KANU representatives argued, however, that the whole structure of Kenya government was changing, that the machinery of government would be established to suit Kenya's interests, and that the CDC and the IBRD would have to work within the framework Kenya established. The party insisted that the Kenya government expected to face the difficult task of denying loans to African farmers. It was not sympathetic with the CDC's argument that an independent administering authority was desirable to shield

27. The authorizing legislation for the old LDSB empowered the minister for agriculture to give specific directions to the board should he choose. McKenzie found it necessary to do so, and this was one reason why he was determined to have it changed. The new Central Land Board included no such provision for ministerial direction.

the Kenya government from an unpopular responsibility. Agriculture spokesmen reiterated that the economic development pursued by the lenders was that being adopted increasingly by the Kenya government. The representatives of KANU thus sought to persuade the lenders to accept indications of compatibility between the lenders and the Kenya government on the nature and importance of economic policy as a substitute for institutional safeguards which were undergoing change. The lenders, for the time being, considered the LDSB in its original form to be "an essential condition" of the Loan Agreement.

The Colonial Office entered the dispute when it feared that the CDC and/or the IBRD might decide to withdraw. In order to preserve the agreement, the Colonial Office indicated it was prepared to insist on the Kenya government's acquiescence to the IBRD and CDC requirements as a condition for Kenya's receiving any further British government money. Thus fortified, the CDC, on behalf of the IBRD and itself, was prepared to insist that their project be maintained as a separate entity along the lines originally approved. As a second line of defense, the lenders were prepared to approve the seconding of a loan officer attached directly to the chairman of the CLB rather than to the permanent secretary of the Ministry of Lands and Settlement (as the Kenya government wished). The lenders' position was that, although the abolition of the LDSB would create difficulties, they would not absolutely insist on its retention as a condition for continuing their loan if suitable alternative machinery were set up. The CDC explained to the IBRD.that the CLB would be a "high-level" constitutional body, lacking the technical expertise to manage the settlement schemes financed by IBRD and CDC. Consequently, CDC proposed, a small committee of experienced farmers with the lenders' own loan officer (attached directly to the chairman of the CLB) would be desirable.

In September, representatives of these groups came to terms. KANU and KADU, after some disagreement, had agreed to a division of responsibility between the new CLB and the Department of Settlement. The terms of the accord were that CLB would handle the land purchase while the Department of Settlement would handle the implementation. This was a contravention of the Lancaster House Conference constitutional framework—a discrepancy that came to light six months later in the public furor surrounding the appointment of General Sir Geoffrey Bourne as CLB chairman.[28] The modified LDSB had already begun operating pending the introduction of the CLB. This modified LDSB was given the task of advising on the boundaries of tribal spheres of influence for the purpose of allocating areas to particular ethnic groups.[29]

Finally, KANU again sought to persuade the lenders to accept the new Kenya constitutional arrangements by explaining that African leaders were increasingly coming to accept a set of values similar to those held by the lenders: i.e., subordination of the process of allocating social values to the objective of achieving the most efficient allocation of material resources. The party leaders explained that, after the first year of purchase, the need for high-density schemes would lapse and the IBRD and CDC Yeoman and Peasant Low-Density Schemes would be given preference. In their opinion Africans were beginning to prefer IBRD and CDC schemes to the High-Density Scheme as they realized how much more than the High-Density Scheme they contributed to the country's economy.[30] In subsequent conversations with the lenders they reiterated their wish for the CDC and the IBRD to lend funds to the Kenya Land and Agricultural Bank because they wanted the bank to have the money it would need to maintain a market for productive large-scale farms whether the buyers were European or African. They indicated a willingness to help efficient European farmers in the settlement-scheme areas to purchase large-scale farms elsewhere with Land Bank assistance. Finally, they urged upon the lenders a program to enable skilled technical personnel to remain in Kenya to assist post-independence agricultural development.[31] (Virtually every one of the senior European officials who have left the Department of Settlement

---

28. See chapter 4.
29. *Ibid.*
30. *Ibid.*
31. *Ibid.* As the concluding chapter will show, this use of technical personnel was virtually forced on the Kenya government later by the leaders at the expense of Britain's Ministry of Overseas Development.

have been hired by the IBRD and reposted to Kenya, where they continue to be available for consultation and advice.) KANU sought to prevent a firm Kenya position on constitutional structure, in conjunction with the view that the emerging similarity of outlook between the lenders and the principal African political leaders on the nature and importance of economic development strategy obviated the need for the special institutional safeguards the lenders desired.

The lenders, however, were of one mind, insisting that the modified LDSB and the CLB did not suitably protect IBRD's and CDC's interests. They still wished their schemes to be insulated against political influence. In this apparent impasse, it was the lenders who finally relented. They eventually agreed that a separate Ministry of Settlement, independent of the vast Ministry of Agriculture and working in combination with the CLB along the lines agreed upon by the two major parties, would be satisfactory. They accepted the agriculture officials' argument that the LDSB as presently constituted was inefficient. (In arguing for a separate ministry the lenders, perhaps without their knowledge, supported the views of KADU.)[32] The Kenya government in return agreed to the appointment of special officials whose particular responsibility would be the implementation of the CDC and IBRD schemes. The constitutional separation of the CLB and the Ministry of Settlement would be more theoretical than practical. The CLB retained the right to approve settlement schemes before the Department of Settlement implemented them, but the CLB would consult with the ministry on its proposed land purchases. The British government subsequently accepted the revised arrangements.[33] All but the Kenya Coalition were

32. KADU in fact preferred the separate ministry as part of its strategy of dividing power at the central government level between the two houses of Parliament and between the CLB and the regular government ministries. KADU was prepared to accept the division of responsibility between the CLB and the Department of Settlement if the latter were placed in a separate Ministry of Lands independent of agriculture and independent of local government, with which it had in the past been combined.

33. The Colonial Office, the CDC, and the IBRD took turns expressing dismay and lack of confidence in the constitutional changes taking place in Kenya. Initially the CDC and the World Bank found the European participation in the settlement organization to be excessive, while the Colonial Office agreed. When the project first was being implemented the IBRD had an internal debate over the wisdom of continuing, which was resolved in favor of continued

a party to the changed role of the new Central Land Board.[34] That they could be kept ignorant for as long as six months was an indication of the declining importance of the right-wing European element as well as of the increasing agreement among the other main political groups in Kenya. The Kenya government had demonstrated to the lenders that its responsibility for the settlement program was now too large to permit delegating authority for the program's implementation to an independent authority outside the government's control.

The agreement that was reached encountered some opposition. The staffs in the lenders' headquarters were still concerned about maintaining the autonomy of the IBRD/CDC enterprise; simultaneously, the Colonial Office was intent on maintaining the original idea of a Central Land Board with full powers of implementation as well as land purchase and scheme approval. Eventually these difficulties were resolved along the lines of the Nairobi accord. Perhaps the parties all realized what one official of the lenders observed: "There is no doubt that the Government has unrestricted control over settlement in all its aspects and that settlement is one of the central political issues and will remain so for many years." The lenders had essentially agreed to build a scheme dedicated to economic development within a political framework established by the Kenya government, despite their initial protestations implying that they would accept only the reverse. Perhaps one major reason for their willingness to compromise was evidence supporting McKenzie's contention that at least the major African leaders were coming to share the values of the lenders themselves. The report of the IBRD mission was in the process of being written as the 1962 Kenya Constitutional Conference at Lancaster House took place, and the mission

---

participation at about the time the Colonial Office became disenchanted with the change in the functions of the CLB to which the banks and the Kenya government had subsequently agreed. During the renegotiation of the settlement program, the Colonial Office felt it necessary to persuade the CDC to stay with the program, while the IBRD appeared to be prepared to work within the changed circumstances.

34. The Kenya Coalition regarded the change in the function and structure of the CLB as yet another example of Perfidious Albion at work. See chapter 4.

was therefore in touch with the participants at that conference. Arthur Gaitskill's views had been made known to KANU by the time of the critical meetings in August and September of 1962. Thus, representatives of both lenders were in a position to know the thinking of senior African political leaders and to be aware of the Kenya leaders' concern for the state of the economy.

High-Density Schemes.   The High-Density Settlement Scheme program was inaugurated in late 1962 by the British government in response to substantial European pressure and threats. It was part of the general program begun at the 1962 Lancaster House Conference to protect the political and economic interests of Kenya's various racial and ethnic minorities as independence approached. In essence, the purpose of the program was to accommodate the needs of some of Kenya's large numbers of landless and unemployed Africans, whose situation was too desperate for the slow healing processes of economic development and whose numbers and poverty were too great for them to be accommodated in the IBRD/CDC apparatus. The High-Density Scheme was in essence an enlargement of the "New" Scheme announced in late 1961 and was designed to accommodate 25,000 to 30,000 families on plots designed to yield net incomes of from £25 to £70 per year.

The meetings with the lenders in August and September of 1962 had resulted in a restructuring of the settlement organization. After the reorganization there were three principal organizations: the Central Land Board; the Department of Settlement, operating within the ministry of Lands and Settlement and Water, which also contained Departments of Lands, Land Consolidation, and Town Planning; and the Settlement Fund Trustees—a committee consisting of the ministers of agriculture, settlement, and finance—whose job was to oversee the operations of the settlement program and, in particular, to watch over its financial aspects. The Department of Settlement, headed by two veteran agricultural officers, was a very comprehensive department. In addition to administrative staff assigned to manage the legal and financial aspects of the settlement program, compile and record settlement-scheme statistics, and handle the program's

marketing problems, there were a number of specialist officers seconded from other ministries to look after particular aspects of the
settlement program. There were representatives of the Departments
of Cooperative Development, Veterinary Services, and Works, as
well as the Ministry of Agriculture. The Departments of Lands and
Town Planning, both in the Ministry of Lands and Settlement, assisted with the documentation and scheme layouts.

The field organization was designed to give intensive supervision
to the new settlers over at least the first two and one-half years of
the program, after which settlers would be advised in the same way
as other African farmers. This period was later extended. Only since
late 1966 has the Department of Settlement started to withdraw
officers from the field.[35] The settlement program in the field was
divided into four areas, each headed by an area controller and a
deputy area controller. These areas did not correspond to the regular
provincial boundaries, and the area controllers were not included in
the "provincial teams" consisting of the provincial commissioner
(the chief administrative officer) and the various specialist officers
from other ministries.[36] The structure indicates clearly the Department of Settlement's essential independence from the administrative
structure of the country. Each settlement area was divided among
two or more "senior settlement officers," each in charge of overseeing
a group of individual settlement schemes. Each individual settlement

35. This process involved withdrawing settlement officers from individual schemes, leaving
a group of schemes under the direct responsibility of the senior settlement officer. The official
explanation was that the funds were beginning to run out, since the settlement organization
was to be dismantled and the schemes placed under the authority of the Ministry of Agriculture on the same basis after twenty-seven months under the Settlement Department. In reality,
the Ministry of Agriculture has withdrawn seconded agricultural officers from settlement and
also from its soil conservation unit. The minister, McKenzie, is directly responsible for the
decision. Part of the reason concerns his personal feud with the minister of lands and settlement, Jackson Angaine. But this may in turn derive from McKenzie's belief that Kenya's
general agricultural program is suffering from the concentration of qualified personnel in the
Settlement Department.

36. The initial idea was that the settlements would be located on the fringes of the White
Highlands to facilitate their inclusion within particular ethnic spheres of influence. The idea
was dropped with the expansion of the settlement schemes, in part because it became apparent
that the settlers would need greater attention than other farmers and in part because the
lenders, the British government, and the outgoing Kenya government recognized the need to
keep those farmers responsible for Kenya's external debts administratively separate.

scheme was under the supervision of a "settlement officer" assisted by clerical staff. The field administration, like the head office, was supplemented by officers seconded from other departments. The settlement officer was assisted by agricultural instructors, veterinary assistants, health assistants, and tribal policemen. In spite of this assistance, the settlement officers were required to be men of many skills. In the early days especially, they gave first aid in matters ranging from agricultural advice and installing roads and bridges to administering the law, settling marital fracases, and delivering babies.[37] Settlement officers are still generalists. Those who have been less able have become in effect lords of the manor, frequently living in the houses of departed European settlers and doing relatively little, in the eyes of the new African settlers, to earn their keep. Those who are more competent have gained an almost filial respect from the African settlers because of the variety of services which they performed. Such officers have received a kind of professional identity from the comprehensiveness of their responsibility for the settlers' interests. In addition, the Department of Settlement has engaged in farming operations of its own by caring for land and livestock between the departure of European farmers and the arrival of new settlers. Finally, the field administration of the land-resettlement program has been reinforced by nearly sixty Peace Corps volunteers from the United States who have served the individual settlements and the settlers in a variety of capacities.[38]

Implementation has been essentially similar for the low-density and the high-density schemes: a complicated and comprehensive process involving assistance and personnel from a great number of ministries in the government. Given the comprehensiveness of the process and the insulation of the Settlement Department from the government as a whole, the settlement institutions and personnel

37. Interviews with approximately 200 settler farmers and twenty settlement officers in the field. Perhaps the most enlightening interviews with settlement officers bearing on this point were those with J. R. Ojwang and M. W. Opi, settlement officers in the Northern Area.

38. The settlement schemes had the benefit of nearly sixty Peace Corps volunteers of the 200 in Kenya as a whole. They represent between 25 and 30 percent of the Settlement Department staff. Perhaps their most valuable function has been in overseeing the activities of the cooperative societies on the settlements.

have in effect been a government unto themselves—a government within a government. On the whole, the settlement "government" has been characterized by a closer and more rigorous relationship between governors and governed than is the case outside the settlement program.

LAND PURCHASE

Land purchase is the first step in the settlement process. In theory this has been the sole responsibility of the Central Land Board. In practice there has been a working relationship between the Department of Settlement and the CLB on the matter of land purchase.[39] The theoretical division of power served the Department of Settlement well; complaints, frequently from Europeans, concerning land purchase could be directed to the board, thus sparing the department much correspondence and potential political trouble and allowing it to get on with the business of implementing the program. The practical cooperation between the ministry and the board was mutually beneficial. The ministry's former permanent secretary observed that "although independent, the Board derives its finance from the Government which therefore has some ultimate say in what happens and, in practice, the staff of the Board and the Government's settlement staff work in close concert, so that land which is useless for settlement is not bought and so that major political issues and developments are taken into account by the Board."[40] Land purchase involved at least three distinct subprocesses: classification of the land on agricultural and technical grounds; consideration of the political parameters that dictated placement of the settlement schemes; and actual valuation, negotiation, sale, and transfer. Only the last was

39. Interviews with J. Nimmo, executive officer of the CLB; N. S. Carey Jones, former permanent secretary, Ministry of Lands and Settlement; James Maina, director of settlement 1965–67; and James Mburu, director 1967–. Also, interviews with the Hon. James Gachago, assistant minister for lands and settlement; the Hon. J. H. Angaine, minister for lands and settlement; and Peter Shiyukah, permanent secretary, Ministry of Lands and Settlement.

40. N. S. Carey Jones, "Land Resettlement Schemes in Kenya," *Africa Quarterly* (April–June, 1964), p. 4.

in fact executed almost entirely by the Central Land Board.

In classifying the agricultural potential of the land, the government and the board were confronted by the basic agricultural fact that the European farming areas contained only about 20 percent of Kenya's high-potential agricultural land (land with an annual average rainfall of 30 to 35 inches).[41] On the other hand, only about 20 percent of the land in European possession was high-potential agricultural land. Perhaps 500,000 to 600,000 acres of European farmland was of this top quality. Land was also classified according to suitability for high-density settlement, low-density settlement, or ranching and plantation agriculture. The last category was excluded from purchase for settlement; consequently, the coffee, tea, and sisal plantation interests have been a moderating influence in the European farming community. They were more inclined to view the prospect of an African government with equanimity because they were reasonably certain that no Kenya government would want to interfere with their highly productive operations. Tea and sisal have, however, been introduced on some of the high- and low-density settlements, with considerable success in the case of tea. The ranching lands were generally excluded, although ranching settlement schemes have been started in the Kamba country of Eastern Province.[42]

The principal political requirement governing the purchase of land was that the traditional "spheres of influence" of Kenya's various African communities should be determined and respected. Further, each major African community was to be given at least one IBRD/CDC settlement scheme and one British government settlement scheme. The settlement schemes served different political purposes in each major African sphere of influence. The Kamba settlements in Eastern Province were primarily to accommodate overpopulation in a generally poor area of the country. Here the European settlers were on better than usual terms with the Afri-

41. Great Britain, *East Africa Royal Commission, 1953–1955: Report*, British Sessional Papers, 1956, Vol. XIII (397), Cmd. 9475 (London: H.M.S.O., 1956), map insert.

42. Interviews with A. Storrar, V. E. M. Burke, and G. R. Henderson.

cans.[43] The vast majority of the Kikuyu settlement schemes were in Nyandarua District, to the west of traditional Kikuyuland, and were to provide expansion room for unemployed and landless Kikuyu. Their landlessness and unemployment resulted from land consolidation in Kikuyuland, from the release of detainees, and from personnel dismissed from European farms as development on them was suspended.[44] European employees who had been retained to the last were also to be included. Nyandarua was a controversial settlement project, partly because the European farmers in this area included some of the most prominent and most outspoken members of the European community, and partly because the Masai claimed several thousand acres of Nyandarua on the grounds that this land had previously been theirs rather than the Kikuyu's.[45] The Masai were not numerous enough to require settlement schemes, and the presence of Kikuyu in Nyandarua prevented the Masai from continuing to use the area for ceremonial purposes as they had done under the European regime. The Masai, including the Masai assistant ministers in the government, continue to express their dissatisfaction and resentment over this whenever the opportunity presents itself.[46] The remainder of the Kikuyu settlement schemes were in Nyeri, the northernmost of the Kikuyu districts in Central Province, and in this district they were designed to accommodate overpopulation in the Kikuyu districts of Fort Hall and Kiambu and to absorb those Kikuyu "repatriated" from other districts in Eastern Province and elsewhere.[47]

43. Interviews with settlers on the Mua Hills settlement scheme; the district commissioner of Machakos District, Isaiah Cheluget; and L. E. K. Lawrence-Brown, settlement officer for Mua Hills complex.

44. Interview with R. J. M. Swynnerton.

45. The Masai assistant ministers in the government do not hesitate even today to embarrass their cabinet colleagues by reasserting this claim.

46. J. L. N. Konchellah and S. N. Oloitipitip are perhaps the most outspoken on this subject.

47. A very substantial percentage of the settlers in the Nyeri area were Kikuyu repatriated from Embu and Meru spheres of influence to the north and east. Neither of these peoples wished to be associated with the Kikuyu in the same region at independence (see Great Britain, Colonial Office, *Kenya: Report of the Regional Boundaries Commission,* British Sessional Papers, 1962, Vol. X [543], Cmnd. 1899 [London: H.M.S.O., 1962]), and these settlers expressed a desire to return to Central Province in part because of the feelings of the Embu and Meru.

The settlement schemes on the western side of the Rift Valley bore witness to one function that European settlement had served: the creation of a buffer zone between African communities that were not always on the best of terms. The area around Sotik in southwestern Kenya was divided between the Kisii and the Kipsigis peoples. Settlement here seems primarily to have served the political purpose of maintaining a buffer, since the area was not attractive on agricultural grounds. In addition, the settlement was isolated, unlike others, from any significant urban center. When independence approached, the Kericho branch of the Kenya Cooperative Creameries (KCC) announced that it would not continue to serve the area, so that the dairy products upon which the new African settlers were to be primarily dependent would have to be transported much further to Nakuru with consequent losses in income and delays in payment. Although KCC has recently been persuaded to reestablish its Kericho branch, settlers in the area, particularly the Kipsigis, resent the government's failure to provide them with any marketable and profitable cash crop.[48] This is an interesting indication of how far the Kipsigis have come from their earlier reliance upon a purely pastoral existence. In west central Kenya, the Luo were provided with low-density settlement schemes budgeted for sugar production. Luo land is densely populated and required some form of settlement scheme to help relieve the resulting pressures. The only solution was to place the Luo schemes at the eastern edge of Nyanza Province, in an area that the Nandi peoples living to the northeast had long considered to be a part of their sphere of influence.[49] To the north, land was set aside for the Abaluhya peoples in the eastern section of Western

48. One of the most interesting recent developments is the economic progress of the Kipsigis and their relative exclusion from major political posts in the government. There are no Kipsigis ministers or assistant ministers. The Kipsigis were among the first to express an interest in land reform and to enclose their holdings. On the other hand, today they have been passed up by the Kikuyu and many others, including the Kisii. Their interest in land reform and agricultural development proved temporary. The Kipsigis settlement schemes lack the cash crops that their neighbors the Kisii and other ethnic groups on other settlement schemes enjoy.

49. See B. J. Walter, "The Territorial Expansion and Organization of the Nandi, 1850–1905" (Ph.D. diss., University of Wisconsin, Madison, 1968).

Province to ease their overpopulation problem. Finally, on the other side of the Western Province–Rift Valley border, some settlement-scheme land was reserved for the Nandi people. The Nandi were settled on the farms of Europeans of South African origin, whose relations with the Africans were perhaps the worst in Kenya.[50] Shortly before independence, more of the European farms in this area were actually abandoned than elsewhere.

Valuation, negotiation, sale, and transfer of the land were under-taken by the Central Land Board. Farms were to be sold at the prices of 1959, the last year before land prices were adversely affected by the prospect of political change. The value of all permanent improve-ments relating to the profitability of each European farm was taken into account. A maximum of £1,300 was allowed for the departing farmer's house, but the figure could be raised to £2,500 if the house had any value to the settlement schemes. This allowance was in most cases substantially below the house's value, given normal times and a transfer of the farm intact to another owner, but the allowance was often above the house's worth to the settlement operation. Specula-tion was prevented by a directive from the minister of settlement to the old LDSB that, where land under consideration for settlement-scheme purposes had been sold after January 1, 1961, the price would be that of the last sale. Notice of the farms to be purchased was published several months in advance. European farmers were given the option of selling or not selling. Most sold voluntarily, though there are some allegations, difficult to document, that government valuers panicked settlers into selling against their wishes.[51] Once a farmer had agreed to sell, valuation was carried out and he was made a preliminary offer. The CLB's chief executive officer was empow-

---

50. There were several instances of abandoned farms or "mined" farms, probably more than in any other areas of European settlement, in this area.

51. It is impossible to evaluate these claims. The allegations, not surprisingly, all come from European settlers or present and former European civil servants. Some of these same people also now realize that their panic at the prospect of independence was not fully justified, notwithstanding the widespread instance of looting that took place before the new government was able to establish its position. Such people now feel some need to explain their insistence on selling. On the other hand, the ability of the Settlement Department and the CLB to obtain large contiguous blocs of land for settlement suggests either that the government saw to it that everyone in a given area was persuaded to sell or, alternatively, that once some had decided to sell, others sold in order not to be left alone.

ered to raise or lower the valuation by as much as 5 percent on the basis of representations from the prospective seller and the government's valuer.[52] Mortgage claims on the properties were cleared and the vendor was given the remainder. At first farmers were paid in installments, but the British government finally agreed to lump-sum payments when it discovered there was no financial advantage to installment payments.

Between the time of purchase and the transfer of plots to African smallholders, the Department of Settlement undertook the operations necessary to maintain the farm's productivity, including maintaining stock holding grounds from which settlers could draw cattle at prices related to their value to the settlers, thus sparing the new settlers from making unwise purchases on their own. The cost of the cattle and the cost of an initial plowing for the settlers prior to their takeover were charged against their development loans. A major objective of these interim farming operations, in addition to defraying the cost of the program, was to prevent members of the Land Freedom Army or squatters from occupying the land.[53]

In planning the subdivision of the European farms into African smallholdings, the principal objective was to maintain the gross production in the settlement area at the level achieved by the previous occupants. The settlement schemes were to accomplish this by budgeting the farms in such a way that the farmers would be able to produce subsistence, to pay the due amount of the loan payment, and to net £25 to £100 income. The subsistence figure on the low-density schemes was set at £40 per family, and on the high-density schemes it was the produce from two acres.[54] It was assumed that the net income figure would provide a source for investment in the further development of the plots.

The settlements' boundaries were drawn so that the average high-

---

52. The records have not yet been made available to indicate how often reevaluation actually took place. The pressures on the CLB were more substantial from the European than from the African side, to judge from appearances. Hence it is possible that upward reevaluation of the houses was fairly common.

53. The Land Freedom Army was an organization of forest fighters and others seeking free land for Africans. Both African and government leaders feared that they would take over unused or underdeveloped land. See chapter 3.

54. Interviews with A. Storrar and N. S. Carey Jones.

density one ranged over 10,000 acres, while the average low-density settlement was about 5,000 acres. The differences in size are extreme, ranging from the 624-acre Mathatani settlement to the 41,000-acre Lukenya ranching settlement—both within fifty miles of Nairobi. Similarly, the number of plotholders varies tremendously, from the 54 families living on the Lietego scheme in southwest Kenya to the 907-family South Kinangop scheme. The settlement areas were subdivided on the basis of contour maps, prepared by aerial photography for the larger land blocs and by plane table survey for small units.[55] The areas were analyzed for soil type and water availability. The plans included provision for village centers, schools, roads, and watering points for livestock. The haste of planning and implementation, necessitated by the pressures from both Europeans and landless Africans prior to independence, resulted in inadequate provision at first. It is now one of the Department of Settlement's principal responsibilities to complete the process of scheme implementation by providing these services now that more time is available—even though the department has less staff and fewer funds than previously.[56]

With the areas demarcated and subdivided and the budgets prepared, the schemes were ready for actual settlement. Under the constitution devised at Lancaster House shortly before independence, selection of their settlers was to be made under the scrutiny of the president of each Regional Assembly to insure that no ethnic spheres of influence would be breached. With the end of the *Majimbo* Constitution, the provincial commissioners of the provinces in which the schemes were to be placed assumed the responsibility of passing on the roster of prospective African settlers. (The provincial commissioners, incidentally, are seldom of the predominant ethnic group in

55. Numerous mistakes were made in the course of hasty surveying. Correcting such mistakes is one of the Department of Settlement's principal tasks in "tidying up" the hastily assembled settlement operation now that the settlements are on the ground and the pressure of time is no longer a factor.

56. One of the main complaints of the settlement critics is not only that the settlers were charged for the land, or charged too much too soon, but that services have not been adequately provided. Some settlement officers themselves hold this view.

the regions they administer.) [57] Settler selection has been different on the low-density and the high-density settlement schemes. In the high-density areas, the matter is largely in the hands of the same local committees which were established to ascertain the ethnic group and the character of the prospective settlers and to determine whether they are landless and unemployed.[58] The provincial commissioner then passes on the recommended list. On the low-density settlements, prospective settlers must establish their farming experience and their capital resources. They must have the approval of the district agricultural officer; a committee consisting of the district agricultural officer and two settlement officers makes the final selection. Once selected, the new settlers are expected to find their own means of moving themselves, their families, and their belongings to the settlements, and then to construct a dwelling, plow at least an acre, make the first payment on their loan, help in the establishment of a cooperative society, and seek training either at one of the local Farmers Training Centres or from the agricultural instructors or officers—all within six months to a year of their arrival. Individually and/or collectively, the settlers are expected to arrange for the marketing of their produce.

PROBLEMS OF IMPLEMENTATION

We have analyzed the process of implementing the settlement-scheme program as it evolved over a period of approximately four years, from late 1962 to 1966. It would be a colossal misunderstanding if it were assumed that the process was completely orderly and smoothly conducted from the start or that it took place without serious mistakes. An accurate assessment of the process must include the substantial evidence that the settlement schemes were imple-

57. None of the provincial commissioners, for example, of June, 1967, was from ethnic groups within the province he administered.
58. There were, of course, many exceptions. Many M.P.'s and members of the Kenya cabinet have plots on the settlements. Their relatives have also obtained plots; few of these people qualified as unemployed, though they have been landless.

mented with commendable zeal, dedication, and ingenuity by a significant percentage of the settlement personnel. But it must also include the evidence that many of the early field officers of the Department of Settlement did considerable harm to the program by their malfeasance, their apparent underlying resentment that the program was taking place at all, and in some cases their dishonesty.[59] Mistakes were made, and those responsible for the program may not have drawn as much as they could have on the experience of earlier settlement schemes established within the former African areas themselves. On the other hand, there were significant differences between these earlier schemes and the Million Acre Scheme; also, the program was necessarily undertaken with considerable haste, which precluded serious study of the older schemes. There are some important problems in the settlement schemes as they now function. Nevertheless, the schemes have undoubtedly served to help restore a market in agricultural land, to relieve the seriousness of rural and urban unemployment, and to breach the unwanted European enclave in the Highlands. These factors must be borne in mind in the discussion of the problems of settlement implementation that follows here and in the next chapter.

There have been three major problems in the process of getting the schemes on the ground. These have arisen in connection with land purchase, selection of settlers, and relationships between the Department of Settlement and the other departments involved in the program both directly and through seconded personnel. The problems involved in land purchase concerned the compassionate case farms, the Ol Kalou Salient, and some of the European farms of the Kinangop plateau composing much of Nyandarua District. Those concerning settler selection arose because of the necessity for a "crash" program of settlement shortly before independence and because of the existence of African resident laborers on European

---

59. The evidence for this charge is to be found in the files of the resident magistrates who preside over the courts of first resort. Many settlement officers and other settlement personnel, both European and African, have been convicted on charges involving petty thievery or embezzlement. I am grateful to the resident magistrates for making their files available to me.

farms. The difficulties in relations with other departments involved the conflict of development strategies employed by the Departments of Settlement, Cooperative Development, Agriculture, and the Ministry of Economic Planning and Development, as their programs came together in the creation of the settlement schemes.

The Department of Settlement wanted land that was suitable for development by smallholders for the high-density as well as the low-density schemes. The high-density requirements were less strict, but given the narrow margins on which the high-density settlers were to operate, it was important that the land be chosen carefully. Difficulties arose because the interests of the European settlers who were selling and the African settlers who were buying did not entirely correspond.[60] The Regional Boundaries Commission had extended the boundaries of Central Province westward to include what was to be the Nyandarua District. All the area in Nyandarua was to be given over to settlement schemes except for Ol Kalou Salient, a section covering 102,000 acres in the northern part of the district which was unsuitable for anything but large-scale ranching and possibly wheat-growing. The 100 European families farming in this area, however, were unwilling to continue to farm because they would be surrounded on two sides by African farmers in the settlement schemes. These Europeans were not content, therefore, merely to have their land excluded from the settlement-scheme land purchases. They observed the growing land pressure in the Kikuyu area and the increasing unemployment among Kikuyu both in Central Province (then Region) to the east and in Rift Valley Province to the west. They believed the Kikuyu would regard the whole of Nyandarua, including the Salient, as a simple addition to their sphere of influence—that they would squat on the Salient farms in great numbers, destroy the economic productivity of those farms, and drive out the European proprietors without suitable compensation for their land, which the squatters' presence might render unsalable. Ol Kalou was in the Central Region, which under the *Majimbo* Constitution would

---

60. Interview with T. A. Watts, former executive officer, Land Development and Settlement Board.

be Kikuyu-dominated, and land not in the schemes was to belong to the regions. There was no certainty that the Central Regional government would be willing or able to restrain such an invasion. The Ol Kalou deliberations arose from the fact that the Salient opened onto the Rift Valley in the southwest. This geography contributed to the likelihood that the Salient would become an area of conflict among Central Province Kikuyu, returning Kikuyu from the Rift Valley and elsewhere (seeking land and/or new employment), and perhaps Masai, who continued to believe that much of the Nyandarua District in which the Salient was located was theirs. The Kenya government was also influenced by the formation of the Land Freedom Army *inter alia,* which suggested to some in authority the recrudescence of Mau Mau–like insurgency born of frustrations over land and promises of free land by some politicians. The government reasoned that abandoned land, such as that which might have appeared in the Salient if the European farmers had left abruptly, would become outposts for such restless African groups.[61]

In December, 1963, after discussions with the British government, Prime Minister Kenyatta announced a special program for the transfer of the Ol Kalou Salient to African farmers. The Ol Kalou Salient was thus included in the settlement program primarily because the European farmers there were able to exert the same kind of pressure that contributed very substantially to the establishment of the Million Acre Scheme. Afraid of being surrounded by Kikuyu settlement schemes, they persuaded the British government, and presumably the nearly independent Kenya government, that they were prepared to leave their farms precipitately. The KANU government and its main leaders were determined not to permit wholesale seizure of European land, both for security reasons and for the ideological reason that acceptance of such seizure would constitute *de facto* acceptance of free land. In return for assurances by Kikuyu political leaders that they would restrain unauthorized squatting, the

---

61. I am grateful to N. S. Carey Jones for making available to me his files, which include a great deal of information on the evolution of the Ol Kalou Salient program of land resettlement.

Kenya government undertook to accelerate the settlement of landless Kikuyu, a further indication that major African leaders were committed to preventing unauthorized invasions. But the Salient was not appropriate for smallholdings. Failing the adoption of some new form of agricultural organization in the settlement-scheme program, the transfer of the Salient was more in the interests of the departing European farmers than in the interests of the Africans who would replace them. The fears of Europeans and the concern of the British and Kenya governments for what might happen if the Europeans suddenly abandoned their farms was a major factor in driving both governments to accept a program that was not suitable for individual African smallholdings.[62]

The condition of the Salient caused serious problems for the Kenya government both in the purchase of the land and in its resettlement by Africans. The Ministry of Agriculture and the Central Land Board differed so sharply in their valuations of the property that their differences had to be resolved by arbitration in London.[63] Part of the difficulty can be traced to the different valuation systems employed by the board and the ministry; however, at least as important was the state of underdevelopment and disrepair on the Salient farms, which made it hard to evaluate them fairly from the standpoint of the purposes to which the land would be put by the new settlers. Although eighty-three of the ninety-nine farmers involved eventually accepted offers from the Department of Settlement, the process of settling the Salient has been colored by considerable grumbling about prices by the European settlers.

In the Salient the peculiar distress felt by the European settlers and the particular problem experienced by the government and the settlers in the negotiations for farm purchases have been followed by an unusually difficult resettlement operation from the point of view of both the government and the African settlers. The £1.38 million from the British government for the Salient project is entirely

---

62. As observed above, many settlers did do just this, particularly those of South African origin living in the Eldoret area, now part of the Northern Area Settlement Schemes. Many of these now belong to Nandi settlers.

63. Kenya, Central Land Board, *Final Report, 1964–1965* (Nairobi: Government Printer, 1965).

loan capital, whereas one-third of the purchase price of land in the IBRD/CDC scheme and the British Million Acre Scheme is financed by a grant from the British government. The Department of Settlement's own estimates show that an additional £0.5 million is required if the project is to be fully financed. Furthermore, the Salient is to be divided into nineteen cooperative farming units employing just under 2,000 families. Each family is to have a subsistence plot which it will maintain in addition to working as a member of the cooperative on unsubdivided land devoted both to livestock and to crops such as wheat, barley, and oats. It is anticipated that each settler will derive an income of £100 or more from the cooperative society after its expenses have been met. Each of these local cooperative societies will be under the control of an organization covering the entire Salient. The members of the Salient cooperative societies have been selected carefully; priority has been given to laborers who had worked on European farms in the Salient. Such places as remain have gone to skilled craftsmen capable of making valuable contributions to the cooperative farms and to laborers displaced by settlement schemes elsewhere in Nyandarua. All machinery and vehicles are centrally controlled by the Salient organization and are to be operated under the supervision of trained staff. Finally, elaborate measures have been designed to provide for the welfare of Salient farmers in the form of medical facilities and to educate the settlers on their roles in the new cooperative societies. By contrast, settlers elsewhere have individual plots for subsistence and cash crops with cooperative societies fulfilling only certain collective needs, and medical and educational facilities have not been emphasized. From the standpoint of the Salient settlers the burdens of loan repayment are heavier, because of the absence of a grant element, and the institutional adjustments required of them are far greater than for the other settlers in Nyandarua.

Similar land-purchase problems were created by the position of elderly and/or infirm Europeans on farms not in areas scheduled for resettlement. These Europeans considered that they and their farms would be unsafe under an African government because they would be unable to protect their farms against intrusion by African squatters.[64] The British government agreed to an additional £1.33 million program to purchase these farms for resale as units to individuals or groups, usually African. Again, the inability of European owners to develop their farms adequately to prevent their takeover by squatters dictated to the government the conditions of, and need for, the so-called compassionate case resettlement program, rather than any judgment that the land in question was suitable for African settlement.

Finally, a general problem arose in the transfer of the land from European farms of substantial size to African smallholdings, because the value of these farms to the Europeans as large-scale units did not coincide with their collective value to Africans when subdivided for smallholdings. Some areas, notably the South Kinangop in Nyandarua, were best suited for large-scale wheat-growing. When such an area is subdivided into smallholdings, wheat is a less economical crop, and instead crops must be planted which are of less value and for which the land is less well suited. The Land Development and Settlement Board and, after it, the Central Land Board confronted the difficult task of balancing the interests of the Africans with those of the departing European farmers. Vociferous complaints were made, particularly by the Europeans, that the prices they received did not reflect the full value of their farms.[65] These complaints were reinforced by the Europeans' dissatisfaction at usually being unable to recover more than £1,300 for their homes. The Central Land Board itself agreed, in its final report, that the prices paid—averaging 184s. ($21) per acre—for developed land made the Highlands some of the cheapest land in the world.[66]

64. Their position also reflected a belief that there would be no possibility of selling their farms except through the settlement program.

65. It may perhaps be to the credit of the CLB that neither Africans nor European farmers were satisfied with the prices. The prices were higher than Africans thought appropriate (if they thought any price at all appropriate) and higher than the lenders considered appropriate. The Europeans had a different view. Part of the problem was created by the dual value of a given piece of land: as a unit operated by a single farmer and as a collection of small plots operated by many farmers.

66. An indication, perhaps, of the CLB's sensitivity to the European position. Kenya, *Final Report, 1964–1965.*

The second group of problems came in the selection of settlers for the schemes, especially for the high-density schemes. The normal process has undergone a change since the beginning of settlement. Most settlers report having been chosen by lot under a system in which the district commissioner drew names out of a hat. More recently, the system has involved the appointment of selection committees to interview applicants and make choices on the basis of evidence of unemployment, lack of land, and agricultural education or knowledge. Selection committees are activated when the Settlement Department informs the Provincial Administration that plots are available for settlement by persons in a given province. After district committees have been established and the choices made, the lists are forwarded to the minister for lands and settlement for final approval. These processes appear to have been developed in their present form after the biggest group of settlers had joined the schemes, to judge from the settlers' own recollections of how they were chosen.

Under the *Majimbo* Constitution, the regional and central governments shared responsibility for the administration of the settlement schemes, so that the presidents of the various regional assemblies would be given the power to approve lists of prospective settlers for the high-density schemes in their individual regions. Such procedures were designed to preserve the integrity of African ethnic spheres of influence. The screening of applicants for the high-density schemes by elected officials proved disadvantageous in some respects, particularly in Central Province where the Kikuyu reside. The Regional Boundaries Commission extended the boundaries of Central Province to include part of the Rift Valley, and this became known as Nyandarua District. Its purpose in so doing, against the expressed preference of KANU, was to provide expansion room for the Kikuyu without moving them into the Rift Valley District where they would have had to share a regional government with the Kalenjin peoples who supported KADU. The growing numbers of landless and unemployed had increasingly become a source of concern to African leaders as well as to Europeans, for the dissatisfied were pushing local African leaders to make good on the long-held nationalist objective of recovering lands lost to Europeans. Faced with the dilemma of too many demands and too little land, KANU leaders in Central Province did not hesitate to say "go to Nyandarua." But in addition to landless and unemployed Kikuyu in Central Province, there were also Kikuyu employed on farms outside Central Province, particularly on European farms scheduled for African resettlement in the Nyandarua area itself. The government estimated that there were some 25,000 Africans, almost all Kikuyu, employed by European farms in Nyandarua when the high-density settlement program began and that this could only be increased by another 8,000, far fewer than the number of additional Kikuyu in Central Province and elsewhere who qualified for high-density schemes.

The government's intention, on Prime Minister Kenyatta's directions, was that laborers legally employed four years or more on European farms were to have priority and that special arrangements were to be made for forest fighters who were involved in Mau Mau and for servicemen, presumably including loyalist forces. The prime minister thus indicated his intention of caring for the interests of Africans on both sides of Mau Mau. But the pressure of landlessness and the partial autonomy given the regions under the *Majimbo* Constitution were enough to block the implementation of his instructions. Instead of the entire eligible existing labor force in Nyandarua being given priority, only about 25 percent of them were settled, the rest of the settlers coming from Central Province.[67]

The principal cause of this displacement was the necessity for a crash program of settlement in the weeks just before independence. The prime minister himself is said to have inquired about the timetable for settling Nyandarua and, on being told, replied that it must be settled before independence, then only a month away.[68] As a consequence, nearly 3,800 families were settled in the southern part of Nyandarua District in the three weeks preceding independence.[69] This was five times the rate of settlement following the crash program and more than five times the rate of earlier program settlement. The entire area of Nyandarua south of Ol Kalou—the southern

---

67. Interview with N. S. Carey Jones.
68. Interview with A. Storrar and with James Gichuru, minister of finance.
69. Kenya, Department of Settlement, *Annual Report 1964–1965.*

two-thirds of the district—was opened up, and 60 percent of the families settled in this area of Nyandarua by June 30, 1966, were placed on the settlement schemes during those three weeks. The government's policy was to give resident labor priority, but the pressure of landlessness and unemployment in the weeks preceding independence made rigid adherence to this policy a politically expensive luxury that could not be afforded then.

The signs of the crash program and of the failure to give priority to resident laborers during the early phase of the resettlement program are still present. On some settlements one finds small villages of huts with only enough land per hut and family to raise a few staples, the equivalent of a small garden. These belong to the resident laborers who did not receive plots and who refuse to leave, believing that their only chance for land is in the area where they were employed. Many of them have been away from Central Province long enough to have lost contact with friends or relatives who might have helped them establish a livelihood there. The government has set aside a single plot on some settlements for these people, who gain their livelihood by working as occasional laborers for the new settlers. They are a visible symbol that the problem of landlessness in Kenya has by no means been eliminated, only ameliorated, by the settlement-scheme program. The continuing presence of landlessness and unemployment in heavily settled districts has been translated by the government into pressure on the Masai peoples to develop their land, which surrounds the Kikuyu districts to the south and west. The Masai continue to be a nomadic people, not much interested in modernization and content to gain necessary cash from the tourists who travel through game preserves in their area. The Masai are, however, roaming over some of the best wheat-growing land, and other good agricultural land, in Kenya. The Masai have only slowly taken an interest in developing the agricultural potential of the land, while President Kenyatta and KANU resist pressures to settle other more industrious agricultural peoples in Masai country.

Even after the crash program, the president of the Central Region refused to implement the policy of giving resident labor priority in the settlement of the schemes, with the result that the central government first threatened to take over the process of settler selection from the regional authorities, and then actually did so.[70] Selection thus became the task of administrative officers rather than of elected officials. Even before the *Majimbo* Constitution was formally scrapped in favor of a strong national government, the central government had made inroads on the autonomy of the regional assemblies on matters to which the central government attached particular importance.[71]

The failure of officials to implement the central government's priorities in the selection of settlers has been criticized. Objections have also been raised to the arbitrary process by which settlers were selected for the high-density schemes. One early student of the settlement schemes, for example, argued that they should not be used as welfare institutions and permitted to become rural slums by the indiscriminate and random selection of settlers for the high-density ones. D. M. Etherington argued that "the careful selection of the very best settlers for all schemes must be considered a major priority." [72] This point of view was gaining increasing support, since some of the local officials of the CDC and the IBRD were prepared to relax rigorous selection procedures even for the low-density schemes, in the belief that the lenders could still help to finance the settlement schemes and contribute to the creation of new economic assets without reliance upon carefully screened settlers.[73] Etherington argued that the process of random selection did not result in a careful determination that candidates were both landless and unemployed rather than simply one or the other, that such a process did not screen out the unemployable as distinct from the unemployed, and that cooperative institutions necessary for the collective well-being of the settlers could not be operated effectively without carefully chosen settlers. He also felt that the low budgeted income of £25 to £40 per settler was not sufficient to attract truly qualified settlers.

70. Details of this reassignment of functions were obtained from the files of Carey Jones.

71. See Cherry Gertzel, "Regionalism in Kenya" (Kampala, East African Institute for Social Research, conference paper, 1965).

72. D. M. Etherington, "Land Resettlement in Kenya: Policy and Practice," *East African Economics Review,* December, 1962.

73. *Ibid.*

While Etherington was not specifically attacking the political process as a means of selecting settlers, he might as well have done so. It would have been difficult for the regional assemblies or even the elected leaders of the central government to enforce rigorous selection procedures, as indicated by the difficulty the political leaders had in enforcing the relatively simple policy of protecting established resident laborers and by the decision to leave the more rigorous low-density settler selection processes to the local settlement and agricultural administrative officers. Etherington's implicit assumption that randomly selected settlers cannot be counted on to make the schemes economically progressive is a view that the Kenya government has itself come to accept since independence. Faced with the need to show quick and substantial results from the scarce and limited development assistance funds procured from foreign governments, the Kenya government has concentrated upon the already progressive farmers, who can be counted on to use the funds responsibly and productively.

The fundamental issue is whether economic institutions designed to foster economic development can make effective new contributors to the economy out of persons without substantial previous experience in managing even a smallholding and without substantial funds to contribute to doing so. The settlement schemes are based on the assumption not that the settlers are welfare recipients but that they can be made effective new participants in the process of building the modern economy by contributing to the maintenance of previous levels of production established by the European settlers. It has been the assumption of Kenya nationalism and of the settlement schemes that induction into the modern economy is a step in the process of building an identification with independent Kenya. On the other hand, the Kenya government in recent years has assumed that primary reliance for the development of the economy must be placed upon established farmers and upon those who have at least come to acquire what amounts to private individual tenure made effective by land consolidation and registration. The working theory of the government today is, then, that development of the economy must be undertaken by those who have already acquired an interest in that economy. Given the emphasis on economic development and the general deemphasis on political institutions and processes per se, it is difficult to see how those who do not already have a stake in the economy can be made to achieve political identification with the new and independent Kenya. This is the problem to which the settlement schemes were particularly addressed and which will continue to bother the Kenya government as long as there are substantial numbers of landless and unemployed. Reliance upon the traditional sector to absorb those not yet employable in the modern economy may yield diminishing returns. Absorption of these people as farm laborers, failing any serious industrialization in Kenya, will not yield economic benefits to the country unless efforts are made to make them knowledgeable farm laborers, and it will not yield political benefits unless the government mounts a concerted program to teach people that landownership is not the only way to achieve a place in society. Such programs would themselves require substantial financial outlays that the economists argue could be used more productively elsewhere.

The third group of problems has involved the interrelationship of the various departments of the central government in the implementation of the settlement schemes. This would make a separate study in itself—when the records of the departments involved enter the public domain. Certain generalizations based upon limited evidence may be advanced at this stage.

First, the views of senior personnel in the Department of Settlement have not always been in accord with those of their opposite numbers in the Ministry of Economic Planning and Development and the Department of Agriculture, because the Planning Ministry does not consider the high-density schemes in particular to be a good investment and because the Department of Agriculture has had to give up considerable numbers of skilled technical personnel to the Department of Settlement who, from its point of view, could have been used more effectively elsewhere.[74] The field officers of the Department of Agriculture have remained skeptical that the new farm-

---

74. Interviews with James Maina, director of settlement, 1965–67, and James Mburu, director of agriculture, 1963–67 (succeeded Maina, with whom he traded positions in 1967).

ers will make efficient use of the land, quite apart from the fact that the department was skeptical whether the new farmers would be able to maintain the level of production in the agricultural economy. One reason why the decision was made to encourage the large-scale European farmers around Kitale and Nakuru to remain was to provide support for the agricultural economy during the process of resettlement elsewhere. Despite the fact that many senior personnel in the Department of Settlement have come from the ranks of the Department of Agriculture, the two departments have clashed over the establishment of farm budgets for the new settlers.[75] A number of senior officials in the Department of Agriculture were vigorously opposed to high-density settlement per se and so had difficulty coming to terms with the Department of Settlement, which had no choice but to put such schemes into operation. Finally, the two departments have differed over whether to permit settlers to grow certain crops on which Kenya is particularly dependent for foreign exchange. Some doubts were expressed about tea-growing, but the big issue was whether to permit settlers on the Kinangop plateau in Nyandarua to grow pyrethrum. There were reliable indications that the Kenya cabinet engaged in a bitter controversy over whether the settlers could successfully grow quality pyrethrum which would sustain the valuable international market Kenya had developed for its crop. Eventually the settlers were permitted to grow pyrethrum because of its appropriateness to the otherwise difficult farming land in many parts of the area. After initially discouraging results, the settlers have succeeded in equaling or surpassing their production quota, although the Pyrethrum Board of Kenya still complains that they have not yet learned to process their crops efficiently.[76]

Second, the relationship between the Department of Cooperative Development and the Department of Settlement has been influenced by the different objectives each tries to achieve through the cooperative societies on the individual schemes. The Department of Settle-

75. Interviews with A. Storrar, G. R. Henderson, and R. D. A. Bennison, provincial agriculture officer. Articles by L. H. Brown, "The Settlement Schemes," *Kenya Weekly News,* July to November, 1965. Interview with R. J. M. Swynnerton.

76. Correspondence with H. J. Lucking, executive officer, Pyrethrum Board of Kenya.

ment, in addition to wanting the societies to arrange for the marketing and, in some cases, the processing of settlement produce, wants the societies to be its local agents for collecting the individual loan payments due from settlers and to purchase, on behalf of the settlers, equipment taken over by the department from the farms of the departed European farmers. The Cooperative Department has on occasion chafed at the Department of Settlement's willingness to overlook its own policy of limiting the loan ceiling of the societies to £10 per settler and has questioned whether the societies are not being given too much responsibility too fast.[77] On other occasions, impatient settlement officers have, in the view of the Cooperative Department field officers, misused the societies by attempting to short-cut established society procedures. In addition, there is inevitably some jurisdictional difficulty between the field cooperative officers and the settlement officers, arising from their overlapping responsibilities for individual schemes.[78] However, these problems have not become so serious as those between the Departments of Agriculture and Settlement, to judge from available information.

Third, a good deal concerning the relationship of the Department of Settlement to these other departments has come to light in the process of reviewing the progress of the settlement schemes that began with the Stamp Mission in 1965. The Stamp Mission urged that further studies be conducted to follow up on its report. The Ministry of Economic Planning considered the possibility of appointing a team of scholars at the University of Nairobi to examine in detail the economic and administrative operations and consequences of the settlement schemes and to make recommendations for facilitating the schemes' efficient operation and maximizing their contri-

77. From the records of settlement cooperative societies made available by the Department of Cooperative Development. Interviews with D. Nyanjom, deputy commissioner of cooperative development; P. Lal, former assistant secretary, Ministry of Cooperatives and Community Development; and R. G. Ngala, minister for cooperative development.
78. Many of the early settlement officers did not respect the jurisdiction of the cooperative officers of the Department of Cooperative Development. This arose in part from genuine confusion over the relative responsibilities of the two departments but also in part from the impatience of settlement officers with the performance and procedures of fledgling cooperative societies.

bution to the economy. The study was to be jointly sponsored by the Ministry of Economic Planning, the Ministry of Agriculture, and the Ministry of Lands and Settlement. Among other things, it was to reflect the stimulation of a closer relationship between the government and the University faculty that both desired. This study was eventually conducted, but by a somewhat different team of researchers—one economist in the Ministry of Economic Planning and Development, another who had formerly been employed by the Ministry of Overseas Development in London, the principal of one of East Africa's leading agricultural training schools, and a sociologist from Makerere University College in Uganda. The change in composition of this research team arose largely from the refusal of the Department of Settlement to approve the initial team, because the Ministry of Planning and the Ministry of Agriculture had not consulted the British government or the IBRD and CDC about its composition. The team as reconstituted included as its chairman a former employee of the Ministry of Overseas Development in London, Brian Van Arkadie.

These maneuvers provide a practical example of a peculiar problem of the Department of Settlement: its perceived sense of responsibility to the lenders for the successful execution of the program as well as to the Kenya government. Because it was established independently of the Department of Agriculture partly at the request of the lenders, who were anxious about the transfer of power, the Department of Settlement as well as the program may be viewed by other departments of the government as a vestige of the pre-independence government, and the Settlement Department itself could be in an embarrassing position when its responsibility to the Kenya government runs afoul of the preference of the lenders.[79]

This chapter has traced the evolution of policy-making concerning land resettlement, the processes of implementing the program, and the problems encountered by the Kenya government in so doing. The processes of implementation demonstrate clearly the extent to

---

79. From the personal experience of the author, who was involved in these negotiations.

which the settlement program was adapted to the political exigencies of the transfer of power, just as one of its main purposes was to enable European farmers to depart and landless Africans to receive land to facilitate that transfer of power. The settlement schemes lack purpose today because the political institutions thought necessary at the time of the transfer of power have, in most cases, been removed, and because today the Kenya government's emphasis on maximizing the use of scarce resources to achieve economic growth is not subordinated to any particular values concerning the way in which social values should be authoritatively allocated. The schemes' lack of relevance to the government's present economic strategies, their institutional isolation established during the transfer of power, and the particular circumstances of the new settlers work effectively to maintain an economic and political distinction between the former African and the former European areas—a distinction which had originally developed and been maintained on racial grounds. As long as this continues, the ideal of integrating the country in the pursuit of economic development will go unrealized. As the next chapter will show, the economic health of the settlements and the settlers' ability to repay the British government and CDC/IBRD loans, as well as the political and economic integration of the country, may depend on the Kenya government's applying the same strategies to the settlers on the schemes as they apply to other African farmers from whom contributions to the modern rural economy are expected.

6

LAND RESETTLEMENT AT THE GRASS ROOTS: INTERNAL DEMANDS AND SUPPORT

> The general will is always right and tends to the
> public advantage: but it does not follow that the
> deliberations of the people are always equally
> correct. Our will is always for our own good but
> we do not always see what that is; the people is
> never corrupted, but it is often deceived.
> —JEAN-JACQUES ROUSSEAU, 1762

THE DECOLONIZATION OF THE WHITE HIGHLANDS during the transfer of power ceased to be an objective of African nationalism in Kenya because the European settlers and the colonial administration made the process a condition for their acquiescence to immediate political independence for the country under an African government.[1] For the African government and the participants in the reset-

---

1. This study is based on interviews with 180 African farmers participating in the settlement program, and on data collected by the Farm Economics Survey Unit of the Kenya

tlement program, the transfer of political power will not be complete until the economic vestiges of this European colonial administration–inspired program are removed. Their removal will also make the government less susceptible to criticism from African leaders like Odinga, and the unemployed Africans for whom he attempts to speak, for assuming economic responsibility for a program inspired by those not in sympathy with African nationalism. The settlement program is an example of the way the government does *not* propose to build the economy of independent Kenya; it wishes to allocate its development resources so that productivity rather than Africanization becomes the chief objective, and within that framework it seeks to involve as many Africans as possible in the building of the economy. It believes that only in this way can political independence be given tangible economic and social content. The government wants the settlement program to contribute to this process primarily by maintaining or surpassing the levels of employment and productivity that the European farmers reached and by repaying promptly the development funds invested in the program by the British government, the CDC, and the World Bank.

The 30,000 African families participating in the settlement schemes have a double public responsibility. They are obliged by the government to become productive on their farms and repay their debts in order simultaneously to free the country from a weighty political and economic burden imposed by a foreign government and people and to assist in the realization of the government's nation-building program. In Kenya's official ideology, its development strategy, and the structure of the settlement program itself, there is an implicit assumption that these public responsibilities are compatible with the private interests and responsibilities of enlightened African farmers. A progressive African farmer is expected to want to become the full owner of a plot of land, economically prosperous, and free

Ministry of Economic Planning and Development. Settlers were selected to include representatives of each major ethnic group, high- and low-density farmers, prosperous and not so prosperous settlers, schemes with relatively high as well as low repayment percentages, and schemes with different cash-crop patterns.

of debt. If he is educated, it is assumed that he can appreciate the relationship between his farming activities and the creation of a viable, economically integrated, and independent Kenya nation. This Rousseauean assumption requires examination. First, how valid is the government's belief that emphasis on efficient development of the country's economy constitutes the wisest nation-building strategy, given its ideological commitments and the circumstances of the country? Part of the answer can be derived from an analysis of the progress of the resettlement program from the standpoint of the government and the program's participants. Second, how does the structure of the program at the grass roots provide for mediation between what the government seeks from the program and what the participants want to achieve? How far does the local program structure permit adjustment between the role patterns which the structure implies and the perceptions and behavior patterns which the settlers themselves tend to adopt? We will consider the local program structure here, then analyze the settlers' responses to it.

GRASS-ROOTS STRUCTURE OF THE SETTLEMENT PROGRAM

Land. The settlement schemes have generally been placed on good land suitable for profitable smallholder farming by capable settlers. The selection of land and the demarcation of individual plots have appeared to attempt to honor both the economic objectives of African nationalism in Kenya and the economic requirements and objectives of post-independence nation-building. The Kenya government, for example, has tried to divert ambitious African farmers from the White Highlands to high-quality underutilized lands within their own areas that are suitable for profitable smallholder farming at less expense than the Highlands. At the same time, the Kenya government has met the objectives of African nationalism not only by creating the schemes but also by subdividing the formerly European farms into small-scale intensively farmed units for the benefit of landless persons from the former reserves. The land has been divided into units capable of earning $70 to $280 over and above expenses, loan charges, and subsistence needs. The Kenya government has thus sought to insure, as far as possible, that the aims of African nationalism regarding land would not be achieved at the expense of uneconomic farming of the Highlands—which would jeopardize the economic objectives of nation-building. The Kenya government and the Central Land Board initially resisted the purchase of poor land like the Ol Kalou Salient. There is no evidence that the division of land for potentially equal income, rather than for equal acreages, is misunderstood by settlers or is a major grievance among them.

An important initial result of the demarcation and allocation of plots to the settlers has been the differentiation and individualization of their environmental conditions and, consequently, problems in adjusting to the requirements of participation in the modern sector of the rural economy. The settlements vary considerably in rainfall, altitude, and soil quality, for example. Nearly all of them are on land which averages better than thirty inches of rainfall per year, the amount considered essential if land is to be classified as having high agricultural potential. However, the settlement-scheme areas vary greatly, as indicated in table I.

These varying ecological conditions between and within settlement areas dictate divergent agricultural programs, which in turn establish divergent patterns of farming behavior for the new settlers to emulate. Defining appropriate model patterns of farming behavior is partly a technical problem for agricultural officers, who must establish the best procedures for growing a given crop in a particular locale. However, these are also determined by the selection of appropriate crops by settlement and agricultural officials on the basis not only of ecological conditions but also of marketing prospects and to some extent of the known working patterns and political dispositions of given ethnic groups. Since the settlers have only imprecise knowledge of these determining factors, and since the government cannot easily force the growing of particular crops in particular ways under pain of fine or imprisonment or even deprivation of land, acceptance of particular crops and farming techniques becomes a matter of trust between the settlers and the local settlement officials. Whether or not the settlers trust the officials is a function of the degree of change from previous farming patterns that is required and the persuasive power of the particular officials. Advertised market prospects are not by themselves always sufficient to induce the prescribed behavior. Pyrethrum, for example, was not welcomed by the Kikuyu initially despite its profit-making potential.

The growing of maize as a cash crop demands fundamental behavioral changes on the part of the settlers. Maize is a familiar crop and is grown by thousands of African farmers both for subsistence and for profit. Because it is not new to the settlers and has been raised and sold profitably in African markets in the past, the government has had difficulty persuading settlers of the necessity and desirability of raising and selling maize in new and different ways. The government would like to integrate the settlers and other African farmers into the national system for marketing and distributing maize by employing local cooperative societies as the initial marketing agents for them. At the same time, the government has sought to use the cooperative societies, on the settlement schemes and elsewhere, to deduct amounts sufficient to repay gradually the farmers' individual land and development loans as well as loans made to cooperative society members collectively for investment in farm machinery and equipment, from the price paid to the farmers for their maize. The settlers have not been easily persuaded that participation in the national agricultural marketing and distribution system and satisfaction of individual and collective loan obligations justify their accepting a lower net price for their crop than they would gain by selling it through traditional channels where no such deductions are made. The government believes, in effect, that its system is more modern because it causes the farmers to work together in the spirit of African socialism, because it causes them to use higher quality seeds and more efficient farming techniques and equipment, and because their participation in the marketing and distribution system helps to weld the country into an economic unit and/or facilitate crop export and generate foreign exchange. The settlers' reluctance to participate fully in this process challenges the government with the idea that the pursuit of individual economic self-interest may lead to the greater good of the whole country. They ask whether the

Table I
SELECTED SETTLEMENT SCHEMES: BASIC DATA

Schemes	Ethnic Groups	Altitude (in feet)	Rainfall (in inches where given)	Predominant Soil Type	Farm Program	Type
Cherangani	Intertribal	6,600–8,000	good*	brown forest loam	t, c, d	LD
Kabisi	Baluhya	5,000–6,500	45–55	red loam	m, b, si, d	HD
Kabuyefwe	Baluhya	5,000–6,500	45–55	sandy loam	m, b, si, d	HD
Mautuma	Baluhya	5,000–6,500	45–55	sandy-murram and rock out crops	m, d, si	HD
Lumukanda	Baluhya	5,000–6,500	45–55	vlei	m, d, si	HD
Ndalat	Nandi	6,500	good*	red-sandy loam	m, d	HD
Elgeyo Border	Elgeyo	7,500–8,000	47	?	m, py, d	HD
Lessos	Nandi	6,500–8,000	45–60	?	py, d, m	LD
Ainabkoi East	Elgeyo, Tugen	8,000–9,000	50	high altitude veldt and vlei	py, d, sh, po	LD
Songhor	Luo	4,500	68	some poorly drained	su, d	HD
Muhoroni	Luo	4,500	60	some black cotton	su, m, d	LD
Sotik East	Kipsigis	6,200–6,700	adequate*	Kikuyu star grass & vlei	m, pf, d, c	HD
Manga	Kisii	6,100–7,100	50–60	Kikuyu star grass & vlei	py, pf, d, t	HD
Gelegele	Kipsigis	6,000–7,000	45–55	star grass and vlei	m, pf, d	LD
Koyet	Kipsigis	6,000–7,000	45–55	star grass and vlei	m, pf, d	LD
Lietego	Kisii	6,100–7,100	50–60	star grass and vlei	m, pf, d	LD
Perkerra	Tugen	6,400–7,400	50	?	py, c, m, d	HD
Sabatia	Tugen	6,400–7,400	41	?	py, c, d	HD
Passenga	Kikuyu	7,800–9,000	52	medium red loams	py, d, sh	LD
Silanga	Kikuyu	7,800–9,000	52	medium red loams	py, d, sh	LD

Schemes	Ethnic Groups	Altitude (in feet)	Rainfall (in inches where given)	Predominant Soil Type	Farm Program	Type
Kipipiri	Kikuyu	7,700–9,000	good*	forest loam, slopes steep	py, po, d, sh	HD
Mawingo	Kikuyu	7,400–8,500	adequate*	forest loams, waterlogging	py, po, d, sh	HD
Nandarasi†	Kikuyu	7,400–8,500	adequate*	forest loams, waterlogging	py, d, sh	HD
Kitiri†	Kikuyu	7,900–9,000	60–80	red-gray loams	py, po, d, sh	HD
Tulaga†	Kikuyu	7,900–9,000	60–80	red-gray loams	py, po, d, sh	HD
Karati†	Kikuyu	7,900–9,000	adequate*	volcanic gray-impeded drain	py, d, sh	HD
S. Kinangop	Kikuyu	8,500	adequate*	forest to vlei, impeded drain	py, d, sh, po	HD
Endarasha	Kikuyu	6,300–8,000	adequate*	red and forest loams/black cotton	py, m, d, sh	HD
Naro Moru	Kikuyu	6,300–7,700	25–40	Kikuyu star grass & vlei/black cotton	py, w, d	HD
Uaso Nyiro	Kikuyu	6,300–8,000	good*	red and forest loam/black cotton	py, w, d, m	HD
Mua Hills	Kamba	5,000–6,900	adequate*	bush, red loams/black cotton	m, c, d, b	HD

* No records; reports of local agriculturalists used.
† Part of the crash program of settlement preceding independence.
b = beans, c = coffee, d = dairy, m = maize, pf = passion fruit, po = potatoes, py = pyrethrum, sh = sheep, si = sisal, su = sugar, t = tea, w = wheat

LD = low-density schemes
HD = high-density schemes

operation of Adam Smith's "unseen hand" is not an equally "modern" concept.

The sense of urgency experienced by both the government and the settlers makes mediation of this difference in perspective more difficult. The Kenya government believes that the building of a viable economy is crucial and that making the most efficient use of scarce resources and manpower is the only path to meeting the demands for employment, schools, medical facilities, and a variety of consumer goods. It believes that these demands must be deferred in the short term in order to meet them eventually as the economy grows. The settlers are equally anxious to secure full ownership of their land and education and medical facilities for their families in order to gain a sense of economic and social security. As the resettlement program provided land in great haste for large numbers of destitute Africans, those same Africans believe their demands for other social amenities should be met with equal dispatch.

Farm Patterns. Settlers on the Kinangop are unable to grow maize successfully because of the high altitude—over 8,000 feet above sea level in most places. As maize is one of the standard subsistence crops of the Kikuyu, the settlers on the Kinangop must develop a diet different from that to which their ancestors and their neighbors on the other side of the Aberdares have been accustomed. Since the Kinangop is difficult to farm, its settlers have been encouraged to diversify their production of cash crops by commercially marketing those vegetables they do not consume. Producers must cope with the relatively high perishability of vegetable crops. Unlike maize, vegetables are harvested regularly over a considerable period of time each year. These two characteristics of truck farming impose on the African settlers the requirements of continuous, efficient, and prompt collection and conveyance of the crops to the commercial processing points. They must also work more closely with the commercial marketing organizations than those settlers who harvest other crops more infrequently. Each of these requirements distinguishes truck farmers from producers of other cash crops and from their kinsmen who are not truck farmers.

The sometime truck farmers rely primarily upon pyrethrum production for cash. Pyrethrum is clearly distinguishable from subsistence crops and has little or no market in the former African reserves to compete with the Pyrethrum Board of Kenya and the settlement cooperative societies. Pyrethrum is initially processed on the settlement schemes. Officers and employees of the cooperative societies must be trained in the techniques of drying the flowers so that the maximum pyrethrum content is obtained. Unsuccessful drying or delay in drying the pyrethrum results in smaller returns per unit of production and deterioration of the crop respectively. Greater demands are thus made of the cooperative societies relative to the commercial marketing organizations. Poor performance creates political trouble between the societies and their employees, on the one hand, and the settler-producers on the other hand, and the societies are not so easily able to pass the blame further along the line to the commercial processors. Pyrethrum shares with milk and vegetables the advantage of yielding a regular income over a substantial part of the year.

On a broader political plane, the large annual production of pyrethrum by the Kinangop settlers has symbolized the largely successful conversion of an area from one of large-scale European wheat-farming and sheep-raising to one in which thousands of smallholder African farmers have (from an agricultural point of view) successfully developed a completely different crop. The greatest pressure for free land, the most controversial conversion of large-scale to small-scale farming, and some of the most outspoken European critics of African political advances were concentrated in the Kinangop. Consequently, the success or failure of the transition in this area was to be symbolic of the success or failure of the settlement program as a whole and to some extent of the transfer of power as well.

On the Kipsigis and Kisii settlement schemes in southwestern Kenya, the government has begun to introduce passion fruit as the principal cash crop. Much of this product is purchased by British candy producers. The problem is that the government, having decided to encourage the growth of passion fruit, must now take steps to restrict the acreage because the popularity of the crop has led to the danger of serious overproduction. The Kisii in particular rushed to plant the crop, and settlers on one of their areas, Lietego, in 1964–65 made an average of $252 apiece from an average of 1.5 acres apiece. The Kipsigis were somewhat slower to take to the crop, and Gelegele and Koyet settlements, next door to Lietego, made only an average of $6.25 apiece from an average of .06 acres apiece. Part of the difference in the return lay in the greater efficiency of the Lietego farmers, who produced an average of 8,000 pounds per acre, while the Gelegele and Koyet farmers were averaging only 6,000 pounds per acre. The Kipsigis settlers have been asked to accept the fact that passion fruit cannot be encouraged on their areas, even though the government cannot find other good cash crops except maize and milk and is under pressure from the lenders to emphasize cash-crop production rather than livestock development. The Kipsigis were among the first to voluntarily enclose and consolidate individual landholdings, but they have not as a whole continued to be in the forefront of agricultural development. Still, many Kipsigis settlers want to develop a relatively high-priced cash crop such as passion fruit, and they do not understand the economic rationale for their being deprived of funds and assistance for this while their neighbors of a different ethnic group on Lietego are prospering with it. The idea of restricted and unevenly allocated acreages for high-priced cash crops is not one that stimulates participation in the modern economy on the part of those who do not receive the larger allocations. One consequence is that the Kipsigis are reluctant to change from production of milk and maize for traditional markets to production for modern commercial markets.

Sugar has been made the principal crop of the Luo settlement schemes. Uganda has been the chief producer over the years, and the World Bank was reluctant to finance the development of sugar in another East African country, preferring to leave Uganda as very nearly the only producer for East Africa. During the colonial period, the Luo people were not very responsive to suggestions that they consolidate individual landholdings and produce goods for the commercial markets, and therefore the lenders were reluctant to entrust the development of such a valuable crop to them.[2] The Kenya government insisted, on the grounds that sugar could be grown in the area and that the Luo would feel discriminated against if they were not given opportunities to develop lucrative cash crops. The Luo were the second biggest supporters of KANU after the Kikuyu, and not to have given them treatment approximately equivalent to that given the Kikuyu would have added strains to the already uneasy coalition between the two groups. Finally, the government considered that sugar was a particularly appropriate crop for the Luo people, because it believed the crop could be produced without threatening some well-established Luo social and economic behavior patterns. Sugar is best grown on large patches rather than separately on individual plots, and thus was amenable to collective economic activity to which the Luo were assumed to be accustomed. The settlers were then given small plots for raising subsistence crops individually. In addition, the settlement officials believed that, since sugar required relatively little care on the part of the ordinary producers and concentrated responsibility in the hands of the scheme managers and processing factories, it would not disrupt the tendency of Luo men to leave for substantial periods of time to go to Mombasa and Nairobi in search of wage labor. A consequence, however, has been that there has been more trouble than elsewhere in persuading the settlers to maintain their primary residence on the settlements, since less of their time is demanded. Perhaps the principal obligation incumbent on the Luo is to accept the need to maintain their basic residence on the settlement. On all settlement schemes dual residence has been a problem, but in attempting to fit the Luo crop to the Luo customs, the government has made the conversion problem more difficult.

This discussion of cash-crop development on the settlement schemes suggests that the presumed natural superiority of "modern" marketing arrangements, the appeal of consumer goods for the mod-

2. The preliminary conclusion of a Ph.D. dissertation being prepared by Jean Hay at the University of Wisconsin, Madison.

ern sector of the economy, and the attraction of hard cash over dealing with traditional markets are not apparent to the settlers, even when the government, with the assistance of international finance, has attempted to bring all the advantages of modernity to the settlers, and even in a situation where many settlers have been among those considered most receptive to modernization. In addition, the different types of behavioral changes required of settlers as a result of the requirements of different cash crops suggest the inadvisability of broad classifications of individual ethnic groups as modernizing, transitional, or traditional. Such differences may reflect not so much differences in responsiveness as differences in the meaning of modernization in particular circumstances or differences in real opportunity.

People. Many studies of political development and modernization rest upon what may prove to be erroneous assumptions about the political culture of developing nations or important segments of them. Such analyses frequently appear to assume the presence of what Almond and Verba have termed "participant" political culture. They assume, for example, that the governments of modernizing countries must prove the extent of their political development by their capacity to perform extractive, regulative, distributive, symbolic, and responsive functions on behalf of a citizenry that does not hesitate to make demands directly upon the decision-making elites for measures to distribute the perquisites of a "modern" society. Even Professor Huntington, in his criticism of contemporary studies, seems to make the same assumption, arguing that governments and studies of such governments should focus to a greater extent on restraining popular participation in the interests of establishing sound governmental processes.[3] The presence of large and persistent demand inputs on governments of new nations is seldom examined or tested. The greatest attention is usually given to the question of whether governmental outputs in response to such demands will

3. Samuel P. Huntington, "Political Development and Political Decay," *World Politics,* XVII, no. 3 (April, 1965), 386–430.

generate support needed to keep demand input within the bounds with which the government is able to cope. Left unexamined are the degree to which these inputs are actually present and the sources from which they emanate, and the nature and extent of compliance with government outputs that is required to make them a reality and generate the input of support. These problems will be examined in the context of Kenya land resettlement by looking at the cultural predispositions of the settlers and the structures created to channel participation and generate the nature and degree of compliance required by governmental outputs. In the second half of this chapter, the kind of compliance and participation actually elicited will be examined.

A majority of the settlers came from ethnic groups which were subject to severe population densities and consequent land shortage. The Luhya, Kamba, and Kikuyu settlers all came from the most densely populated rural areas of Kenya. The largest single ethnic group among the settlers are the Kikuyu, who were in the forefront of Kenya nationalism and who are most conspicuous in the Kenya government today. We have emphasized the importance of land in the emergence of Kenya nationalism and the role of the Kikuyu in the development of that nationalism. Land reform and redistribution formed much of the social content of Kenya nationalism and represented one of the chief purposes for seeking political independence from Britain. Prior to independence, therefore, the Kikuyu pressed the colonial authorities for land and land reform in a way similar to the manner in which students of post-independence modernization assume that African peoples are pressing their governments for some of the accoutrements of "modernization." [4] Thus an examination of the attitudes of Kikuyu settlers, in particular, toward the land-resettlement program should indicate the attitudes toward attempts at modernizing members of a group whose leaders have been in the forefront of modernization demands.

---

4. For example, Daniel Lerner, *The Passing of Traditional Society* (Glencoe, Ill.: Free Press, 1958); David Apter, *The Politics of Modernization* (Chicago: University of Chicago Press, 1965); and Lucian Pye, *Aspects of Political Development* (Boston: Little, Brown, 1966).

Cultural predispositions. The quality of settlers' participation in the processes of modernization through the input of demands and support for governmental programs is a function not only of the settlement program itself but of the resources and dispositions of the settlers at the time they joined the scheme. Knowledge about the latter is necessary in determining the net impact of the program on the behavior, perceptions, and material condition of the settlers. It is difficult to acquire this knowledge, since little study was given to the profiles of the settlers when they joined the settlement schemes, and one must exercise considerable caution in attempting to determine how far their present attitudes and behavior are products of their pre-settlement rather than their post-settlement experiences. A few generalizations may, however, be risked about the settlers' motivations, resources, and perceptions at the time they became members of the schemes.

The original motivations of the settlers may be compared to those that appear to be implicit in the Kenya government's development strategy as well as to those implicit in various academically conceived models of modernization. The Kenya government's ambivalence toward the schemes is reflected in its development strategy, outlined in chapter 4. On the one hand, the Kenya government assumes that the attraction of consumer goods available in the monetary economy will motivate Africans to acquire the skills needed to produce for that economy. It assumes that modifications in social institutions and behavior patterns will be accomplished in the pursuit of this objective. On the other hand, as noted in chapter 4, the government believes that too many resources have been poured into the schemes relative to their economic potential and with disregard for the interests of the African people of Kenya as a whole. The government also accepts continued economic discrimination between the formerly European areas where the settlements are located and the rest of rural Kenya. Such considerations have affected the government's expectations of the motivational patterns of the settlers, mostly in the period after the bulk of them joined the schemes. Most of the settlers received their plots at the time when the government still saw the settlement program as a major exercise in improving the condition of a substantial number of landless and unemployed Africans, an integral part of the government's nation-building effort. It expected the settlers to be motivated to become productive farmers and, as a corollary, to receive educational, medical, and other social benefits. While the African farmers were not expected on the average to reach incomes above those of 90 percent of Kenya's African income-earners, the possession of land was expected to motivate them to build and participate in thriving small-scale rural societies. Each settlement was to have land set aside for the creation of a "township" bearing more than passing resemblance to an idyllic English rural community—possessing schools, medical facilities, meeting places, shops, a church, a cemetery, and sanitary facilities. It is very difficult to determine how much the ambivalence of many of the first settlement officers in the field obstructed the communication of these motivations to the settlers. Many of the first settlement officers had been European settlers, and a number of them were less than fully committed to the interests of the new African settlers.

The current motivations of the settlers differ considerably from the government's present expectations, as we shall show. The discrepancies were probably less apparent when the settlement program began, but perhaps there were subtle differences even then. All the settlers were expected to demonstrate commitment to the schemes by full-time residence on their plots. A great many of the settlers, especially those on the low-density schemes, kept other employment in addition to their farms, a natural result of the fact that they were not required to be landless or unemployed to receive a plot. Even on the high-density schemes, where lack of employment or of access to land were conditions for selection, many settlers today are willing to admit that they have other land or sources of income. There may also have been a difference between the actual economic motivations of the settlers and the expectations of the Kenya government. The government saw the distribution of land as providing an economic resource for participation in the modern economy. The settlers then—as today—may have seen the acquisition of land as a means of gaining social security more than as an instrument of economic upward mobility. Many settlers today explain that they wanted land as security for their old age, while very few see the possession of land primarily as a means of acquiring monetary income. Commitment to participation in the modern economy did not necessarily mean, as the government may have assumed then as well as now, participation in the institutions set up by the government or private enterprise to process and market crops for the whole country as distinct from local African traders. Finally, there is no particular evidence to suggest that the settlers came inclined to participate in community development as outlined by the government's plans for townships on the schemes. The settlers may have seen such social facilities more in terms of assistance for the immediate family than as means and symbols of wider community interaction.

Differences between the settlers' real and expected motivational patterns have a bearing on academically designed theories of modernization. One common ingredient in many of these theories is individual willingness to participate in a common effort, involving a wider social group than previously, toward achieving new social goals. Such willingness may be more apparent than real, since people may indicate a willingness to be mobilized while entertaining objectives quite different from the national leaders' attempts to accomplish mobilization for modernization. While the settlement program might well appear to be an example of national mobilization for modernization (given the numbers of Africans involved, the urgency of its undertaking, and the extent of resource commitment to the program), the settlers' real motivations and those attributed to them by the government may well have been quite different even at the outset of the program—which must be taken into account in measuring the amount of mobilization actually achieved.

Resources. The settlers' resources for modernization at the beginning are also significant in determining to what degree they were prepared for effective participation in the settlement program. What resources beyond motivation, if any, are needed for participation in some form of modernization is a matter on which differences of opinion exist. It can, of course, be argued that mere distribution of some of these resources is in fact the responsibility of the government that seeks to achieve modernization. Among the resources that may have some bearing on success in modernizing are age, education, occupational experience, financial resources, and responsibilities. The settlers we are considering here were in the great majority of cases in age brackets that made them physically able to engage in the long hard work necessary to create new farms and new communities. Most of the settlers were in their thirties and forties, with a significant number in their twenties. Few were in their fifties, and only a very small number were sixty or over. Those settlers who were also officers of the settlement cooperative societies were slightly younger than those who were not. More officers were in their thirties, and almost none were over fifty.

In a country where only half of the primary school age population is actually enrolled, according to 1965 statistics, the educational background of the settlers would not appear to be vastly different from the African rural population at large. Few settlers had had more than elementary education, but then only a small proportion of all African schoolchildren are able to acquire more than an elementary school formal education. There appeared to be a discernible difference in this study between the educational backgrounds of those settlers who were elected cooperative society officers and those who were not. The majority of the office-holding settlers had completed more than 50 percent of their elementary education. Nearly half of the regular settlers had had no formal education of any kind, but an equal number had had more than half of their formal elementary schooling. The presence, for Kenya as a whole, of 50 percent of elementary school age children in school gives no indication of the percentage that actually complete elementary school, nor does it correct for probable differences between urban and rural Kenya. Hence it is likely that the educational profile of the settlers, and especially of their leaders, does not differ greatly from the national pattern, at least in the rural areas.

The high-density settlement schemes were designed for the landless and unemployed Africans. The government sought where possible to obtain unemployed and landless Africans with some previous agricultural experience. Thus the schemes were aimed not at down and out Africans but at those who were without land or employment as a result of land consolidation, the departure of European settlers, or the general decline in the country's economy following the 1960 Lancaster House Conference. Also included were the underemployed rural Africans and the adult members of large families on small plots in generally overcrowded areas of Central and Western Provinces and elsewhere. More difficult to verify is the hypothesis that local leaders used the settlement schemes as receptacles for undesirables in their locales. This hypothesis, based on observations by people not especially sympathetic to the schemes, would appear to be confirmed only insofar as proclivity for political infighting is included within the definition of "undesirable." We shall discuss political infighting on the settlement schemes later in this chapter. In any event, almost none of the settlers admitted to being unemployed prior to entering the settlement schemes. Of those settlers who were not office-holders, the largest number (30 percent) claimed employment as farm laborers. The next largest number (25 percent) claimed to have farmland of their own; this category includes tenants as well as "owners" but excludes squatters on European farms. Third in importance were those (15 percent) who claimed employment in various unskilled positions: drivers, cooks, etc. Another 15 percent claimed employment in what could be termed skilled positions or minor clerical posts. The remainder claimed to be teachers (6 percent) and traders (2 percent). Only 6 percent claimed no employment of any kind. Among the settlers who were office-holders at the time of this study, a different pattern of prior employment emerges. The largest number (33 percent) had served in clerical, minor managerial, or skilled positions. Most of the others were distributed fairly equally among farmers, teachers, and unskilled farm and nonfarm positions. About 10 percent were involved in trade or shopkeeping. Only one office-holder claimed no previous employment. The difference in educational background and in occupational background between "ordinary" settlers and those elected to office suggests a substantial tendency on the part of the settlers to voluntarily choose office-holders with more preparation for the managerial requirements of cooperative positions than they themselves possess, or to select from their ranks those with the most preparation. Finally, 33 percent of the settlers on the high-density schemes admitted to having profitable employment in addition to maintaining their scheme plots—a remarkable percentage, since this is illegal. These figures seem to demonstrate that a rather substantial proportion of the settlers did not lack the experience of responsible employment within the modern sector of the economy. For these persons, the settlement schemes merely provided employment of a somewhat different nature to replace jobs lost as a result of the transfer of power. For many the financial improvement, if any, may not have been very great. This may help to explain why many settlers continue to have additional jobs and why many did not see the settlement schemes as a vehicle for economic upward mobility.

The financial resources and obligations of the settlers at the time they joined the settlements probably cannot be accurately estimated now. One can infer from the record of previous employment that perhaps most of the settlers were not penniless then, and it is widely believed among settlement officials that settlers' relatives came to their assistance to help them get plots. It is known that many settlers had partial interest in family livestock which they liquidated to gain funds. The financial obligations of the settlers are equally hard to assess, even at the present time. What can be observed is the number of dependents present on the settlers' plots. The FESU statistics indicate ratios of between five and ten dependents for every settler plotholder. These ratios may well be higher than those elsewhere in rural Kenya, but perhaps not higher than in those areas whence the settlers came.

This educational and employment information suggests that the settlers are not without qualifications for contributing to rural development, but the record of past and present employment, together with the articulated motivations of the individual settlers, suggest the absence of motivations desired by the government and reasons for their absence, factors which may well have been present at the time the settlers took over their plots. The educational background of the settlers also indicates the presence of people with a modicum of education and a propensity for them to elect those with more education as their spokesmen in the cooperative societies. The settlers are not without articulate spokesmen, whether or not such spokesmen fulfill other requirements for effective grass-roots leadership.

In a unique category are those settlers who have been given special hundred-acre plots. In transferring the land from European to African hands, the settlement administration had to dispose of the rather substantial homes built by many of the settlers. In one category were placed "state houses," especially large and finely constructed homes that were not distributed to settlers but retained by the state for special public functions. The very poor houses or buildings were destroyed or given to the settlers on whose plots they happened to fall. In a third category were the so-called standard houses, which were substantial but less pretentious than the state houses. The government decided to surround these homes with hundred-acre plots and dispose of the houses and plots to selected individuals who could develop the plots and meet the financial obligations entailed. The intention was to give these homes and plots to leaders of the community, political and otherwise, who would, by their example, inspire the settlers on regular—far more modest—plots. A number of members of Parliament, local leaders, and relatives of the president and his cabinet ministers have acquired an interest in the settlement schemes through purchasing these special plots. These plots were also seen as a means of giving the political leadership a stake in the new Kenya. It was believed that they would be more likely to remain content with the political course of the country after independence, and with their roles in it, if they were given the prestige, security, and reward of a substantial piece of land and an attractive home.

Many of the purposes of this hundred-acre program have not been realized. It proved unpopular politically, especially among those political gladiators who did not receive plots. Criticisms of the settlement program as a whole have made this particular aspect of it more vulnerable to attack, for the program of distributing special plots, like the program as a whole, makes the government responsible, on behalf of the settlers in these special plots, to Great Britain for an unpopular loan benefiting relatively few Africans and for the allocation of public resources disproportionately to the number of beneficiaries. In early 1967 the government announced that the program of special plots would be discontinued. There is no evidence, furthermore, that the holders have done more than inspire envy among the ordinary settlers, and they have been more laggard than the other settlers in repaying their land and development loans.

Settlement-Scheme Structure at the Grass Roots. The nature and quality of the settlers' responses to their new environment are not only a function of the economic potential of the area and the backgrounds of the settlers themselves. The arrangements for structuring the settlers' participation in the new setting are also of central importance. The most important arrangements concern land tenure, development loan obligations, and the cooperative societies. Collectively, these define the intended balance between administrative control of settler activities, collective initiative and responsibility by the settlers, and individual settler obligations and opportunities. It will become apparent that steps taken at the grass roots to meet the major nation-building crises of legitimacy, identity, penetration, distribution, participation, and integration are conflicting rather than complementary. Not only will the results of development efforts meet these crises differentially, but the strategies themselves must reflect choices between the demands arising from these various crises.

The settlers have only limited security of tenure on their land. Upon entering, they were required to participate in a number of agreements. They were expected to accept a "Letter of Allotment" which gave them what may best be described as conditional freehold tenure. This Letter of Allotment was not a grant or conveyance of freehold title but a promise of freehold tenure provided certain conditions were met. The major conditions were that the land be used for agricultural purposes only, that subdivision, charges on the land, transfer, or lease not be undertaken without the prior written consent of the Central Land Board (now the Department of Settlement), and that each settler develop a portion of his land (cultivate one acre, build a house, fence his land) within six months of entry. Failure to comply with these conditions after due warning may result in the settler's eviction. The settlers were required to agree to repay the loan for the purchase of the land over a thirty-year period at 6 percent interest and agree again to many of the conditions in the Letter of Allotment. In addition they had to agree to reside personally on the plot, to keep only such livestock on the plot as are approved by the settlement fund trustees, to farm the land according to rules of good husbandry as determined by the trustees, and to pay all taxes and other assessments charged against the land. A tenant's failure to comply may result in the trustees' spending funds necessary to meet these conditions and charging them, with interest, to the settler. The settlers were required to accept development loans of varying amounts as determined by what the government believed necessary to enable each settler to meet his budgeted income. The settlers apparently had no option but to accept a development loan, since possession of the land was tied to undertaking its development along lines specified by the settlement administration. The settlers undertook to repay this loan in six-month installments over a period of ten years. If they did not meet these payments, the whole loan could be recalled immediately and/or the land in question could be forfeited. The settlers are in reality tenants on sufferance of the settlement administration. They are required to accept developmental obligations as a condition for gaining plots, and the actual titles to the lands are held by the Central Land Board and are to become the possession of the settlers only when they meet their financial and developmental obligations. The settlers, finally, have no legal recourse in case the settlement administration tries to recall loans or repossess plots. Their tenure on the land is only as secure as their ability and willingness to meet their obligations, and it depends on the satisfaction of the settlement fund trustees and their administrators, the Department of Settlement, with their performance.

The settlers' legal position in regard to their land is at variance with the motivations many of them had in seeking to acquire plots. Despite instructions to administrative personnel involved in land transfer to make certain the new tenants understood their position, a very substantial number of settlers we interviewed claim not to have fully understood their position at the time they entered their plots and to have been surprised and disappointed to learn of their obligations later. Some of these claims may well be rationalizations for subsequent deficient performance, but, considering the haste with which the program was necessarily implemented, many may be valid. The educational qualifications of the settlers appear to be such that most of them could have understood their position if given a reasonably thorough explanation, but they are not such that the settlers could be expected to grasp the particulars immediately and automatically. An observed tendency among some Africans to indicate comprehension and agreement without really having either, in order not to anger a superior, could well have contributed to a lack of communication between the settlers and the administrators of the transfer. Perhaps it is even more important that the settlers characteristically sought plots of land to provide social security for themselves and their families, while in reality the conditions of their tenure withhold the actual security of full ownership and they can be evicted at the discretion of the settlement administration if they fail to live up to the developmental expectations implied in the loan agreements.

The conditions of tenure pose a genuine developmental dilemma. On one hand, the settlement authorities can be forgiven for protecting themselves against any settler failure to perform to expectations. The settlement loan agreements are among the British government, the CDC, the World Bank, and the Kenya government. The Kenya government then lends the funds to individual settlers. The government wants to meet the loan obligations in order to establish its international credit. Similarly, it believes that inexperienced settlers cannot be fully trusted to meet their obligations because of lack of skill and through general failure to accept the new responsibilities. The Kenya government has sought to put itself in a sound financial position vis-à-vis both the international financiers of the program and the settlers rather than accept the viewpoint of politicians like Odinga, Kaggia, and Oneko. These leaders believe that the land should be free to the settlers because it was theirs prior to colonial rule, and that the Kenya government should not demean itself by honoring a loan which Britain forced on Kenya in the interest of the European rather than the African settlers. On the other hand, the distribution of potential rewards and threatened deprivations appears to have distressed rather than motivated the settlers in a great many instances. Development planning in Kenya, as we have seen, assumes that Africans behave like Europeans where economic theory is concerned. A basic tenet of economic theory is that individuals are inspired to produce efficiently both by the opportunity to profit and by the risk of economic loss—that is, by the simultaneous presence of the carrot and the stick. Accordingly, the settlers are asked to risk losing their land for the chance of achieving some other objective, such as gaining a larger income through increasing their means of producing such an income. They are offered only the stick and no carrot. The settlers, however, are risking the very possession for which they came to the schemes to achieve no other purpose, in most cases, than to gain full control of what they have risked. In the balance is not only an economic asset but status and old age security as well. The settlers' lack of previous experience with fulfilling loan obligations of this sort may well reduce the probability that they will carry the risk successfully and perhaps makes them in their own minds less willing to do so. Fear of the consequences of failure and/or dissatisfaction with the arrangements may in turn further decrease the likelihood that the settlers will meet their obligations successfully. Since the settlers place more than simple economic value on the land and are more interested in secure possession than in capitalizing on the land's income-producing capabilities, their perception of the distribution of potential rewards and threatened deprivations differs from that of the government and the lenders. In most instances, they face a choice between what they seem to believe is an unattractive proposition on the settlements and unemployment.

The conditions of land tenure involve the government in dealing with the problems of penetration at the expense of measures for dealing with each of the other crises of nation-building identified by Pye. The settlers' security of tenure is substantially less than that of the Africans involved in the land-consolidation programs and even of those who have access to land according to traditional rules of tenure. The objective of the government continues to be to put land tenure on the same basis throughout Kenya. Having the settlers on a substantially different basis does not contribute to solving the problems of integration described at the conclusion of chapter 4. By giving settlers access to the land but withholding realization of their objectives in seeking the land, the settlement program's contribution to resolving the crises of distribution may be substantially lessened. The settlers' attitudes toward the conditions of their tenure suggest that their sense of participation in the benefits and processes of post-independence nation-building is also diminished. The settlers' identification with the new nation and their recognition of the government's legitimacy do not appear to have been shaken, in part because of the position of the cooperative societies. While the land-consolidation program was undertaken with the explicit objectives of giving the participants a stake in the community and a reason for not challenging the existing regime, the settlement of Africans has per se contributed less to these objectives. The settlers do not admit to wishing they had never come, but neither do they appear to have formed any greater commitment to the government or the nation simply by their occupation of a plot.

The cooperative societies play a critical role in the structure and functioning of the settlement schemes at the grass-roots level. Their use on the schemes reflects an attempt to harmoniously merge considerations of practicality, ideology, and pre-colonial African tradition in Kenya. The settlers needed to realize economies of scale in order to make possible the purchase of tractors, trucks, and processing equipment. Collaboration could also facilitate the marketing of their products. The cooperative societies were also seen to be in line with African leaders' calls for institutions appropriate to African socialism, even though cooperative societies of the kind employed in the settlements were initially introduced after World War II to reflect the socialist views of Britain's new Labour government. Finally, the cooperative societies were intended to reflect vaguely the cooperative traditions of African peoples prior to colonial rule.

The functions of the societies have been to supervise any necessary local processing of the settlers' crops, to provide for marketing them, to assume responsibility for collecting the settlers' individual loan repayments, and to manage the settlers' collective obligations to repay loans for common property such as tractors and trucks. The collection of loan repayments has been one of the most troublesome responsibilities of the societies and is one that the government gave to the societies somewhat later than the others. The bylaws common to cooperative societies under the Cooperative Societies Act as revised in 1963 did not include this function. It is important to remember that these societies were established for fewer than 1,000 settlers —as few as fifty-four in one case—rather than for a whole district. They operate with no more than ten paid employees and often with only two or three. Their capital and equipment are customarily minimal. Their leaders are not far removed from the members and share most of the same concerns. These societies, in short, perform their functions at a very grass-roots level.

Membership in the cooperative societies is nearly universal in the settlement schemes. Normally each has its own cooperative. Settlers were not compelled to join the cooperatives as a condition for receiving a plot, but the administrative personnel on each scheme gave high priority to gaining 100 percent membership of settlers in the cooperatives and have virtually succeeded in this task. In fact, the settlers have no real option but to remain as members. Only the cooperatives are able to provide such services as artificial insemination and dip cleansing for cattle, and failure to have one's cattle cleansed can result in repossession of the animals by the Settlement Department, loss of means of repaying land and development loans, and, therefore, expulsion from the plot. A few settlers have fallen victim to these circumstances. In principle, the bylaws common to these societies provide that membership may be refused to an applicant by the cooperative society officers without a stated reason and that members may be expelled by the general membership or the cooperative officers for criminal behavior or "acts in any way against the interests of the Society." [5] The actual freedom of action of the societies is considerably limited by field officers of the Department of Coopera-

5. Based on the Cooperative Societies Act 1966, Republic of Kenya, No. 39 of 1966 (Nairobi: Government Printer, 1966).

tive Development in ways and for reasons that will be explained shortly. One manifestation of this administrative supervision is not only the settlers' lack of freedom regarding membership in the cooperative society but their lack of freedom to refuse members or expel them unless the government settlement officers and Cooperative Department officers determine that a settler's behavior justifies his expulsion from his plot.

The real business of each cooperative society is conducted by a committee elected for staggered two-year terms by the general membership. The committee includes a chairman, vice chairman, secretary, treasurer, and normally five other members. The committees, assisted usually by two or more paid employees, are entrusted with the tasks of overseeing the processing of crops on the schemes, the marketing of the crops, the care of livestock, keeping records of individual society members with respect to amounts of marketed produce and loan repayments, and acting generally as liaison among the cooperative officers, settlement officers, general membership of the cooperative societies, and the settlements. Any expenditure by the cooperative must be authorized specifically by the general membership unless it is included in the annual budget, which the general membership must also approve. Most of the cooperative societies have felt the need for more executive leadership and have been encouraged by the cooperative and settlement officers to select managers. The managers are often but not always settlers themselves, with appropriate educational and occupational qualifications, usually full primary education and some administrative experience, who are responsible to the elected committee and through the committee to the general membership. The structure of such societies is very much like a miniature of the city-manager form of government in the United States. It also resembles the relationship between stockholders, the board of directors, and the executives of a corporation. The managers are paid a modest salary, while the elected committee members are paid only a five-shilling allowance for each general meeting and committee meeting, which the cooperative officers try to limit in number, since the funds come from the societies themselves.

The business of the cooperative societies, like matters of membership, is largely removed from the discretion of the committees and general membership of the cooperatives. The cooperative societies were in fact established not through any grass-roots initiative or even through the initiative of local or national political leaders; they were created because the Department of Settlement believed that only some such institution could provide for the collective needs of the settlers. The cooperative societies are responsible for implementing those policies which the government believes essential to the economic success of the settlement schemes individually and the settlement program as a whole. The government also needs the societies in order to complete the process of land transfer. The Settlement Department took over possession of numerous farm buildings and houses, and some equipment, along with the land which was subdivided into small plots. After the settlers were on the schemes and the cooperative societies were established, the department began to sell these permanent improvements to the individual settlements on which they were located. The government provided the societies with capital to purchase these improvements by requiring each settler to buy at least one share in the cooperative society, leaving the individual settlers' development loans to be used only for their personal requirements. At the same time, the government took steps to protect the financial position of the societies by placing a ceiling on the cooperatives' borrowing power ($28 per member), by requiring Cooperative Department approval of any proposed borrowing, by limiting to one-fifth the percentage of shares which any one settler might own, and by forbidding the purchase of these shares by anyone other than settlers on the area in which a given cooperative is located. Similarly, loans by the society to individual members were placed under the supervision of the Cooperative Department. Yearly audits and monthly financial statements are required by the department.

In practice, control over the financial transactions of the cooperatives has proved difficult to maintain according to the letter of the bylaws. The government has been involved in a conflict of interest concerning the disposal of permanent improvements taken over with the transfer of land. The government has an interest in maintaining the financial stability and soundness of the cooperatives, but, as the middleman between European settlers and the new African settlers, it also has had an interest in selling these permanent improvements. The Settlement Department has been anxious to dispose of these improvements even at the expense of exceeding the cooperatives' borrowing limit, especially if the improvements were badly needed by the members individually and collectively in order to improve their economic position. The Cooperative Department has been more concerned with safeguarding the interests of the cooperative societies and has clashed frequently with the Settlement Department, which it believes has been straining the resources of the cooperatives unduly when they are young and vulnerable. Consequently, the borrowing ceiling has not been consistently, or even sensibly, maintained.

Control over the loan structure of cooperative societies has been difficult to maintain, because the Settlement Department has been unable to control loans made to the settlers and the cooperatives by outside groups. On the low-density settlements especially, where members were required to have some working capital, the government has been unable to prevent the *de facto* involvement of outsiders in the financial structure of the cooperatives, because it has been unable to ascertain in advance to whom the settlers may be informally indebted for this working capital. Commercial firms in towns near the settlements appear not to have understood that borrowing by the societies requires administrative approval, and in a number of instances the cooperative societies have purchased equipment on credit from these firms without the prior knowledge of the cooperative officer or the settlement office. Sometimes such loans have created a dilemma for the administration. The equipment purchased on credit has in some cases been clearly needed by the settlements to enhance their production capacity or marketing efficiency, but at the same time the societies have also lacked the necessary financial backing to safely contract such purchases on credit.

Since independence, the government has found it necessary to strengthen its control of the cooperative societies. The increase in administrative supervision was a response to problems arising not solely or even primarily as a result of experience with settlement scheme cooperative societies (as distinct from those outside the settlements). Examples of misappropriation of large amounts of society money by cooperative officers and members had become common knowledge even prior to independence. Instances of misappropriation, unwise use of funds, poor record-keeping, and general ignorance of essential cooperative procedures had become legion, and problems of this nature had occurred in every settlement cooperative society investigated here. The Settlement Department had maintained closer control over its societies than the Cooperative Department had over cooperatives outside the Settlement Department, in part because the settlement cooperatives bore responsibility for channeling the repayment of the large loan employed to finance the program. One effect of the New Cooperative Societies Act of December, 1966, was in part to increase the Cooperative Department's control over non-settlement cooperatives to a level commensurate with the Settlement Department's *de facto* supervision of its cooperatives. There was little recognition of the fact that greater supervision had not relieved the settlement cooperatives of the misfortunes that had befallen non-settlement cooperatives.

The revision of the Cooperative Societies Act in the direction of more centralized administrative control over cooperatives did more than give statutory backing to existing supervision of settlement cooperatives by the Department of Settlement. The nature of the revisions provides a catalogue of the problems which cooperative societies both in and out of settlements had experienced. The new act gave the commissioner of cooperative development direct control over the budget and expenditures of the societies and authorized him to require the appointment of an accountant at an appropriate fee or salary for a given society or societies. Any charges on the cooperative society property made as security for its purchases required the approval of the commissioner to be valid. The commissioner was given control over remuneration of society officers and employees, who were made subject to fine and/or imprisonment for illegal receipt of society funds (funds dispersed without the prior knowledge of the commissioner or not provided for in the budget), and over loans by the cooperative societies to their individual members. Finally, appointment of any paid employees of the society required the approval of the commissioner if they were to be graded as civil servants. Willful impersonation of officers or submission of erroneous financial reports was made punishable by fine and/or imprisonment. The Settlement Department, in addition, decided on its own to encourage the appointment of cooperative society managers for individual societies, leaving the committees with supervisory rather than direct executive responsibility for society affairs.

The government also decided to expand considerably the educational opportunities for its own cooperative officers as well as for the elected leaders and paid employees of the societies themselves. The Scandinavian countries and Japan have recently sent teams to analyze the problems of Kenya's cooperatives and to assist in reshaping them and expanding cooperative education. A cooperative college has been built in Nairobi, and cooperative centers in the various provinces are being developed to provide appropriate educational opportunities. These programs are aimed primarily at the cooperative society leadership rather than at the individual members, in part because of the still limited availability of educational facilities and in part on the theory that the leaders and employees of the societies can subsequently pass on their insights to the general membership.

Despite the increased centralization and administrative supervision of cooperative societies in and out of the settlement schemes, the government has sought to maintain a balance between such supervision and the principle that cooperative society leaders must be elected by and responsible to the individual members. Maintenance of this principle satisfies the ideological purposes of the cooperative movement: to exemplify socialism, democracy, and traditional patterns of cooperation among Africans. The need to strike this balance between central administrative supervision and local democracy, and yet to give new emphasis to the former, testifies to the disparity between the requirements of ideology and those of efficiency and sound local contributions to economic development, which have become the government's primary objectives. The need to satisfy all these requirements has been responsible for many of the difficulties which continue to beset the cooperative societies, at least on the settlement schemes and probably elsewhere as well. As the second half of this chapter will demonstrate, the existing allocation of responsibilities has amounted in reality to a new version of the colonial notion of indirect rule. The government has succeeded in maintaining its legitimacy in the eyes of the settlers by using the accepted authority of elected leaders of cooperative societies to carry out functions, such as collecting loan repayments, that might impair the legitimacy of the government were its own officers to assume them. It is perhaps more palatable to have leaders of one's own choosing carry out unpopular tasks, but the government has benefited by having criticism of its policies diverted elsewhere.

One very important further assumption behind the government's structuring the cooperative societies both in and out of the settlement schemes has been that politics, or political interference, can and should be kept from impairing the smooth functioning of these societies. In part this reflects the desirability of keeping cooperative societies independent of political parties, members of Parliament, and others who have or seek elective positions. The purpose is to maintain administrative rationality, but the price may be to sacrifice the assistance of persons who could possibly have a real (and beneficial) influence over the members. In any event, the depoliticization of the cooperative societies is not matched by other channels for articulating and aggregating demands and supports by the members. The assumption also has the corollary that the political structure of the societies themselves not be permitted to interfere with their rational and impartial administration. The first assumption has been generally substantiated in the settlement cooperatives; the corollary has not proved to be realistic and perhaps could not be.

GRASS-ROOTS RESPONSES TO THE SETTLEMENT PROGRAM

The grass-roots responses to the settlement program may be examined from the standpoint of tangible material progress on the individual settlements and from the perspective of individual settlers' and cooperative leaders' perceptions of the program and its progress.

The two are, of course, a function of each other: settlers' perceptions of the program will be affected by their economic and administrative success, but they will also influence the nature and degree of such progress.

Condition of the New Environment. The tangible progress of the settlement schemes can be evaluated by examining three important determinants: the economic situation of the settlement schemes and the individual settlers, the extent of community development in the individual settlements, and the condition of the cooperative societies. A general and comparative statement may be attempted at the outset: the economic condition of the schemes has been uneven, ranging from destitution to very strong progress; the development of communities on the schemes has generally been minimal; the cooperative societies remain generally troubled and unsatisfactory for reasons having to do with the structure of the cooperative movement there, the special responsibilities of the settlers, and the settlers' general lack of previous experience with such institutions.

The economic data available at the time of writing attempted to explain the progress of the schemes through the first three to four years of the settlement program, i.e., through the condition of typical settlers in the second or third year of operation. Some data were available for 1966 as well. The data came from two sources, the Department of Settlement's records, available in annual reports and in unpublished monthly reports from individual schemes, and the Farm Economics Survey Unit of the Kenya Ministry of Economic Planning and Development. The Settlement Department's data appear to be quite reliable, because they are based on aggregate data for individual schemes and on the written records of the cooperative societies, checked monthly by officers of the Department of Cooperative Development. The FESU data are less reliable because they are more ambitious: they attempt to depict the economic progress of a random sample of settlers in selected areas, based on interviews with the settlers and written records which they were asked to keep. In addition to the risk involved with the written records of settlers, especially those on the high-density settlements who are unused to such procedures, there are certain questions which the settlers are unlikely to answer accurately because of what they believe to be their self-interest. For example, the nature and extent of nonfarm employment and even, perhaps, their incomes, may not be reported accurately. Settlers may have a bias in favor of underreporting these items because the nonfarm employment is illegal on high-density settlements and the level of income is an important determinant of government tolerance of delinquent loan repayments.

Economic data on the settlers and the schemes in the first years of the program are important, because they indicate the likelihood that the settlers or the schemes will attain economic viability in the future. Those settlements and settlers that do poorly in the first years are caught in a downward spiral that is difficult to reverse in subsequent years. Lack of productivity leads to delinquency on loan repayments, and such delinquencies result in a more rapid increase in the subsequent annual loan repayment bills than in the ability to repay. Poor crops or loss of cattle leads to a lack of the income necessary not only for subsistence but for developing crops in the future. Although the Department of Settlement in individual instances has supplied "rescue loans" for settlements beset by natural disasters, this practice is not universal and the funds available are limited. On the other hand, those settlements and settlers that make a good beginning in the first years build a foundation and reserves that will make future success more likely and will provide a cushion against poor years. The Kenya government's desire to repay the lenders promptly and its intention not to invest large amounts of additional money in the settlement schemes tend, therefore, to make the critical initial years of the program difficult ones for the settlements and the individual settlers.

The settlement schemes showed uneven economic progress in the first full years of their existence. The eleven low-density ones included in the initial FESU survey averaged a net income, assuming full loan repayment, of approximately 47 percent of budgeted income figures; the six low-density settlements in this group that were examined most closely in this study averaged about 36 percent of the budgeted figure. These figures are less depressing than they appear, because most of the settlement schemes were not budgeted to achieve the target net income before the third year, and some of these schemes were in only their second year of operation. Nevertheless, the figures are on the average below expectations. The thirty-nine high-density schemes in the FESU survey average a negative net income, as did the twenty in this group examined here. A number of the high-density areas, including Kipipiri, Mawingo, Nandarasi, Kitiri, Tulaga, Karati, and South Kinangop, did much better in the latter half of the 1964–65 survey year and in the next year because of their pyrethrum production. It is probable that all these high-density areas came out of the category of negative income as a result of the development of this crop. Lietego also began to grow substantial quantities of passion fruit in the year following the FESU survey and probably also left the negative classification. For the other, low-density settlements in the negative category, there is no particular reason to believe that their position has improved substantially since the survey. The belated introduction of profitable cash crops like pyrethrum can be explained by the lack of trust placed in the settlement schemes by government officials outside of the Department of Settlement. There was strenuous opposition within the government to growing pyrethrum on the Kinangop settlements for fear that low-quality products or low output would endanger Kenya's export markets for pyrethrum. However, it is these very settlements, settled during the crash program, which contain the settlers most associated with the freedom fighters during the Emergency. For them to suffer economically for lack of a viable cash crop would have entailed major political risks. No such risks were foreseen on the Baluhya settlements, Kabisi, Kabuyefwe, Mautuma, and Lumakanda. These were to have grown sisal, and the collapse of sisal on the world market has not been counteracted by the introduction of a new and more substantial cash crop.

These income figures, it must be emphasized, reflect net income, or income after repayment of loans. Before the loan repayment, the average settler is in the black. Consequently, part of the delinquency in loan repayment may be attributed to inability to produce sufficient income, unwillingness to reduce the proportion of production con-

Table 2
ESTIMATED AVERAGE NET INCOME ON SELECTED SETTLEMENT SCHEMES 1964–1965

Settlement	Date Started	High- or Low-Density Scheme	Budget Net Income (shillings)	Estimated Actual Income	Actual Percentage of Budgeted Income (minimum)
Kabisi	Sept. 1963	High	500–800	139.54	27.9
Kabuyefwe	March 1964	High	500–800	−268.00	0.0
Mautuma	March 1963	High	500–800	−14.61	0.0
Lumakanda	Sept. 1963	High	500–800	−74.39	0.0
Ndalat	Sept. 1962	High	500–800	1053.71	210.7
Elgeyo Border	Sept. 1962	High	800	677.96	84.7
Sotik East	March 1963	High	800–1,400	−133.68	0.0
Manga	March 1964	High	800–1,400	185.19	23.1
Sabatia	March 1963	High	800	271.11	33.9
Kipipiri	June 1962	High	500	239.48	47.9
*Mawingo	Dec. 1963	High	500–800	−435.09	0.0
*Nandarasi	Dec. 1963	High	500–800	−536.24	0.0
*Kitiri	Dec. 1963	High	500–800	−795.30	0.0
*Tulaga	Dec. 1963	High	500–800	−806.17	0.0
*Karati	Dec. 1963	High	500–800	−754.27	0.0
South Kinangop	June 1963	High	500–800	−444.22	0.0
Endarasha	Dec. 1962	High	500–1,400	−317.20	0.0

Settlement	Date Started	High- or Low-Density Scheme	Budget Net Income (shillings)	Estimated Actual Income	Actual Percentage of Budgeted Income (minimum)
*Uaso Nyiro	Dec. 1963	High	500–1,400	403.55	80.7
Naro Moru	Dec. 1962	High	500–800	−965.02	0.0
Mua Hills	Sept. 1962	High	500–1,400	−137.36	0.0
Lessos	March 1964	Low	2,000	916.16	45.8
Ainabkoi East	Sept. 1962	Low	2,000	703.26	35.2
Gelegele-Koyet	Mar., Sept. 1962	Low	2,000	675.41	33.8
Lietego	March 1962	Low	2,000	−152.81	0.0
Passenga	June 1963	Low	2,000	−235.71	0.0
Silanga	June 1963	Low	2,000	2400.68	120.0

* Crash Program
Compiled and calculated from Farm Economics Survey Unit and Settlement Department data.

sumed on the farm, or inability to find other sources of income to relieve the position. Only part of the delinquency can be so accounted, however. When nonfarm income is included, the settlers on the average possess the financial resources to meet the loan bill, and the explanation for delinquency must be sought elsewhere. Many settlers feel imprisoned by their debt. They may feel that the debt should not be repaid, that the land should be theirs, that the funds are for other things, or that the debt is a kind of sentence upon them which they lack the power to remove.

The repayment percentages show a decline from the initial percentages and a slight recovery on the Kikuyu high-density settlements (Kipipiri through Naro Moru). The initial higher percentages reflect the fact that, on many settlements, the first billing came before a crop was in the ground. Consequently, the settlers had no alternative but to pay for their land out of the money lent to develop it. This practice was widely reported by the settlers and must have taken place with the concurrence of the Settlement Department, which retained control of disbursement of development loan funds. The early billing and the practice of permitting development loan funds to be reduced in order to reduce a settler's indebtedness was economically wrong and has been denounced by the settlers themselves, who had no choice, and by the many critics of the settlement program. The reason for these practices lay in the fear that the settlers, unless required to pay something early in their tenure, would develop the belief that the land and facilites had been given them free. There were a great many critics of KANU's decision to support the principle of buying back European land, both within and outside KANU, and the retiring colonial government and Settlement Department officials were anxious above all not to lend the appearance of reality to wishes for free land. One political objective, however, was achieved at the cost of another, for the early billings put many of the settlers in a difficult position from the start, and their serious indebtedness has given fuel to political and economic critics of the program. In fact, some of the same African spokesmen who demanded that the land be free at the outset have used the position of the indebted settlers as a vindication of their earlier arguments and as ammunition for their present attacks upon the government.

Many individuals on the low-density settlements admit that they preferred to repay their development and land loans by canceling part of the former rather than to go deeper into debt in the interests of building up their farms. The prevalence of such attitudes attests to the lack of economic motivation of the relatively prosperous low-density settlers as well as the more impoverished high-density settlers.

The slight improvement of loan repayments on the Kikuyu high-density settlements during the most recent year for which we have data is in contrast to the slight continued decline on most of the other settlements. The continued decline on the non-Kikuyu high-density areas and on the low-density settlements reflects both depleted development capital and unfortunate growing seasons. The Kikuyu improvement would appear to reflect in part the impact of the new pyrethrum crop and in part the government's determination to collect the loan on these settlements. This emphasis on collecting the Kikuyu loans reflects the fact that it is from the Kikuyu, and especially those associated with the freedom fighters of the Emergency, that the government most fears the continued belief that the land should be free to the settlers.

The over-all repayment percentages remain very low. (The reasons for the settlers' nonpayment even where repayment appears to be financially possible will be explored in the next section of this chapter.) It is very important to observe the continued low repayment figures at the same time that the government has increased its determination to recover the loan monies and has armed itself with new powers to deal firmly with defaulters. The government insisted that 50 percent of cooperative society throughput be charged against the loan repayment billings, which has not improved the position of the cooperative societies with the settlers. Zealous settlement administrative officers in the field have attempted to improve their standing with the home office by going beyond the 50 percent requirement. For example, one senior settlement officer saw to it that the settlements near Mount Kenya (Endarasha, Naro Moru, and Uaso Nyiro) raised their repayments to 60 percent. In 1966 a siftings committee, comprising the director of settlement as chairman and eleven members of Parliament, including the assistant minister for lands and settlement, toured the settlements and attempted to identify those chronic defaulters who had the means to repay. Ten settlers lost their plots for failure either to repay or to observe the conditions in their Letter of Allotment. One thousand others were warned to take steps to repay and/or conform with the conditions of their tenure or face eviction. Of these, 486 settlers complied with the demands upon them and escaped eviction. The remainder continued under threat of eviction. These settlers had recourse only through the political process, for the government had armed itself with powers to summarily attach their plots as well as their movable property to satisfy the debts. With full freehold title, the government presumably would have had to go through the courts to obtain the evictions. However, despite this increased pressure, the loan repayment position has not improved. Part of the explanation is that accumulated overdue repayments depress the settlers' cumulative repayment percentage even if they meet a large percentage of the most recent billings. The longer the indebtedness continues, the more effort the government will have to expend to achieve substantial improvement in the over-all position, and this is certain to put strains on the government's public image. An indication of such pressure came in early 1967, when President Kenyatta surprised his own government by announcing a two-year moratorium on loan repayments for new settlers. The probable price of this relief will be to weaken the determination of the older settlers to repay, because they will think they are included in the moratorium or that they should be.

An important reason for continuing low repayment percentages lies in the settlers' "safety in numbers." The government cannot and would not replace all the settlers on the settlements. It has no reason to think new tenants would accept repayment responsibilities with any more alacrity than the present settlers, and it could not begin to accept the political price of evicting 30,000 settlers even if it had the administrative resources to do so (which it probably does not). The settlers' repayment behavior indicates a tendency on their part to pay a part of their bill rather than to ignore it entirely. Some prevalent practices suggest—and a number of settlers were prepared to admit as much—the belief that a partial payment will establish their good faith and enable them to avoid eviction. They think that collectively and individually the odds of their being evicted decrease if they make partial payments rather than none at all. Consequently, from the perspective both of the settlers themselves and of the government's realistic options, obtaining full repayment is a matter not of command but of persuasion. The government can only persuade the settlers to do what they are legally required to do by way of repayment. For both settlers and government, the repayment question is largely one not of economic facts or physical force but of political support or nonsupport. Settlers who understand and accept their obligations, recognize that the loan should be repaid, and accept the authority of the government and the cooperative societies will repay well. Those who do not support the cooperatives or do not recognize the validity of the loan and its importance vis-à-vis other possible uses of the funds, demonstrate their political disaffection by nonpayment.

One form of political protest is coupled with economic self-interest. A substantial portion of the settlers' production on the farms does not pass through the cooperative society and therefore is not subject to the deductions which the cooperatives make for repayment of individual settler loans and collective loans for cooperative equipment. The farmers on most of the settlements have ready access to traders of Asian or African origin whom the cooperatives were intended to supplant. Their prices are higher than those which the cooperatives pay because they make no deductions. The situation is paradoxical, since one classic justification for cooperatives is that they eliminate the profiteering of middlemen and bring more of the profits to the producers. But since the cooperatives are also intended to create economies of scale in the use of expensive farm machinery, and the settlers must pay for these investments, the old middleman actually has an economic advantage. The cooperative societies also presume a degree of community that did not exist at the outset on the settlements. The noncompetitive prices received by settlers marketing produce through the societies prevented the cooperatives from creating that sense of community. Consequently most settlers admit a distaste for the economic possibilities of cooperative societies, are not won over by the economies of scale and bookkeeping assistance offered, and do not hesitate to sell substantial portions of their crops outside the cooperatives. Repayments become delinquent because settlers prefer to market substantial portions of their crops outside the cooperatives—whatever the consequences, economic, social, or political, for the community represented by the cooperative societies.

The settlers' genuine economic hardships are partly of political origin. Lack of income-producing animals promised in the budgets, inability, unwillingness, or lack of resources to cultivate full acreages called for by budgets, and simple inefficiency in the developing and marketing of crops help to explain some of the economic difficulties. But deficiencies in the number of cattle may be attributed in large measure to a serious depletion of the national herd by European farmers, who translated political fears into stark economic reality during the transfer of power by selling stock for slaughter in order to realize their cash value before departing. After three years of settlement, the number of mature dairy cattle had reached only 70 percent of the budgeted figure. Stock differences among the settlements arise in part from unequal success with artificial insemination and in part from loss of cattle through death and disease, especially in the Kipsigis and Kisii areas (Sotik East through Lietego). Even at the outset of settlement, however, there were substantial inequalities in the distribution of dairy cattle. It is possible, though admittedly difficult to prove, that these inequalities resulted in part from a pattern of ethnic discrimination in favor of the Kikuyu, for there is a discernible difference between their positions (Passenga through Naro Moru) and the other settlements. If such discrimination occurred, it need not be attributed primarily to the Kikuyu predominance in the independent government, for the inequalities were present before the new government had real control of the settlements. The attitude of the retiring colonial government, which feared the impact of the Kikuyu after independence, led to the crash program and to the demand that loan repayments be started before any production had occurred. This fear may well have led the government also to obviate the possibility of economic distress among Kikuyu settlers by keeping them well supplied with money-earning, prestigious cattle.

Milk is the largest single product of the settlements, yet production is far below target figures because of circumstances related to the politics of the transfer of power as well as to the political structure of settlements themselves. In 1966 dairy cattle were still at only 70 percent of the target figure, though this represented a 15 percent improvement over 1965. Production increased by 10 percent but still represented only 31 percent of the budgeted target. Production figures are deflated because of sales outside the cooperative societies; however, production also falls short because of inefficient production techniques.

Many schemes and many settlers have achieved genuine economic success. One of the principal reasons has been the development of pyrethrum, which has become the second-largest income producer in the settlement program. The success of pyrethrum can be explained in large measure by the political circumstances surrounding its production. Pyrethrum is a new crop in the Highlands and its present development, unlike that of milk production, is not tied in any way to the politically inspired economic behavior of the departing European settlers. The new African settlers can make a fresh start with pyrethrum unimpeded by past political circumstances. At the same time, the crop has been a boon to cooperative societies. The only buyer is the Pyrethrum Board of Kenya (PBK), which sells almost the entire crop abroad. It will not buy from individual settlers, and individual settlers have no market other than the PBK. Since they thus must sell through the cooperative societies, they have been forced to place their confidence in the cooperatives. The crop yields a steady revenue throughout the year, which facilitates repayment of loans whenever payments happen to come due, and contributes to a feeling of security on the part of the settlers that other crop production patterns do not. That security may be reflected not only in further confidence in the cooperatives but in responses to the structure of the program as a whole, including the loan repayment requirements. Some of the perceptible increase on the Kikuyu settlements in loan repayment percentages during 1966 may have resulted from the increased confidence generated by pyrethrum production. Great optimism is not justified in this regard, however, because the crop appears to be agriculturally suitable for only some of the settlements, especially the Kikuyu ones. More uneven economic development and increased political jealousies may result. The substantial increase in production was achieved by raising crop acreages well beyond budget figures. There has been a great deal of inefficient production, some of which results from poor processing on the settlements. The cooperative societies are responsible for local processing and have been widely blamed by settlers for resulting losses of income.

Finally, the economic success of the settlement schemes is affected not only by factors on the production side but also by patterns of expenditure. Of primary importance is the percentage of production that is consumed on the farm, which in turn is affected by population patterns on the settlement schemes. The FESU studies recorded the size of families on the schemes and estimated the proportions of output sold, used for subsistence needs, and remaining as stocks or increased livestock value.

The cash income of the settlement farmers is in part a function of the percentage of production consumed on the farm, but these percentages do not tally closely with the average size of families on the schemes. The figures suggest a behavior pattern widely reported by the settlers themselves: a tendency to rely on outside employment, including support from friends and relatives farming nearby outside the settlement. This tendency was most conspicuous among the Kikuyu high-density settlers and among the Baluhya schemes in Western Province. In such situations it is likely that the financial burdens of establishing settlement farms have been borne in part not only by the settlers' farming operations but by their own outside earnings and those of their friends and relatives. The recent economic improvements on the Kikuyu settlements, relating to pyrethrum development, may lessen this pattern of dependence there. The low-density settlements demonstrated a pattern of production which also featured dependence upon outside employment, but in these cases there was a tendency to use the additional income to develop hold-ings and to increase the sales from the farm rather than for subsist-ence needs. Because the low-density settlers had more profitable means of employment both in and out of the settlements, the relative importance of expenditure on subsistence needs was reduced.

The Kenya government and the lenders have still not rendered a final judgment on the economic success of the settlement program as a whole. The economic judgments offered have often reflected the same political biases that have influenced the economic progress of the schemes themselves. The Kenya government has already con-cluded that, even if the production and employment figures are comparable to those achieved outside settlements, the cost has been much greater. The political circumstances that led to the creation of the settlement schemes have influenced this judgment, just as they have affected the economic development of the settlements. For example, unfavorable comparisons have been made between settle-ment production and pre-settlement production. While this can val-idly be done in many instances, it ignores the underdevelopment of the Highlands by the Europeans. This negative comparison is often made by Europeans, like Leslie Brown, who fundamentally regret that political change forced the demise of profitable European farm-ing operations. The settlement schemes were also hampered in their early stages by the need to use as administrators European former settlers who for reasons far more emotional and personal than Brown's also regretted the economic and social consequences of political change. The reports of the Stamp and Van Arkadie missions are freer of this kind of bias. But they have both been dominated by the thinking of economists and statisticians, as is the *Development Plan* of Kenya in regard to the schemes. The contributions of the program, or the lack of them, to political requirements of post-independence Kenya (as distinct from the successful conclusion of the transfer of power) have generally been ignored. Both political and economic considerations and their interrelationship must be fully involved in any such assessment. In fairness to these reports, we admit that such an assessment is not easy to make.

The progress of the settlements toward becoming viable communities has been slow. The settlers themselves were strangers to one another when they came to the settlements. They came to satisfy the pressing and immediate needs of their families rather than to participate in new communities. During their tenure, the settlers have been preoccupied with establishing their farms and have not had much time, by their accounts, to devote to wider social concerns. The government's determination not to spend large additional sums on the settlement schemes has also contributed to delays in the development of the townships originally planned for most of the schemes. The settlers' limited resources have prevented them from setting up businesses on the settlements and have perhaps discouraged outside commercial interests from establishing themselves there. Finally, the cooperative societies have driven the settlers to look outside rather than within the settlements for economic relationships, because of the societies' inefficiency and responsibility for loan repayments. These difficulties reflect two basic problems: Where in the order of priorities does community development properly belong? And how should these communities be developed when they command a high priority? The government has taken the position that settlers will build communities and appreciate them as soon as they develop the necessary resources and initiative and no sooner; it does not believe that a substantial outlay of funds to build these facilities for the settlers would even be appreciated by them. The settlers themselves pointed to limited educational and health facilities when they listed their difficulties, but such deficiencies were not given so much weight as problems connected with loan repayment, tractors, and marketing facilities for their crops. It is possible that if loan funds were to be made available to Africans other than the settlers themselves, for the development of the markets, health facilities, schools, etc., such an infrastructure might help to weld settlers into viable communities, which in turn might strengthen the cooperative societies. But the decision to take such a step would presume that the settlers should form independent communities rather than be integrated with the surrounding communities.

The question of whether the schemes should become largely self-sufficient, semiautonomous units or should be absorbed in the surrounding society has not been fully answered either in policy statements or in practice. The government has not clarified the degree to which the local municipal and district authorities should be responsible for the provisions of social services to the settlers. The settlers have paid taxes to these local authorities but have not had much to show for it—in terms of the condition of settlement roads, for example. On the other hand, the position of the cooperative societies has not encouraged development of political units or local government activity within the settlements. The settlers have peculiar responsibilities which lead both the settlements and the Department of Settlement to be largely independent of the surrounding communities and the rest of the government, respectively. Paradoxically, one of the purposes of the settlement program was to destroy the distinction between the formerly European Highlands and the rest of the countryside—an objective which the independence of the settlers and the Department of Settlement does not encourage.

Settler Perceptions of the Settlement Program.   Our analysis of the condition of the settlement schemes at the grass roots has suggested three broad problem areas in which the perspectives of the settlers themselves must be considered: (1) the manner in which resources have been introduced to assist the settlements and the individual settlers in getting going; (2) the relationships of the settlers to the surrounding communities and their former environments; and (3) the legitimacy of the program and the grass-roots political and economic structure in the eyes of the settlers.

The total investment in the settlement schemes has revealed a set of government attitudes toward the settlers which have not been lost on them. The investment was undertaken in great haste amid the anxieties of the transfer of power, but the attitudes conveyed to and evoked from the settlers nevertheless remain part of the basic contour of the settlement operation. An essential feature of the investment of these resources was a basic lack of trust in the settlers, indicated clearly by requiring them to begin loan repayments before many of them could have had any new crops from which to earn the necessary funds. The retiring colonial government was not convinced that the settlers would accept the obligation to repay. The independent African government has also put repayment at the top of its priority list for the settlement schemes. Nevertheless, 1964–65 repayment figures suggested that the settlers have been repaying less since independence. Part of the reason for this decline lay in the initial decision to force early repayment, since the settlers responded to early pressure for loan repayment by paying out of development capital rather than income. In some cases, settlement officers made this decision for the settlers.

The settlers have given the government some cause to believe they oppose repayment of the land and development loans, but only partly for the reasons attributed to them by the government and political leaders. The settlers' limited resources have forced them to choose between the benefits and the obligations of economic modernization. They perceive that if they sell produce via the cooperative societies and repay their loans, they must sacrifice (at least in part) the income necessary to achieve the security they sought in coming to the settlement: education for their children, medical facilities for their families, and automobiles and trucks to allow them to function independently of middlemen, who were until very recently frequently European or Asian. This conflict appears to be uppermost in the settlers' minds, rather than the historical concern over whether "stolen lands" should be returned free of charge to Africans that was discussed in the published utterances of many present and former political spokesmen for African nationalism.

The conflict is in part a result of the economic condition of the settlement schemes. Those low-density settlers who attain their budgeted net income can easily afford to pay school fees for the three to five children for whom they characteristically bear responsibility. High-density settlers who achieve their income targets can do so at greater cost in terms of other benefits. The many settlers, especially on high-density settlements, who do not achieve budgeted incomes can contribute to meeting these social needs only by resorting to outside employment, thereby lessening their commitment to their settlement, or by not repaying a portion of their loan on time, thereby indicating to the government their political disaffection with the settlement program. The settlers are also subject to graduated personal taxes payable to local government authorities. The main responsibility of local governments with respect to the settlement schemes is the provision of adequate roads, which may be regarded as a precondition for economic development rather than as a benefit of economic development. Local taxes are not included in the settlers' budgets; they amount to about 10 percent of high-density settlers' budgeted income and not always reduced in proportion to inability to earn the budgeted income. Finally, even the means of producing the income necessary to pay for the benefits of economic development have been refused for a settler's failure to meet repayment deadlines. The records of the cooperative societies show that the director of settlement denied water reticulation projects, the purchase of tractors, and/or other investments to some schemes until repayment percentages reached 75 to 90 percent of amounts due. More recently this hard line has been softened, and a number of settlements have been allocated funds for water reticulation projects.

The conflict between the benefits and the responsibilities of modernization is political as well as economic and is reinforced by the perceptions the settlers and the government have of each other. The government and its local functionaries (cooperative and settlement officers) fear that the settlers will not repay their loans. Their interpretation of nonpayment as political opposition to the structure of the settlements, based on the early political claims to free land, has led these officers to emphasize loan repayment at the expense of very nearly all else. This arrangement of priorities conflicts with the settlers' main purpose and would cause them to believe that the government was acting against their interests were it not for the position of the cooperative societies as intervening scapegoats. As explained earlier, the government must in reality rely on its persuasive rather than its coercive powers to gain acceptance of loan repayment and other obligations associated with economic progress. Such persuasion becomes difficult when the settlers believe acquiescence is contrary to their interests.

The settlers' willingness to participate in the economic development of the schemes, their belief in the legitimacy of the settlement program and the government, and their sense of identification with the new order are weakened by the clash of interests they perceive between the government and themselves. However, it is the cooperative societies rather than the government which have taken the brunt of settler dissatisfaction. The settlers say they believe that the cooperative societies are harming their interests and express the wish that the government take more responsibility for the societies' activities. The weak legitimacy of the cooperatives, and the settlers' half-hearted participation and identification with the new environment, are not blamed on the government. It is possible that the settlers said "cooperative societies" when they meant "the government," but if so they gave no hint of any such intentional obfuscation.[6]

One of the main difficulties in inducing settlers to invest in the settlement program, from the settlers' standpoint, is that they have seen so little hard cash as a reward for their efforts. The deduction system of the cooperative societies is partly responsible, enlarged by the fact that the societies deduct not only for individual settler repayments and repayments on cooperative society purchase but also for repayment of Minimal Financial Return (MFR) loans. On a number of the settlements, the settlers have been provided during the planting season with funds for seeds, preparation of their plots through tractor plowing, and other production expenses which are to be deducted at the time of harvest. This system was designed to help the settlers at a time when funds are particularly short, and it allows those who have lost money in previous seasons to do better in the new season; otherwise, they would be without reserves to cover bad seasons. But the risks involved in this well-meant program are considerable. The price of failure is increased debt and increased displeasure from the Department of Settlement, which had to guarantee

---

6. The conflict described here is a perceived conflict of interests. Without a complete breakdown of the way in which settlers spend their gross incomes, it is impossible to say with certainty that the settlers actually spend their money on education and other amenities instead of on loan repayments. They may spend money in other ways not directly associated with the benefits of modernization. Settlers who earned negative farm incomes after full allowance has been made for scheduled repayments did, however, report spending substantial sums of money on the education of their children.

repayment to the Agricultural Finance Corporation, the source of the MFR loans. The risks are also increased by the fact that the settlers appear to be made insecure and discouraged by their indebtedness more than they are motivated to turn loans into healthy profits. Since the settlers' motivation in coming to the schemes seems characteristically to have been the achievement of social security rather than economic upward mobility, the carrot of potential profit and the stick of potential loss associated with the new loans only serve to deny the settlers the security they sought in coming to the settlements—security represented by the absence of debts making them vulnerable to eviction.

Where the loans are repaid on schedule, the consequence of the substantial burden of debt is the denial of hard cash to the settlers. This, too, increases their discontent and insecurity. Consider the situation of a high-density settler on one of the Baluhya schemes in Western Province in 1966:

Maize price paid by marketing board	37s.
20% deduction for cooperative society expenses (8s.)	29s. remaining
50% deduction for loan repayment (15s.)	14s. remaining
Deduction for repayment of MFR (10s.)	4s. remaining

Other deductions may also be made for cooperative society investments. The result is that various deductions not figured in the budgets for the settlers combine to reduce the amount of money that actually reaches them. They then feel an oppression similar to that of peasant farmers victimized by profiteering middlemen elsewhere. The failure of the cooperative societies to make the full deductions, the settlers' practice of selling produce outside the societies for closer to the full published price, and their general delinquency in loan repayments all result from their desire to have the security of cash on hand.

The same kind of dissatisfaction has been caused by the policies and procedures involved in issuing the loans and acknowledging receipt of loan monies repaid. Many settlers never saw their development loans. In part this was because they were credited to loan repayment, but it also resulted because the Settlement Department obtained an authorization from each individual settler to use the settlers' loan funds to pay for plowing and developing settlers' plots. Money for fencing and for livestock was disbursed in kind on the theory that this would prevent diversion of cash to unauthorized purposes. Delays in payments for produce are understandable results of fairly complicated marketing procedures; delays in acknowledgment of repaid loans are less justifiable and have been criticized by the Van Arkadie report. In addition, the consequence of these delays has been to arouse suspicion among the settlers that theft has occurred somewhere along the line. Furthermore, payment for development materials in kind has given the settlers the feeling that they have not really been given development loans. One reason is that the settlers have manifested the well-documented preference for a number of poor cattle over a few quality dairy cattle. Since they have not been schooled or conditioned to place the same values on the cattle that the government does, they do not believe they have really been given their full loans. One result has been numerous unauthorized sales of quality cattle. Similarly, settlers have not seen the importance of fencing the perimeters of their plots, and fencing has been uneven because fencing materials have been sold or stolen and sold for cash. An additional problem has been that loans do not bear a direct relationship to economic improvement. Fencing and housing loans may be important, but they do not produce income. Furthermore, where crops and cattle suffer during bad seasons, the income-producing resources disappear; the obligation to repay does not.

The settlers' suspicions are justified by the fact that, although the great majority of settlement officers and employees have been honest men, there have been a number of thefts of settlers' funds by settlement personnel. Cooperative society office-holders' thefts of settlement funds have also been numerous, as the records of the resident magistrates near the settlement schemes attest. Where such misappropriations have occurred the damage done is political as well as financial, for the settlers retain a distrust of cooperative societies and of the settlement officers' integrity and motivations. Any delay in payment or acknowledgment of repayment simply reinforces the inclination to work independently of the societies.

The root of the problem has been that the government's procedures and policies in establishing the settlement program have assumed both that settlers possess the motivation and skills to achieve economic upward mobility and that the settlers cannot be left to their own initiative in pursuit of this objective because they might not use the funds correctly. Initially these contradictions were very largely the product of the circumstances of the transfer of power, which prevented development of any program to pre-train or condition the settlers to the obligations of participation in the monetary economy and the reasons for these obligations, as well as to inform them of the opportunities that settlement would present. But the experiences with the settlement program, most particularly criticisms of the program, and the fact that non-African as well as African interests were served by its creation, have influenced the government to channel most rural development funds into the hands of those who have less need for such training and conditioning. The government's attitude toward the settlement program contradicts the assumptions of its own development planning: that all Africans can be assumed to feel motivation to become profitable farmers, and that the appeal of the benefits of economic improvement will motivate Africans to accept the responsibilities of participation in the modern economy. Instead, the government believes that reliance for agricultural development should be placed on those who have already demonstrated a capacity to participate effectively in the development of the cash economy.

The second major problem area concerns the settlers' relationship to the environment surrounding the settlements. The government has never decided whether or to what extent the settlement

schemes are to be social entities isolated and autonomous from surrounding areas or integrated and absorbed by them. One of the main
questions is whether the settlers are able to participate in the surrounding communities without sacrificing, knowingly or unknow-
ingly, their interests. The major difficulty in this regard involves the
settlers' relationships with firms providing tractor services. Characteristically, the settlers have been dependent upon such firms to plow
before the planting, with funds allocated from MFR loans where
these have been issued. The results have been unfortunate. Distrust
has characterized the settlers' relationship with these firms, in part
because the latter have generally been Indian or European. Misunderstandings have exaggerated racial distrust. Some of the contractors involved with plowing for the settlement schemes have been
unreliable. Steps have been taken to remedy this and also to prevent
the resentment felt toward these unreliable contractors from being
focused on the government by associating the settlers with the area
settlement controllers in the selection of contractors each season.
Even under these conditions, however, the plowing has not been
done to specifications, and this has hurt the settlers' crop prospects.
The contractors have claimed that cooperative societies have not
been reliable in making payments, that access routes to the plots are
impenetrable, and that the rough condition of the land has damaged
their vehicles. Settlers have argued that the plowing is done late, that
it is often done at night when shoddy plowing is more likely to result,
that plowers' attitudes have been rough and unfriendly, that they
have had to be bribed to do a decent job, and that they have frequently not come at all while claiming payment. Whoever is to
blame, the settlers lose if the plowing is not done or is done poorly.

The tractor issue has been responsible for cooperative societies'
buying their own tractors with or without cooperative officers' approval. This has often not been the best answer, though it is an
understandable recourse. Cooperative societies and settlers generally
lack the knowledge to run tractors efficiently, and get expensive
repair bills which add to the cooperatives' and the settlers' debt
burden. Mishandling of the tractor problem by the cooperative societies has increased settler disenchantment with the societies, even

though in most instances cooperative society officers are not able to prevent the difficulties from arising and may themselves be victims of the same difficulties.

The settlers' difficulties with purveyors of tractor services encourage those who argue that the settlers are not in a position to deal effectively with outside commercial interests even when they are assisted by Department of Settlement administrative personnel. The same problem of enforcement that faces the government in trying to supervise the farming techniques and loan repayments of 20,000 or more settlers also prevents it from overseeing every part of the plowing operation. Only where some settlers have, through outside employment, gained the funds to purchase their own tractors and to rent out their services to other settlers does the plowing seem to get done to everyone's satisfaction. This has occurred in only a few instances. The result of unsatisfactory dealings with outside contractors has been indebtedness without the means to liquidate it. To the settlers, therefore, debt has come to symbolize not so much the price of economic improvement as the legacy of unsatisfactory dealings with outside commercial interests, the cooperative societies, and the government that collectively deprive them of the security they sought in becoming settlers.

The settlers' tendency to rely on outside employment has been described earlier. Such employment is not strictly illegal on the low-density settlements and is, consequently, widely undertaken. On the high-density settlements it is less prevalent but widespread, considering that the settlers were supposed to be landless and unemployed. One of the main problems that double employment creates is a lessening of commitment to the settlement program. A number of low-density settlers explained that they could not make ends meet without taking outside employment. However, to do so they had to hire laborers to work on their farms—which would otherwise have been unnecessary. Since it is more difficult to develop a plot into a lucrative income-earning enterprise than to maintain an existing plot or hold down some form of salaried employment, there appears to be some tendency to forego full development of settlement plots in favor of greater reliance on outside income. The World Bank and the CDC, in their periodic reviews of their schemes, have noted settler absenteeism. To the extent that there is absenteeism, its real effect is to shift the burden of recovering the investment of the settlement programs to the economy outside the settlements.

The settlers are constantly subjected to competition from economic patterns in the reserves maintained by people who are not fully committed to the development process. For example, the settlers are supposed to use artificial insemination to produce new dairy cattle. Bulls are employed in the reserves, and it is very difficult to prevent settlers from obtaining the services of bulls in the reserves from relatives or friends. Most settlers consider the artificial insemination process unnatural, are dissatisfied when it takes four or five attempts to impregnate the cow, and are not impressed by the need to maintain the stock of quality cattle. Since they are not cut off from the reserves, they are not cut off from the example and the attitudes of African farmers who continue to practice and believe in the old methods. In addition, in the reserves settlers may sell their crops, obtain seeds and bags, get instant payment, and suffer no deductions from traders. Selling produce through the approved cooperative channels and into the modern cash economy has none of these advantages, and settlers frequently do not see that inconveniences are perhaps the necessary price of economic improvement. This is particularly true when such improvement is not their principal objective in coming to the settlement. Also, settlers often prefer to maintain a number of cattle, many of which are not quality, rather than rely on fewer quality cattle, since the numbers of cattle count more than their quality in determining social status. There are frequent instances where settlement-scheme quality cattle have been sold in the reserves for less productive but greater numbers of cattle or for cash to be used in some other way. Since the settlers are not cut off from the reserves, they are not cut off from semitraditional concepts of status and value.

Some progress has been made in the introduction of crops like pyrethrum and in the practice of dipping rather than spraying cattle, both of which entailed departures from outside practices. However, in general the decision not to cut settlers completely off from the reserves, even were that possible, has made it more difficult to convert settlers to practices and beliefs deemed appropriate to the modernizing cash sector of the economy.

There is a fundamental dilemma involved in the relationship of modernizing and relatively less modernizing sectors.

Failure to isolate the settlers from the less modernizing sectors of the rural environment entails the price and problems just identified. To undertake complete separation is difficult for purely administrative reasons where whole geographical areas of settlers are involved. However, what is more important is that complete isolation in the interests of gaining new forms of participation in the modern economy, and screening out influences that might tend to undermine settlers' identification with the new order or their belief in the legitimacy of the program and the sponsoring government, would produce a situation wherein the settlement schemes would perpetuate the dual economy and the dual society created by their European predecessors. Racial separation is gone, but economic and social separatism would be maintained and reinforced by a greater commitment of resources to one sector. The Kenya government has not attempted to isolate the settlements in this way. However, if greater efforts to enlist the participation and support of the settlers are not made, the settlements and the settlers cannot be fully integrated with the surrounding environment without sacrificing the government's heavy investment in the program, an investment that is premised upon complete acceptance of modern means of production, marketing, risk-taking, and profit-seeking.

Ideology is also a factor in the relationships of the settlers to their surrounding environment. "African socialism," which the Kenya political leadership wishes to inculcate in the people and the institutions of the country, seems to contemplate ending inequitable distribution of income and income-producing resources and exploitative economic relationships. It does not, however, appear to include any model or formula for increasing individual and national income that will avoid such inequities. How can Africans become involved in the production of national income without exploitation and inequalities occurring? The Sessional Paper on African Socialism in effect begs this question by postulating that economic inequalities will not disturb political equality. To the extent that economic competition cannot be encouraged without also bringing inequality and exploitation similar to that experienced by Africans at the hands of Europeans in its wake, economic competition appears to the settlers themselves to be out of keeping with the principles of Kenya African socialism. Lacking any socialist alternative to such competition, the settlers have no weapons with which to defend themselves against the influence and the effects of small-scale capitalism in the surrounding environment. The settlers themselves are bothered only by ill effects of their relationship with some outside commercial interests, and not by individualistic trading relationships that provide an attractive alternative to trading through the cooperative societies. Cooperative Department personnel and some of the settlement administrators in the field, on the other hand, are aware of this dilemma and consequently are inhibited in taking initiatives in guiding the settlers' relationship with the outside environment.

The third problem area is the difficulty of establishing the legitimacy of the new environment of the settlements in the minds of the settlers themselves. This results in part from the other two problem areas but comes to a focus in the operation and performance of the settlement-scheme cooperative societies, which serve a mixture of practical, ideological, and historical purposes. It is difficult to establish whether the instigators of the cooperative movement really believed that it was consistent with African traditions. If they did, they overlooked the variety of African traditions and the fact that traditional patterns of cooperation are a long distance from the imported institution of cooperative societies, particularly when involving practical economic purposes as well as the objective of eliminating exploitative interpersonal economic relationships. If they did not really believe that the similarity of African tradition to the requirements for successful management of cooperative societies obviated the need for systematic training in the principles of cooperative societies for the general membership as well as the leadership, then they recognize by now that the exigencies of the transfer of power may also be blamed for the lack of necessary time to train officers and members, either gradually or in advance, in the responsibilities and benefits of cooperative societies.

One major consequence of the settlers' required membership in cooperative societies that they have not fully understood and appreciated has been that cooperatives have not been an effective means of creating "communities" out of the individual settlers. The cooperative and settlement officers have attempted, on their own and on behalf of the government, to use the cooperatives to take on unpopular tasks such as loan repayments as a means of communicating their wishes to the settlers and as a channel for passing along government directives (such as one directing that all settlers must grow one quarter-acre of fodder crops for each productive animal on their plots). Consequently, the meetings of the cooperative society general membership on the individual settlements have served less as a vehicle for settlers to effectively communicate to the government their attitudes, problems, demands, and questions than as a means for the government to communicate its demands, policies, and regulations. The records of the societies show clearly that settlers, ostensibly voluntarily, agree to government requests and demands which many of them basically do not accept. Settlers' real feelings are communicated to each other outside the framework of the cooperative societies at informal *barazas* (meetings). Since it is usually settlers other than those leading the cooperative societies who dissent vocally, they appear to be, and often are, revolutionary within the framework of the society. As a result of these *barazas*, coups and countercoups are organized, grievances are expressed, and letters are written to the president and to leading national political figures.

Experience with the cooperative societies so far would appear to suggest that they cannot serve as a channel for communications both upward from and downward to the grass roots. At present they serve the latter function but not the former. Lacking formal means of upward communications, dissatisfied settlers who have despaired of taking over the cooperative society machinery have tended to form rival cooperative societies or, more frequently, self-help groups and societies, whose members retain only nominal membership and interest in the official cooperative societies. These groups are centered around growers of specific crops who feel the societies are biased against them or, more generally, around individual settlers who stand outside the formal cooperative society leadership. These groups voice some of the points of view which lead the government to fear that the settlers have rejected the settlement program and which cause the government to act firmly to establish the commitment of the other settlers by redoubling its efforts to secure loan repayments and to assure the marketing of settler produce via the cooperative societies. The leaders of the rival cooperative groups voice their concerns in terms of the settlers' right both to free land and to more educational and medical facilities. The settlers themselves tend to speak only in terms of the need for educational and medical facilities, but they appear to demonstrate some support for the demand for free land by withholding loan repayments.

The cooperative society office-holders find themselves in somewhat the same position that was held by traditional chiefs under British colonial administrators. In theory, the office-holders are elected by and responsible to the settlers; in fact, they assist the administration by carrying out tasks which might impair the government's legitimacy were its own officers to carry them out. The office-holders are not, therefore, recognized as spokesmen by the settlers; rather, they are seen only as administrators drawn from their own ranks. As the colonial government undermined traditional institutions by using them and their leaders for its own purposes, the Kenya government today has endangered the legitimacy of the cooperative movement in the eyes of the settlers by turning the democratic structure of the societies into a tool for the communication of its own regulations. The vital difference is that the cooperatives have no real traditional legitimacy to withstand such a threat. The result, however, is that settlers do not seek the elected positions in the cooperative societies because of their unpopularity. As *de facto* administrators for the government, the society office-holders have no means of taking actions which the settlers themselves may demand and thus have no way of becoming the real leaders of the settlers.

Corruption has been a major problem in the cooperative societies. Some of the corruption is plain dishonesty. To some extent, the institution of society office-holders strains the scruples of honest settlers. The position of the office-holders raises an old question of political philosophy: whether to pay elected officers enough to compensate them adequately for their efforts at the risk of leading them to consider their elected positions to be career professions, or to pay them little enough to avoid this problem at the risk of inviting corruption or dependence on wealthy benefactors. The present arrangements reflect a preference for the latter. Office-holders are paid only five shillings per person for each of a limited number of meetings. If they are to do their job effectively they must contribute a great deal more time; consequently they must sacrifice the care of their own plots. With this on their minds, and haunted by the knowledge that their tenure in office is limited by their inevitable unpopularity with the settlers, some office-holders succumb to the temptation to take their "proper" reimbursement into their own hands. It is possible, but difficult to establish, that the present arrangement leads to less scrupulous settlers' seeking offices with this objective in mind. These circumstances do not increase the settlers' confidence in the cooperative societies.

The problem of leadership at the grass roots in a developmental situation is fundamental. If a sense of participation and actual participation in the process of nation-building at the grass roots are both essential, then some means is needed to produce leadership roles at the grass roots that will facilitate upward as well as downward communications, that will allow the incumbents to have sufficient tenure to make the acquisition of necessary skills associated with institutions like cooperative societies economically feasible, and that will provide for the legitimate interests of such settlers without allowing them to become independent of the communities they lead. The establishment of such a system would require that the government risk its own legitimacy by assuming direct responsibility for unpopular tasks rather than straining, at least at the outset, the legitimacy of new leaders in new local institutions. Then cooperative society leaders could speak and act as the representatives of those who elected them. The danger in this, of course, is that cooperative leaders might become spokesmen for their constituents without providing good executive leadership. However, even if this were to happen, the creation of a dialogue between cooperative and government leaders over priorities could create better levels of support for the program and for somewhat revised government strategies than now exist. Specialized personnel must be trained to handle jobs such as providing tractor services, and settlers' families must be trained to assume management of farms when their senior member is involved in community leadership.

At the root of the problems of the cooperative societies is the fact that, by government policy, through their structure, and in the eyes of the participants, the societies merge economic and political responsibilities. As elected leaders, their office-holders are political representatives of the settlers, presumably elected to allocate social values according to the settlers' preferences. Simultaneously, as managers of the cooperative societies, they are expected to allocate scarce resources according to predetermined governmental specifications. While structuring the cooperative societies in such a way that they cannot serve as channels for grass-roots demands regarding the allocation of social values, the government has also discouraged the formation of any other channels to express them. In fact, the basic economic situation of the settlers is shaped according to governmental specifications. Africans involved in rural development elsewhere may have the option of not participating in the political system through the cooperative societies, but the settlers do not have roots in a traditional society to give them that option. The government has in effect made political participation synonymous with economic participation in the process of nation-building by denying the legitimacy of any separate way for settlers to express opinions about the allocation of social values. Support for existing policies is indicated by fulfilling behavioral expectations, such as repaying loans, employing artificial insemination, and selling products through rather than outside the cooperative societies. The settlers can make political demands upon the authorities only by resisting these economic obligations. Since the government lacks the means to coerce settlers *en masse* to participate, it must rely upon persuasion, which may prove more successful if cooperative societies are allowed to become a means for the articulation of settlers' demands and support and for bargaining with the government for adjustments in developmental priorities. While this would require the government to take direct responsibility for relatively unpopular aspects of agrarian development, these changes in the role of the cooperative societies could in the long run strengthen the legitimacy of the government in the eyes of the settlers and encourage them to identify with it.

PART THREE

Conclusions

The continuing personal and social importance of land to both Africans and Europeans and the belief that Kenya's high-potential land
represents the country's best hope for real economic and social progress are fundamental elements of continuity linking the stages of
Kenya's emergence as a new and politically independent nation. The
African peoples have made no secret of their devotion to the land
and their recognition that land is the key to their well-being. But
they were not alone. The British government considered agricultural
development to be the key to making its Indian Ocean strategy
economically viable in the early years of the century. Enlargement
of the European farming enclave in the White Highlands became a
fundamental objective of European politics throughout the colonial
period. Land reforms and rural economic development during the
ten years preceding independence were also employed by European
and colonial political leaders as means to preserve European interests
in the land. While agriculturalists in Kenya were not necessarily
thinking in political terms when they advocated land consolidation,
registration, and cash-crop development for the African rural areas,
they provided the colonial administration and European politicians
with economic reasons for not disturbing the White Highlands. The
agriculturalists said that most of the best land continued to lie in
African hands, and the Europeans reasoned that economic development of the African areas might divert African attention from recovery of the White Highlands. European politicians exacted promises
of land resettlement, under which Africans would be enabled to
purchase and develop subdivided European farms, as their price for

acquiescing in the transfer of political power to an independent African government. Jomo Kenyatta and his government have agreed with missions from the World Bank and the Commonwealth Development Corporation that Kenya's interest lies in developing the land as efficiently as possible by getting the most development for an invested dollar or pound.

The basic political significance of these land reforms has been that their timing, structure, and objectives have been decisively influenced by European settlers, the colonial administration, and international lending agencies, rather than by the African political leaders who made land reform nearly as important an element of African nationalism as political advance itself. The Africans have argued that Europeans gained their land without their consent and without payment of suitable compensation. They have attributed the poverty, excessive population densities, and insecurity found in some African areas like Kikuyuland to colonial policies toward Africans in general and in particular to the reservation of large areas of the Highlands exclusively for European farmers. But the first major land reform, land consolidation and registration of title, was initiated by the colonial administration only after Mau Mau arose and the main spokesmen for African nationalism were in detention or fighting in the forests. Care was taken not to force individual title upon peoples who had not yet evolved individual tenure on their own, yet individual title was set forth as the model on the basis of discussions in colonial and European circles, with no apparent attempt to consult the major African leaders. The objective was in fact to establish the economic basis for the emergence of a new African political leadership cadre, one which would cooperate with Europeans in opposing African nationalist leaders when they were freed and would cooperate with Europeans in furthering economic development in the spirit of multiracialism rather than pressing for more rapid African political advancement.

The second major land reform, African resettlement on land in the White Highlands being sold by departing European farmers, was instituted during the transfer of political power as a critical aspect of the general strategy of placing economic and political checks on the future African government. The strategy was based on the assumption that the independent African government would be formed by the Kenya African National Union led by Jomo Kenyatta and other exponents of African nationalism, and it was founded on the fear that once in power these nationalists would embark on policies detrimental to the fundamental economic and political interests of all communities in Kenya that did not support KANU. European settlers, the British government and its colonial administration, and the Kenya African Democratic Union all contributed to the development of a defensive political and economic strategy comprising two major elements: the establishment of a constitutional structure prior to the formation of a KANU government that would provide institutional safeguards for those communities that feared post-independence threats to their essential interests by a KANU government; and a land-reform program prior to independence that would protect these same groups by making it unnecessary or difficult for the African government subsequently to carry out a reform of its own that might be opposed to their interests. The British government agreed to a *majimbo* constitution in response to the fears of KADU and many Europeans that a KANU government might infringe individual political and property rights; it agreed to a land-resettlement program primarily at the request of moderate and conservative Europeans who anticipated that an African government would seize their land without compensation and distribute it to African landless and unemployed, or that property values under an African government would plummet to unacceptable levels. Europeans who wanted to leave Kenya sought the resettlement program to insure that they would be able to realize the full value of their property. The more moderate Europeans who hoped to remain in Kenya believed the resettlement program would dissipate pressure on the new African government to engage in land reforms at their expense.

As the transfer of political power recedes into the background, it becomes more apparent that the European-colonial defense strategy yielded both benefits and liabilities for the independent government precisely because the Europeans and the colonial administration probably exaggerated the militant tendencies of most of the principal leaders of KANU and underestimated the ability of the more moderate leaders like Kenyatta and Mboya to prevail over more militant spokesmen like Odinga and Kaggia. Rosberg and Nottingham argue that Kenyatta was a moderate leader who was unable to control the growing militancy of his followers, which led to Mau Mau, because the colonial administration was unresponsive to moderately expressed demands for economic and social reform.[1] They dispute the popular European assumption that Kenyatta was the principal perpetrator of Mau Mau, an assumption that may have contributed to a possible similar misjudgment of Kenyatta and most of his ministers during the transfer of power. The evidence for this argument is not to be found in Kenyatta's pre-independence assertions and behavior, because the strategy adopted by Europeans and the colonial administration made very costly a strategy more militant than the one he actually followed. Even Odinga might have found it difficult to do other than follow Kenyatta's line, had he rather than Kenyatta been the principal leader of the independence movement. Knowing that Kenyatta had determined to gain independence at the price of concessions on land policy and constitutional arrangements, Odinga could safely represent what was apparently a minority within the KANU leadership group in taking a more militant line on land policy. Odinga did not have to fear so much as Kenyatta that his views on land policy might jeopardize independence, especially since he was not part of the government during the critical negotiations in late 1961 and the first half of 1962. Kenyatta, for his part, may have been quite content to have someone like Odinga to rally his more militant followers to the KANU banner by somewhat more extreme assertions, as long as there was no evidence to suggest that Odinga might break with him because of Kenyatta's more moderate line.

The main evidence for the moderation of Kenyatta and most of his lieutenants is that they did not seek to couple political independence with immediate subsequent steps to achieve an independent African economy in Kenya by rapidly Africanizing the agricultural

---

1. Carl Rosberg, Jr., and John Nottingham, *The Myth of Mau Mau: Nationalism in Kenya* (New York: Praeger, 1966).

and commercial spheres of the economy and renouncing the obligation to repay the loan given for resettlement. Instead, they remained
content to work on the more long-term objectives of establishing
international credit and building the economy, at the cost of honoring an unpopular debt and forestalling immediate Africanization of
economy and society. After independence, Odinga and his colleagues
were no longer content to acquiesce in Kenyatta's moderation. Had
Kenyatta and his government been concerned only with transferring
economic resources rather than with developing them, the party
could have continued the former policy after independence whether
or not a land-resettlement program took place before independence.
Kenyatta and most of his principal adjutants promised that they
would end *majimbo* if they were given the necessary parliamentary
support, but they insisted that the economic and political rights
majimbo was supposed to defend would be recognized in any event.
Consequently they sought a strong central government, rather than
the regional system established by the *Majimbo* Constitution, in
order to foster unity and economic development and to avoid unnecessary, expensive proliferation of administrative positions. They
did not seek to end individual political and economic rights. Had
Kenyatta and his party been determined to nationalize European
farms, limit political freedom, and end *majimbo,* the establishment
of a *majimbo* constitution before independence would not have presented an insurmountable obstacle. Indeed, his government did take
steps to limit the administrative competence of the regional governments even before the *Majimbo* Constitution was formally scrapped,
but this move was not accompanied by any invasion of individual
rights. Had Kenyatta and his ministers believed that Africans should
not be required to pay for the recovery of "stolen lands," his government could have tolerated rather than opposed the settlers' laxity
in repaying their land and development loans after independence.
His government did in fact do so for the few political notables who
gained special extra-large plots under the settlement program.

In short, Kenya's land policy today, on which much of its development program depends, is a balance of direct and immediate measures to relieve both African destitution and European dominance of

the economy, and more indirect and long-run measures to build the economy by relying on those (European, Asian, or African) who already possess and know how to use economic assets. The more radical and nationalistic measures were taken for the Kenyatta government by those who feared it, thus leaving the complementary, more conservative measures for the independent government to initiate and implement on its own. The proof of Kenyatta's moderation and of the mistaken nature of the basic assumption of the European-colonial defense strategy is that Kenyatta's government has in fact balanced more radical immediate distributive measures with more conservative long-run development programs when it could have continued to emphasize the former. This is reinforced by the fact that the Kenyatta government has adhered to its policy quite tenaciously through the first years of independence, although the economic benefits gained by following it have been obtained at substantial political expense. The costs include loss of support from Odinga, who had been one of Kenyatta's two or three most influential lieutenants, the unpopularity of the debt Kenyatta's government has tried to honor, frustration of Africans' expectations that economic benefits would accrue to them immediately following independence, and continued prominence of Europeans and Asians in the Kenya economy and society.

The early initiation of the land resettlement program was an important key to the realization by the Kenyatta government of some major benefits. Thousands of African families were provided with land and thus employment; the racial exclusiveness of the White Highlands was decisively ended; and those Europeans who wished to liquidate their farming assets were allowed to do so with reasonable compensation for them—all tasks that would have placed a heavy and perhaps even prohibitive financial and administrative burden on Kenyatta's government if they had been left for the new independent government to implement. Kenyatta's moderation was made more credible to those who feared him and his government because the pressure of landless, unemployed Africans for immediate radical measures was diminished. A more credible moderate development strategy in turn helped to make possible the dismantling of *majimbo* and the merger with KANU of the party (KADU) which had sought *majimbo* in the first place. Together, the moderate development strategy and evidence of unforced political unity gave foreign and domestic investors (including remaining Europeans) confidence that their investments in Kenya's economy would be both safe and productive. A more thriving economy has made possible new agricultural and commercial development, new communications facilities, and expanded educational opportunities. The changed view of Kenyatta held by those who had once feared him is perhaps best illustrated by the remarks of Sir Patrick Renison. In an interview just prior to his death in 1965, the former governor, who had called Kenyatta "a leader unto darkness and unto death," was prepared to admit that Kenyatta "is a great statesman." [2]

The benefits of the post-independence development strategy which land resettlement has helped to make possible suggest the possibility of a reciprocal and at least somewhat mutually reinforcing relationship between contributions to the central strategic objectives of political integration and economic development. Land resettlement eased the relationships between larger and smaller African ethnic groups by providing for systematic and limited settlement rather than unregulated and uncontrolled migration from overpopulated lands of the larger groups into the neighboring underpopulated lands of the smaller ones. The program thus made more credible the Kenya government's subsequent focus on economic development, which carried the message that all racial and ethnic communities might participate in, and benefit from, the processes of nation-building without fear that their respective essential group interests might be threatened by the government's land-development strategy. At the same time, the domestic and external development resources made available as a result of the Kenyatta government's focus on economic development promised not only to assist the growth of the economy but to make possible giving more Africans some economic and political stake in Kenya's future. With a wider group of Africans gainfully employed in the building of a modern

2. Interview, October, 1965.

economy and fewer joining the urban unemployed or underemployed, the government hopes that traditional ethnic and racial jealousies may thereby be diminished.

Land resettlement is also responsible in significant measure for the troublesome consequences of the government's present development strategy. One of the most important of these arises from the timing, auspices, and announced purposes of the program itself. Established primarily in response to pressures from European settlers on the assumption that they were the rightful owners of the land they were selling, and implemented as well as largely administered at first by the retiring colonial administration, the program is considered more a European than an African creation by the government, by educated Africans outside the government, and by many of the settlers themselves. The government's legitimacy, insofar as it is based on adherence to the tenets of African nationalism, is thereby weakened.

A second troublesome consequence of the government's present development strategy for which land resettlement is substantially responsible has been that it may have generated *too much* confidence in Kenya on the part of domestic and expatriate investors and businessmen. Land resettlement, by accommodating thousands of landless and unemployed Africans, helped to make credible the government's strategy of developing economic assets rather than transfer for its own sake. The danger is that the establishment of a reputation as a politically stable nation with a degree of potential for economic development, in combination with Kenya's moderate policy on the question of Kenyanizing the economy, will in fact result in increased rather than decreased Europeanization of the economy. The government's former chief manpower planning advisor estimated that 24 percent of professional and technical positions and 29 percent of administrative, executive, and managerial positions were held by Africans in 1964.[3] Within these categories, the percentages were considerably smaller in the private sphere than in the public one. At the

---

3. T. Aldington et al., "The Economics of Kenyanization," mimeographed (Nairobi: Institute for Development Studies, 1968).

same time, he predicted that the increasing supply of trained Africans would not keep pace with the increasing demand for qualified personnel for these posts.

While demand for qualified Africans exceeds supply in the higher managerial and technical positions in the economy, supply far exceeds demand for unskilled positions. The same manpower projection indicated that less than half of the new entrants to the labor force would find employment in the monetary economy. Some of these potentially unemployed persons are being absorbed in the traditional sectors of the economy, but a substantial number may be destined to form the core of an urban unemployed class, sufficiently visible to pose a major political challenge to the government. It is sobering to observe the rate of increase in the labor force outstripping the capacity of a developing economy to provide work, even when all efforts have been concentrated on developing an economy that will generate sufficient employment opportunities. Land resettlement has had its impact on this problem of Kenya nation-building. The program sought to enable thousands of formerly landless and unemployed Africans to reach collectively the production and employment levels achieved by the departing European farmers. Because of its large investment in this program, the government has felt that it must concentrate its other developmental resources on furthering long-term economic development rather than relieving short-term pressures of unemployment and poverty. Without other funds to devote to immediate palliatives for unemployment in the short term, pressures for Kenyanization have become severe, making it difficult for the government to maintain its policy of accomplishing Kenyanization only within the context of increasing economic development. In late 1967 the Kenya government took new steps to restrict the rights of noncitizens to participate in the work force, resulting in a sharply increased rate of exodus by Asians, most of whom apparently did not become citizens. The government angrily reacted to a paper by economists at the University of Nairobi that pointed out that the new policies were not in keeping with what they believed to be a sound policy of economic development, one virtually identical to that which the Kenya government itself had pursued until that time.[4] A government determined to emphasize long-term economic growth is clearly confronting a dilemma in attempting to meet short-term demands for the benefits which long-term economic growth is expected to bestow. A government pursuing long-term strategies clearly needs assistance for somehow meeting short-term demands. However, development funds are seldom available for short-term goals as distinct from long-term economic growth projects. It may be argued that less money should have been poured into land resettlement and that less emphasis should have been placed on meeting production levels set by Europeans. But it is doubtful that funds not used for settlement during the transfer of power would have been available for later programs to relieve unemployment. Perhaps only the anxious demands of European farmers would have been sufficient to elicit these funds from the British government.

The problems caused by Kenya's post-independence development strategy became the potential political assets of Kenya's new opposition party, the Kenya People's Union. Odinga and Kaggia had become alienated from KANU during the transfer of power by differences with Tom Mboya and James Gichuru over land policy. These differences became crystallized when Kenyatta and KANU joined the post-1962 Lancaster House Conference government, after having accepted and agreed to support the land-resettlement program. The colonial administration refused Odinga a ministry in the coalition because he opposed any policy that implied European rights to ownership of land about to be transferred. Although Kenyatta pledged that the colonial administration's tactics would not prevent him from naming Odinga as his right-hand man after independence, subsequent events deepened the alienation of Odinga and his allies from the dominant KANU policies. Odinga became vice president of the country as well as vice president of KANU following independence, but after KADU's merger with KANU in late 1964 the former KADU leaders seemed to replace the militant wing of KANU in key positions. Odinga lost his chairmanship of

4. R. S. Ray, "The Structure of Employment in Kenya." Paper presented at the Conference on Education, Employment and Rural Development, Kericho, Kenya, August, 1966.

the KANU parliamentary party to former KADU leader Ronald Ngala. The parliamentary chief whip, J. D. Kali, who also supported Odinga, lost his post. Achieng Oneko complained that he could no longer control the policies of his own Ministry of Information and Broadcasting. In March, 1966, Odinga was replaced as KANU vice president by seven regional vice presidents, three of whom were former KADU leaders. In May, 1966, Odinga, Kaggia (who had been dismissed in 1964 as an assistant minister), Oneko, and twenty-seven other members of Parliament resigned from KANU and the government to form the opposition Kenya People's Union.

KPU took exception to KANU's basic development strategy because it seemed to stress development of economic resources rather than their redistribution to poor or destitute Africans. The party complained that KANU had failed to provide enough people with land, sufficient educational and medical facilities, or regular employment. The government was blamed rather than praised for the land-resettlement program because too few Africans were accommodated and those who were included were forced to pay too much. Land resettlement and the whole employment picture, as well as the government's general development strategy, seemed to KPU spokesmen to reflect the continuing if not increasing influence of European ideas, funds, and personnel. The government forced through Parliament a bill requiring the KPU members of Parliament to seek reelection. Although it was not entirely free of difficulties, the KANU government managed a generally fair election. Only seven of the thirty KPU candidates, including Odinga, were reelected. An unpublished study of the election suggests that more Africans might have voted for KPU had the party been campaigning for the right to form the government.[5] Perhaps the most disturbing feature of the election was the division of the electorate along ethnic lines. The Luo candidates were generally returned, as well as the two Kamba hopefuls, while Kikuyuland remained solidly in the KANU camp. The over-all effect of the election was to add a political dimension to ethnic tensions be-

5. Based on the results of an unpublished study of the 1966 election, edited by Cherry Gertzel and Lionel Cliffe, in which the author participated.

tween the two largest African communities, the Kikuyu and the Luo.

Land resettlement has illustrated what is perhaps the most fundamental problem of contemporary Kenya politics: the underdevelopment of political input processes, arising from the fact that implementation of the development strategy has been concerned with the generating support for governmental outputs without reference to political input processes. Kenya's leaders have chosen to rule through the bureaucracy rather than through the party. Members of Parliament seldom have an opportunity to do more than debate and discuss policies to which the president's cabinet is already committed, and they lack even the organizational strength of the back-bench caucuses which their counterparts in other Commonwealth parliamentary systems employ to influence their leaders. Local elected municipal councilors and party officials have little opportunity to influence the processes of development, because responsibility for decision-making is concentrated in central government ministries. Elected cooperative society leaders, as in the case of the settlement schemes, are in a poor position to transmit demands upward to the authorities, because the authorities expect these societies to serve as vehicles for the implementation of their own directives. Because of the technical expertise ideally required to establish and execute a development plan, the more educated administrators are inclined to deny that the less educated local party officials and participants have the standing to make demands for program modifications. For example, the view, widespread among the settlers, that many of their financial difficulties arise from their having been forced to start repaying their loans before their crops were even in the ground received little sympathy from the settlement administration until the Van Arkadie Commission raised the point. The view that five shillings each for a restricted number of meetings of the cooperative society does not compensate its office-holders for the greater amount of time necessarily spent away from the development of their own plots has never gained any audience. If we assume that development programs are rationally related to development objectives because they have been, and necessarily are, formulated by trained technicians, there is no room for the presumably irrational demands for changes in those programs advanced by relatively uneducated subjects of the developmental process. Development is, thus taken to involve output generation by trained technicians and relatively well-educated administrators but not responsiveness to inputs by relatively less educated participants in the developmental process and their politician spokesmen.

The failure to engage political input processes in the formulation and implementation of development plans and programs has contributed to the atrophy of these processes, with attendant dangers to the health of Kenya's political system. Without a role to play in articulating and aggregating demands for modifications of development policies and administrative practices, the governing party has begun to lose its usefulness as a contributor to political integration. The assassination of Tom Mboya in July, 1969, further aggravated this problem by removing from the scene one of KANU's most experienced and skillful party leaders, on whom Kenyatta had relied to oversee both the day-to-day work of party organization and periodic party reorganizations. However, the need for the integrative functions of a comprehensive, pragmatic party organization has become increasingly apparent. No clear means is available for establishing a consensus on who should succeed Jomo Kenyatta, what should be done about student unrest at the University of Nairobi, how the various African communities will adapt to one another when Kenyatta's unifying influence is not available, and what should be done to deal with the continuing problem of African unemployment. There is a danger that uncertainty over how these various difficulties can and will be resolved may lead political leaders to fall back on and to reinforce rather than soft-pedal ethnic allegiances. Such may be the significance of the decision of non-Luo members of KPU—party vice president Bildad Kaggia and deputy parliamentary leader Simon Kioko—to return to KANU, the party with which most of the people of their communities are politically identified. In the case of Kaggia and other Kikuyu members, reported increases in rituals reminiscent of Mau Mau may have hastened their decision.

KENYA LAND REFORM AND MODERNIZATION

What is the relationship between Kenya land reform and broader patterns of modernization assumed to be present in African and other developing nations? For answers we must rely on recent formulations of modernization theory that attempt to describe the essence of the social processes at work in the developing part of the world. Empirical studies testing such theories of modernization are too few in number, perhaps in part because such theories are not easy to test in their existing formulations. To examine modernization theory in a given empirical context, two questions must be answered. Before one can determine whether a given set of data confirm or deny one or more hypotheses concerning modernization, the investigator must determine whether the hypotheses involved deal with species of data present in the given research context. In the remaining pages, we shall explore these questions in relating Kenya land reform to selected theories of modernization.

There are many theoretical formulations which might merit attention in answering both questions. There are ideologically oriented theoretical conceptions, those concerned particularly with socialism. A number of African countries have articulated socialist aspirations for their emerging societies, including, as we have seen, Kenya. Land resettlement became the focus of ideological conflict because of the loan repayment issue—was it consistent with Kenya African socialism for settlers to be required to repurchase land allegedly never legally purchased from them? A major difficulty with such ideologically oriented theory from the standpoint of this study is the rather clear discontinuity between socialist aspirations and existing development strategy observable not only in Kenya but elsewhere in Africa.[6] While this discontinuity is not lost on either administrators or participants in the land-resettlement program, it does not appear to be the central problem. It can be argued that the government has not made a sufficient effort to sensitize the new African farmers to

6. Giovanni Arrighi and John Saul, "Socialism and Economic Development," *Journal of Modern African Studies*, VI, no. 2 (1968), 141–70.

the requirements of socialism or that these requirements have not been sufficiently thought out by the country's leaders. But the difficulty, as seen by the designers of the program, its administrators, and its participants, is that of achieving economic growth and creating conditions that will maximize efficient grass-roots contributions to that growth. Problems that arise in this connection are not seen, on the whole, in ideological terms. If they are, the reference is usually to the promise of African nationalism rather than to post-independence ideas of African socialism.

Then, land reform has been linked historically to the emergence of democracies and dictatorships in Europe, America, and Asia. One of the most important recent analyses of land reform and political development is Barrington Moore's *Social Origins of Dictatorship and Democracy*.[7] He outlines five conditions in agrarian development that have been associated historically with the growth of democracy in England, France, and America. Such theoretical analysis has a clear bearing on nation-building in Kenya, since Kenya has sought to maintain democracy as well as achieve agrarian development through land reform. However, Moore's ideas are difficult to apply, not only because the conditions are not stated in a way that facilitates empirical testing, but because it is too early to determine whether some of the conditions Moore identified are going to appear in Kenya, much less to assess their impact if they do. One condition is a balance between the strength of the monarchy and the independence of the landed aristocracy. What is too independent? What is too strong? How much concentration of land and power is necessary to produce a landed aristocracy? Kenya has not experienced anything close to monarchical absolutism, nor have the agrarian landowners become so powerful as to generate permanent fragmentation and serious weakening of the government's authority. A second condition, the development of commercial agriculture, has been marked in Kenya by contrast to Indian experience prior to India's independence. The third and fourth conditions, weakening of the

---

7. Barrington Moore, *Social Origins of Dictatorship and Democracy: Lord and Peasant in the Making of the Modern World* (Boston: Beacon Press, 1966).

landed aristocracy and prevention of an aristocratic-bourgeois coalition against the peasants and workers, have been respectively achieved and prevented thus far. The presence of a visible landed aristocracy in Kenya since the departure of the Europeans is not apparent, except in the sense that high members of the government have purchased large farms since coming to power. Urbanization and industrialization have not advanced much in Kenya, and the presence of an unpopular Asian commercial class has so far prevented any aristocratic-bourgeois alliance. Moore's fifth condition is a revolutionary break with the past. In Kenya, the evidence is contradictory. Mau Mau and land consolidation transformed an important sector of Kenya agriculture, while the departure of most of the European farmers and the completion of the land-resettlement program have further changed the countryside. Yet the total effect of the transfer of power and resettlement has been to influence the present government in the direction of maintaining continuity rather than breaking with the reform policies developed prior to independence. African agrarian society has changed, but the development strategy of the present government bears a close resemblance to the pre-independence Swynnerton plan. With this one possible exception, Kenya would appear not to have violated the conditions Moore found to have produced a link between agrarian development and democracy elsewhere. However, it is still too early to determine whether these favorable conditions are relatively permanent features of Kenya's society, and it is not entirely clear that these are the only relevant conditions. Since mid-1966 Kenya's pattern of democratic stability appears to have been under increasing stress, for reasons that are not immediately related to Moore's conditions. One reason is the difficulty of establishing a likely successor to President Kenyatta. Another is the failure of even this relatively successful agrarian economy to develop fast enough to meet demands made upon it for services and employment.

Samuel Huntington criticizes the equation of modernization with political development.[8] According to him, political development

---

8. Samuel Huntington, "Political Development and Political Decay," *World Politics,* XVII, no. 3 (April, 1965), 386–430.

should be related to the degree of institutionalization in a given country. He conceives institutionalization in terms of progress toward institutional adaptability, complexity, autonomy from social organizations, and coherence. He seems to consider institutionalization as somehow occurring in isolation from secular social forces which he believes political institutions must regulate. At the same time, political organizations are believed to be strong to the extent that they enjoy a wide scope of support. By "adaptability," he means the ability of organizations to respond positively to social change by modifying their functions. Institutional development is certainly not optimal in Kenya, but the problem of land reform does not appear to be primarily one of institutional coherence or complexity. Nor is the problem one of institutional survival and adaptation to changes so much as it is of their capacity to induce such changes in agrarian development. It is possible that one problem of the bureaucracy in achieving this end has been its very attempts to maintain or increase their autonomy in relation to other social organizations, producing lack of empathy with or understanding of the problems, especially by new participants in the developing economy. Huntington does not conceive of political development as taking place in the context of (rather than in isolation from) the social changes a developing political structure must regulate. For this reason, quite apart from difficulties of making his constructs operational, his theory does not appear especially applicable to the subject of this study.

Another set of theories concentrates on social mobilization. Literacy, mass media, urbanization, industrialization, and per capita income are evidence of social mobilization and, therefore, of political development.[9] They are also frequently advanced as being associated with the presence of stable democracy. In addition to Huntington's criticisms of such theories, which the author believes are valid, they characteristically ignore the role of agricultural development in achieving political development, social mobilization, or stable de-

9. For example, Karl Deutsch, "Social Mobilization and Political Development," *American Political Science Review,* LV (September, 1961), 493 ff.; Aristide Zolberg, *One-Party Government in the Ivory Coast* (Princeton: Princeton University Press, 1964); S. M. Lipset, *Political Man* (Garden City, N. Y.: Doubleday, 1960); and James S. Coleman, "Nationalism in Tropical Africa," *American Political Science Review,* XLVIII, no. 2 (June, 1954), 404–26.

mocracy. To the extent that countries like Kenya have determined to concentrate on agricultural development, such theories appear to lead the investigator to conclude that these countries are backward-looking. Moreover, these theories are derived from Western experience and little attempt has been made to modify them in the light of non-Western realities. Such theories do not always explain the significance of particular patterns of evolution among these various indicators of social mobilization.

Finally, there are theories of modernization derived from the work of Talcott Parsons and Edward Shils and others in *Toward a General Theory of Action.*[10] Their ideas have been applied in the works of Almond, Coleman, Eisenstadt, Apter, Holt and Turner, and others. These writers have assumed, where Parsons and Shils in their general theoretical work did not, that role-differentiation, instrumental values, universalistic norms, and recruitment on the basis of achievement are indicators of modernity in contrast to their counterparts—with the qualification that all societies are believed to possess elements of both modernity and nonmodernity. Lacking to date have been (1) a consideration of the relationship between these pattern variables (which have sometimes been assumed to be both universal and inevitable) and the development strategies framed by individual countries in the context of a particular environment; and (2) consideration of the interrelationships of these pattern variables given a particular environment and development strategy. It may be profitable to undertake these tasks, because the underlying pattern variables do not appear inherently ethnocentric in conception or impossible to examine empirically. Most important, the pattern variables of universalism-particularism and role-differentiation–fusion appear to apply directly to the key problems of land reform in post-independence nation-building.

One application of Parsonian pattern variables in the formulation of a theory of political development that has commanded considerable attention has been that of Gabriel Almond and G. Bingham

10. Talcott Parsons and Edward A. Shils, eds., *Toward a General Theory of Action: Theoretical Foundations for the Social Sciences* (New York: Harper & Row, 1951).

Powell. They define political development as "the increased differentiation and specialization of political structures and the increased secularization of the political culture." [11] By "differentiation of political structures," they appear to be referring to what Parsons and Shils mean by differentiation of norms, role-expectations, and need-dispositions. By "secularization," Almond and Powell mean "the process whereby men become increasingly rational, analytical and empirical in their political action." Such a definition appears to correspond closely to what Parsons and Shils mean by universalism as distinct from particularism. In combining these two concepts in one definition of political development, Almond and Powell, like Parsons and Shils, do not examine the relationship to each other of these pattern variables, nor do they inquire about what happens to indicators of these two concepts in the context of a "conventional" development strategy operating in the context of agrarian Kenya.

The results of our study suggest that, where nations adopt a "conventional" agrarian development strategy, the pattern variable alternatives of universalistic norms and differentiated roles and structures may be conflicting rather than complementary. When the government's policy is to emphasize economic development, the development of differentiated political roles and specialized political structure is not encouraged, while existing ones are allowed to atrophy by being isolated from what the government considers to be the essential processes of nation-building. Consequently, participation or nonparticipation in economic processes and structures takes on political significance, and political roles and structures and economic roles and structures tend to become fused rather than differentiated. The secular political culture, of which Almond and Powell speak, tends to become synonymous with an "economic culture" involving rational allocation of material resources to generate efficient contributions to economic development. Rational, analytical, empirical political action, again when the government's emphasis is on economic development, tends to call for the skills of economists and

---

11. Gabriel A. Almond and G. Bingham Powell, *Comparative Politics: A Developmental Approach* (Boston and Toronto: Little, Brown, 1966), p. 105.

technicians rather than the use or creation of roles and structures designed to encourage widespread participation in the transmission, aggregation, and evaluation of demands for reallocation of social resources and therefore values. Under such circumstances, political development as defined by Almond and Powell appears to be composed of two distinct forces working against each other rather than in harmony. This in turn leads to a reconsideration of the relationship of the basic Parsonian pattern variables to each other, since they lie behind the Almond and Powell formulation. When emphasis is on a policy of maximizing economic development, a secular political culture becomes synonymous with a secular "economic culture," which in turn appears to be at odds with the differentiation of political roles or the maintenance of those differentiated political roles and structures that already exist.

As Almond and Powell's idea of development requires modification in the circumstances of a particular country's applying its development strategy to a particular and major social problem, so their idea raises a question which both the investigator and those who shape Kenya's political contours may well consider: whether it is wise to allow the development of universalistic values to occur at the expense of differentiated political roles and structures. Underlying much of the preceding analysis is an assumption that greater emphasis on development of structures and processes to facilitate the articulation and aggregation of inputs would make a positive contribution to Kenya nation-building in general and her agrarian development program in particular. It is difficult to prove that such input orientation would be beneficial.

Three major arguments seem to justify our assumption. One, the general atrophy of input processes is linked with Europeanization of the transfer of power, agrarian reform, and opposition to Kenya African nationalism. If these circumstances were not present, it is possible that the atrophy of political parties as a consequence of the apparent requirements of nation-building would be acceptable provided other channels existed to communicate development problems from the grass roots to decision-makers in Nairobi. Under these circumstances, deemphasis of input processes is more troublesome, because the leadership can be accused more easily of not breaking with the European-colonial past over and above ignoring popular expectations of the benefits that would follow independence.

Second, it is clear that decision-makers and administrators have not established rapport with the intended participants in the developing modern economy. Central government planners and decision-makers have no channels they consider reliable for understanding the problems of grass-roots participants, for distinguishing between legitimate and illegitimate complaints by them, or for establishing any kind of dialogue with them in order to resolve outstanding issues. Decision-makers decide and participants respond largely in ignorance of each other's intentions and points of view. When the grass-roots participants have only rudimentary knowledge of the economic structure into which they are being initiated, this lack of rapport can seriously undermine their positive response to the structure of incentives and admonitions which central government planners try to establish to produce new modernizing farmers.

Finally, behind the Kenya development strategy and its consequences and significance for the progress of the country stands the figure of Jomo Kenyatta, around whom Kenya politics has revolved for a generation and more. In a sense, the respect which he has commanded among his people has made the further development of the political process—related less to nationalism and more to the objectives and requirements of nation-building structures and processes—seem superfluous. Kenyatta has served as the symbol of Kenya African nationalism, as the key figure in piloting Kenya through the transfer of power with the least damage to the country's political stability and economic vitality, and as the symbol of post-independence Kenya nation-building. In the last analysis, however, success in the development of the economy through land reform and other measures may be dependent on continued and increased political, economic, and social integration, in part because eventually this will have to be achieved on some other basis than personal respect for President Kenyatta. Such integration may be achieved only through the further development of the political process to fill a specialized role in the general process of nation-building. Jomo Kenyatta's most important remaining gift to his people may, therefore, be to encourage the development of political processes that will yield future generations of Kenya nation-builders.

BIBLIOGRAPHY

BOOKS, MONOGRAPHS, AND DISSERTATIONS

Ashford, Douglas E. *National Development and Local Reform.* Princeton: Princeton University Press, 1967.

Baker, Richard St. Barbe. *Kabongo, Story of an African Chief.* New York: A. S. Barnes, 1955.

Bennett, George. *Kenya: A Political History; The Colonial Period.* London: Oxford University Press, 1963.

————, and Rosberg, Carl G. *The Kenyatta Election: Kenya 1960–1961.* Published for the Institute of Commonwealth Studies, Oxford. London: Oxford University Press, 1961.

Bernardi, B. *Mugwa: A Failing Prophet of Meru.* London: Oxford University Press, 1959.

Biebuyck, Daniel, ed. *African Agrarian Systems.* Published for the International African Seminar. London: Oxford University Press, 1963.

Bienen, Henry. *Tanzania: Party Transformation and Economic Development.* Princeton: Princeton University Press, 1967.

Blundell, Sir Michael. *So Rough a Wind: The Kenya Memoirs of Sir Michael Blundell.* London: Weidenfeld & Nicolson, 1964.

British African Land Utilization Conference, Jos, Nigeria, 1949. *Final Report.* London: H.M.S.O., 1951.

Brockway, Fenner. *African Journeys.* London: Victor Gollancz, 1955.

An excellent bibliography on Kenya politics is to be found in Carl G. Rosberg, Jr., and John Nottingham, *The Myth of Mau Mau: Nationalism in Kenya* (New York: Praeger, 1966). The bibliographic items appearing below are those not found in that source.

Carey Jones, N. S. *The Anatomy of Uhuru: Dynamics and Problems of African Independence in an Age of Conflict.* New York: Praeger, 1966.

Chandos, Viscount [Oliver Lyttleton]. *Memoirs.* London: Bodley Head, 1962.

Clark, Paul G. *Development Planning in East Africa.* Published for the East African Institute of Social Research. Nairobi: East African Publishing House, 1965.

Clayton, Eric. *Agrarian Development in Peasant Economies.* New York: Macmillan, 1964.

————. *Economic Planning in Peasant Agriculture: A Study of the Optimal Use of Agricultural Resources by Peasant Farmers in Kenya.* London: University of London, Wye College, 1963.

Convention on Social and Economic Development in the Emerging Kenya Nation. *The Kenya We Want.* Report of the Convention held in Nairobi, August 12–17, 1962.

Cox, Richard. *Kenyatta's Country.* London: Hutchinson, 1965.

de Wilde, John C., et al. *Experiences with Agricultural Development in Tropical Africa.* 2 vols. Published for the International Bank for Reconstruction and Development. Baltimore: Johns Hopkins Press, 1967.

East African Institute of Social and Cultural Affairs. *Problems of Economic Development in East Africa: Ten Papers on Economic Planning, Manpower Utilization and Regional Development.* Nairobi: East African Publishing House, 1965.

————. *Racial and Communal Tensions in East Africa.* Nairobi: East African Publishing House, 1966.

The Economic Development of Kenya: Report of a Mission Organized by the International Bank for Reconstruction and Development. Published for the International Bank for Reconstruction and Development. Baltimore: Johns Hopkins Press, 1963.

Fearn, Hugh. *An African Economy: A Study of the Economic Development of the Nyanza Province of Kenya, 1903–1953.* Published for the East African Institute of Social Research. London: Oxford University Press, 1961.

Forrester, Marion W. *Kenya Today: Social Prerequisites for Economic Development.* The Hague: Mouton, 1962.

Gatheru, Jugo. *Child of Two Worlds*. New York: Random House, Vintage Books, 1965.

Goodhart, Philip. *In the Shadow of the Spear*. Sussex: Key Press, 1962.

Hance, William A. *African Economic Development*. Published for the Council on Foreign Relations. 1958; rev. ed. New York: Praeger, 1967.

Hirschman, Albert O. *Development Projects Observed*. Washington, D.C.: The Brookings Institution, 1967.

———. *Journeys toward Progress: Studies of Economic Policy-Making in Latin America*. New York: The Twentieth Century Fund, 1963.

Hobson, Charles, and Brown, George. *Kenya Impressions*. London: Voice of Kenya, 1963.

Holt, Robert T., and Turner, John E. *The Political Basis of Economic Development: An Exploration in Comparative Political Analysis*. Princeton: D. Van Nostrand Co., 1966.

Hughes, A. J. *East Africa: The Search for Unity*. Harmondsworth: Penguin Books, 1963.

Huntingford, G. W. B. *The Eastern Tribes of the Bantu Kavirondo*. The Peoples of Kenya, no. 14. Nairobi: Church Missionary Society, 1944.

———. *The Nandi of Kenya: Tribal Control in a Pastoral Society*. London: Routledge & Kegan Paul, 1953.

———. *The Southern Nilo-Hamites*. Ethnographic Survey of Africa: East Central Africa, Part 7. London: The International African Institute, 1953.

Huntington, Samuel P. *Political Order in Changing Societies*. New Haven: Yale University Press, 1968.

Huxley, Elspeth. *Forks and Hope*. London: Chatto & Windus, 1964.

———. *A New Earth*. New York: Morrow, 1960.

———. *No Easy Way: A History of the Kenya Farmers' Association and the UNGA Limited*. Nairobi: East African Standard, n.d.

———. *Settlers of Kenya*. Nairobi: Highway Press, 1948.

Huxley, Elspeth, and Perham, Margery. *Race and Politics in Kenya*. Rev. ed. London: Faber & Faber, 1955.

Kariuki, Joseph Mwangi. *Mau Mau Detainee: The Account by a Kenya African of His Experiences in Detention Camps, 1953–1960*. London: Oxford University Press, 1963.

Kenyatta, Jomo. *Facing Mount Kenya: The Tribal Life of the Gikuyu.* London: Secker & Warburg, 1953; New York: Random House, 1962.

———. *Harambee! The Prime Minister of Kenya's Speeches, 1963–64.* Nairobi: Oxford University Press, 1964.

Koinange, Mbiyu, with Achieng Oneko. *Land Hunger in Kenya.* London: Union of Democratic Control, 1952.

Lambert, H. E. *Kikuyu Social and Political Institutions.* Published for the International African Institute. London: Oxford University Press, 1956.

———. *The Systems of Land Tenure in the Kikuyu Land Unit.* Communications, School of African Studies, No. 11. Capetown: School of African Studies, 1950.

Maini, Krishan M. *Land Law in East Africa.* Nairobi: Oxford University Press, 1967.

Matheson, J. K., and Bovill, E. W., eds. *East African Agriculture.* London: Oxford University Press, 1950.

Mboya, Tom. *Freedom and After.* London: André Deutsch, 1963.

Middleton, John, and Kershaw, Greet. *The Kikuyu and Kamba of Kenya.* Ethnographic Survey of Africa, ed. by Daryll Forde, East Central Africa, Part 5. London: International African Institute, 1965.

Ngugi, James. *The River Between.* London: Heinemann, 1965.

Pio Gama Pinto: Independent Kenya's First Martyr. Nairobi: Pan African Press, 1966.

Robinson, Ronald, et al. *Africa and the Victorians: The Climax of Imperialism.* Garden City, N.Y.: Doubleday, Anchor Books, 1968.

Rosberg, Carl G., Jr., and Friedland, William H., eds. *African Socialism.* Stanford, Calif.: Stanford University Press, 1964.

———, and Nottingham, John. *The Myth of Mau Mau: Nationalism in Kenya.* Published for the Hoover Institution on War, Revolution, and Peace. New York: Praeger, 1966.

Ruthenberg, Hans. *African Agricultural Production Development Policy in Kenya, 1952–1965.* Berlin: Springer-Verlag, 1966.

Schultz, T. W. *Transforming Traditional Agriculture.* New Haven: Yale University Press, 1964.

Sorrenson, M. P. K. "Land Policy, Legislation and Settlement in the East African Protectorate." D. Phil. dissertation, Oxford University, 1962.

————. *Land Reform in the Kikuyu Country: A Study in Government Policy.* Published on behalf of the East African Institute of Social Research, Makerere University College. Nairobi: Oxford University Press, 1967.

Stolper, Wolfgang F. *Planning without Facts: Lessons in Resource Allocation from Nigeria's Development.* Cambridge: Harvard University Press, 1966.

Walter, B. J. "The Territorial Expansion and Organization of the Nandi, 1850–1905: A Study in Political Geography." Ph.D. dissertation, University of Wisconsin, Madison, 1968.

Waterston, Albert. *Development Planning: Lessons of Experience.* Published for the Economic Development Institute, International Bank for Reconstruction and Development. Baltimore: Johns Hopkins Press, 1965.

Wood, Susan. *Kenya: The Tensions of Progress.* Published for the Institute of Race Relations. London: Oxford University Press, 1960.

ARTICLES AND PAPERS

"Agrarian Policy: Plea for a New Statement." *Kenya Weekly News,* February 18, 1964.

Aldington, T., et al. "The Economics of Kenyanization." Paper prepared by 18 economists at the University College, Nairobi. Institute for Development Studies and Department of Economics, University College, Nairobi, Discussion Paper No. 64, February, 1968. Mimeographed.

Allot, A. N. "Legal Development and Economic Growth." In *Changing Law in Developing Countries,* edited by N. J. Anderson. New York: Humanities Press, 1963.

Alport, C. J. M. "Kenya's Answer to the Mau Mau Challenge." *African Affairs,* LIII (July, 1954), 241–47.

Apthorpe, Raymond, and Odingo, Richard. "Land Settlement and Rural Development." Paper presented at the Conference on Education, Employment and Rural Development, University College, Nairobi, 1967.

Beech, M. W. H. "Kikuyu System of Land Tenure." *Journal of the African Society,* XVII (1917), 46–59, 136–44.

Bennett, George. "The Development of Political Organization in Kenya." *Political Studies,* II (June, 1957), 113–30.

Boswell, C. W. "A Note on Some Changes in the Economy of the Kipsigis Tribe." *Journal of African Administration,* VIII (1956), 95–101.

Brain, James Lewton. "The Changing Role of the European in East Africa." Paper presented to the African Studies Association, 1964.

Branney, L. "Towards the Systematic Individualization of African Land Tenure." *Journal of African Administration,* XI (1959), 208–24.

Brett, E. "Economic Policy in Kenya Colony: A Study in the Politics of Resource Allocation." Paper presented at the East African Institute of Social Research Conference, Kampala, January, 1965.

Brown, Brack. "Problems and Obstacles in Development Administration." Paper presented at the Seminar on Rural Development, Syracuse University and University College, Dar es Salaam, Dar es Salaam, April 4–7, 1966.

Brown, Leslie H. "The Settlement Schemes." 10 parts. *Kenya Weekly News,* July 16–August 27, 1965, October 15–29, 1965.

———. "Under-development and Unemployment." *Kenya Weekly News,* February 28, 1964.

Carey Jones, N. S. "The Decolonization of the White Highlands of Kenya." *The Geographical Journal,* CXXXI, pt. 2 (June, 1965), 186–201.

———. "Land Settlement Schemes in Kenya." *Africa Quarterly* (April–June, 1964). pp. 1–11.

Clayton, E. S. "Alien Enclave and Development—Reply." *East African Economics Review,* XI (1964), 80–81.

———. "A Note on the Alien Enclave and Development." *East African Economics Review,* X (1963), 35–40.

———. "Safeguarding Agricultural Development in Kenya." *Journal of African Administration,* XI (1959), 144–50.

Clough, R. H. "Some Notes on a Recent Economic Survey of Land Settlement in Kenya." *East African Economic Review,* I, n.s. 3 (December, 1965), 78–83.

Etherington, D. M. "Land Resettlement in Kenya: Policy and Practice." *East African Economics Review,* X (June, 1963), 22–35.

———. "Some Thoughts on the Settlement Schemes." *Kenya Weekly News,* April 5, 1963.

Gertzel, C. "Regional Administration in Kenya, 1963–1964." Paper presented at the East African Institute of Social Research Conference, Kampala, January, 1965.

Ghai, D. P. "Economic Development of Kenya: A Critique of Kenya's Development Plan." Centre for Economic Research, University College, Nairobi. Mimeographed, n.d.

Gray, Clive S. "Agricultural Sector Planning in Kenya: Planning without Facts." Paper presented at a Conference on Agricultural Development, University College, Dar es Salaam, April, 1967.

Harbeson, John W. "The Kenya Little General Election: A Study in Problems of Urban Political Integration." Institute for Development Studies, University College, Nairobi, Discussion Paper No. 52, June, 1967. Mimeographed.

———. "Land Resettlement and Development Strategy in Kenya." Institute for Development Studies, University College, Nairobi, Discussion Paper No. 38, January, 1967. Mimeographed.

———. "Land Resettlement and the Politics of Rural Development." Institute for Development Studies, University College, Nairobi, Discussion Paper No. 28, August, 1966. Mimeographed.

———. "The Politics of Land Resettlement in Kenya." Paper presented at the Research Workshop on the Political and Administrative Aspects of Agricultural Development, Molo, Kenya, August 5–7, 1966. Sponsored by the East African Institute of Social Research, Makerere University College, Kampala.

Hennings, R. O. "Some Trends and Problems of African Land Tenure in Kenya." *Journal of African Administration,* IV (1952), 122–34.

Heyer, Judith. "Kenya's Agricultural Development Policy." *East African Economic Review,* II, n.s. 2 (December, 1966), 35–47.

———. "Kenya's Cautious Development Plan." *East Africa Journal* (August, 1966).

Homan, F. D. "Consolidation, Enclosure, and Registration of Title in Kenya." *Journal of Local Administration Overseas,* I (1962), 4–14.

———. "Succession to Registered Land in the African Area of Kenya." *Journal of Local Administration Overseas,* II (1963), 49–54.

Howarth, Fred. "The Role of Co-operatives in Rural Development." Paper presented at the Seminar on Rural Development, Syracuse University and University College, Dar es Salaam, Dar es Salaam, April 4–7, 1966.

Hughes, O. E. B. "Villages in the Kikuyu Country." *Journal of African Administration,* VII (October, 1955), 170–74.

Huntington, Samuel P. "Political Development and Political Decay." *World Politics,* XVII (April, 1965), 386–430.

Kenya, African Affairs Committee. "Land Titles in Native Land Units." *Journal of African Administration,* II (1950), 19–24.

Kibaki, Mwai. "Manpower for Economic Development." In East African Institute of Social and Cultural Affairs, *Problems of Economic Development in East Africa.* Nairobi: East Africa Publishing House, 1965.

———. "Political Economy of Land in Kenya." *Venture,* XI (1959), 6–7.

Kilson, Martin L., Jr. "Land and the Kikuyu: A Study of the Relationship between Land and Kikuyu Political Movements." *Journal of Negro History,* XL (April, 1955), 103–53.

———. "Land and Politics in Kenya: An Analysis of African Politics in a Plural Society." *Western Political Quarterly,* X (September, 1957), 559–81.

"Land and the Bill of Rights." *Kenya Weekly News,* April 3, 1964.

MacArthur, J. D. "The Planning and Evaluation of Agricultural Settlement: The Kenya Experience." Paper presented at the Conference on Agricultural Development, University College, Dar es Salaam, April, 1967.

———. "Some Thoughts on Future Trends in Farm Employment in Kenya." Paper presented at the Conference on Education, Employment and Rural Development, University College, Nairobi, 1967.

Macleod, Iain. "Blundell's Kenya." *Kenya Weekly News,* March 27, 1964.

Maina, J. W. "Settlement Patterns and Prospects." Paper presented at the Seminar on Rural Development, Syracuse University and University College, Dar es Salaam, Dar es Salaam, April 4–7, 1966.

Manners, Robert A. "The Kipsigis—Change with Alacrity." In *Markets in Africa: Eight Subsistence Economies in Transition,* edited by Paul Bohannan and George Dalton, pp. 181–99. New York: Doubleday, 1965.

Marris, Peter. "Lending Money." Paper presented at the University of East Africa Social Science Conference, Nairobi, 1966.

Massell, Benton F. "Farm Management in Peasant Agriculture: An Empirical Study." Institute for Development Studies, University College, Nairobi, Discussion Paper No. 44, February, 1967. Mimeographed.

Moris, Jon R. "Education and Training of the Farmer." Paper presented at the Conference on Education, Employment and Rural Development, University College, Nairobi, 1967.

————. "The Educational Requirements of a Transformational Approach to Agricultural Development." Paper presented at the Seminar on Rural Development, Syracuse University and University College, Dar es Salaam, Dar es Salaam, April 4–7, 1966.

————. "The Evaluation of Settlement Scheme Performance: A Sociological Appraisal." Paper presented at the University of East Africa Social Science Conference, Nairobi, December, 1966.

Mungeam, G. H. "Kikuyu and Masai Responses to the Establishment of British Administration in the East Africa Protectorate." Paper presented at the University of East Africa Social Science Conference, Nairobi, December, 1966.

Ndegwa, Philip. "The Role of Development Banks in Underdeveloped Countries." East Africa Institute of Social Research, Makerere University College, Kampala, EDRP No. 30, April 29, 1964. Mimeographed.

————, and Norbye, O. D. K. "Rural Development: The Strategy of Kenya's Development Plan 1966–1970." Paper presented at the Conference on Education, Employment and Rural Development, University College, Nairobi, 1967.

Nguyo, Wilson. "Some Socio-Economic Aspects of Land Settlement in Kenya." Paper presented at the University of East Africa Social Science Conference, Nairobi, December, 1966.

Oates, C. O. "The Settlement Schemes." *Kenya Weekly News,* July 17, 1964.

Oduor, Herman A. "Land Reform in Kenya." *Kenya Weekly News,* February 28, 1964.

Okai, Matthew. "Field Administration and Agricultural Development." Paper presented at the Research Workshop on the Political and Administrative Aspects of Agricultural Development, Molo, Kenya, August 5–7, 1966.

Okelo-Odongo, T. "Role of Economic Planning in the Context of African Socialism." Paper for the East African Institute for Social and Cultural Affairs, Nairobi, September 4, 1964.

Pedraza, G. J. W. "Land Consolidation in the Kikuyu Areas of Kenya." *Journal of African Administration,* VIII (April, 1956), 82–87.

Penwell, D. J. "A Pilot Scheme for Two Kikuyu Improved Villages Near Nairobi." *Journal of African Administration,* XII (1960), 61–67.

Potekhin, Ivan. "Land Relations in African Countries." *Journal of Modern African Studies,* I (1963), 39–59.

Ray, Robert S. "The Structure of Employment in Kenya." Paper presented at the Conference on Education, Employment and Rural Development, University College, Nairobi, 1967.

Rosberg, Carl G., Jr. "Political Conflict and Change in Kenya." In *Transition in Africa,* edited by Gwendolen Carter and Robert Brown, pp. 90–120. Boston: Boston University Press, 1958.

Ryan, T. C. I. "Rejoinder to Dr. Clayton's Note on the Alien Enclave and Development." *East African Economics Review,* X (1963), 41–47.

Saul, John S. "Notes on Agricultural Politics in Tanzania." Paper presented at the Seminar on Rural Development, Syracuse University and University College, Dar es Salaam, Dar es Salaam, April 4–7, 1966.

Sinclair, Sol. "The Strategy of Kenya's Agricultural Development Plan." Paper presented at the Conference on Education, Employment and Rural Development, University College, Nairobi, 1967.

Sorrenson, M. "Counter Revolution to Mau Mau: Land Consolidation in Kikuyuland, 1952–1960." Paper presented at a Conference at the East African Institute of Social Research, Kampala, June, 1963.

———. "The Official Mind and Kikuyu Land Tenure, 1895–1939." Paper presented at a Conference at the East African Institute of Social Research, Kampala, January, 1963.

Swynnerton, R. J. M. "Kenya's Agricultural Planning." *African Affairs,* LVI (July, 1957), 209–15.

Thomas, Garry. "Effects of New Communities on Rural Areas—the Upper Kitete Example." Paper presented at the Seminar on Rural Development, Syracuse University and University College, Dar es Salaam, Dar es Salaam, April 4–7, 1966.

Van Arkadie, B. R. "The Role of Agriculture in the Strategy of the Plan." Paper presented at the Conference on Education, Employment and Rural Development, University College, Nairobi, 1967.

Wilson, R. G. "Land Consolidation in the Fort Hall District of Kenya." *Journal of African Administration,* VIII (July, 1956), 144–51.

Woods, Roger. "The Dynamics of Land Settlement: Pointers from a Rhodesian Land Settlement Scheme." Paper presented at the University of East Africa Social Science Conference, Nairobi, December, 1966.

GOVERNMENT DOCUMENTS

GREAT BRITAIN

Indians in Kenya: A Memorandum. British Sessional Papers, 1923, Vol. XVIII (4), Cmd. 1922. 1923.

Memorandum of Native Policy in East Africa. British Sessional Papers, 1930, Vol. XXIII (105), Cmd. 3573. 1930.

Report of the Kenya Land Commission. British Sessional Papers, 1934, Vol. X (229), Cmd. 4556. 1934.

Land and Population in East Africa: An Exchange of Correspondence between the Secretary of State for the Colonies and the Government of Kenya on the Appointment of the Royal Commission. Col. 290. 1952.

Baring, Sir Evelyn. *The Kenya Emergency and the Future.* Address to the Kenya Legislative Council on October 20, 1953. Central Office of Information. 1953.

Report to the Secretary of State for the Colonies by the Parliamentary Delegation to Kenya, January 1954. Walter Elliott, Chairman. British Sessional Papers, 1954, Vol. XI (123), Cmd. 9081. 1954.

East Africa Royal Commission, 1953–1955: Report. British Sessional Papers, 1956, Vol. XIII (397), Cmd. 9475. 1956.

Corfield, F. D. *Historical Survey of the Origins and Growth of Mau Mau.* British Sessional Papers, 1959/60, Vol. X (907), Cmnd. 1030. 1960.

Report of the Kenya Constitutional Conference Held in London in January and February, 1960. British Sessional Papers, 1959/60, Vol. X (891), Cmnd. 960. 1960.

Kenya: Report of the Regional Boundaries Commission. British Sessional Papers, 1962, Vol. X (543), Cmnd. 1899. 1962.

Report of the Kenya Constitutional Conference, 1962. British Sessional Papers, 1962, Vol. XI (875), Cmd. 1700. 1962.

Statement by the Rt. Hon. Barbara Castle, M.P., Minister of Overseas Development, on "Kenya Land Purchase and General Development." Issued by the British Information Service. Nairobi, November 19, 1965.

Commonwealth Development Corporation Report and Accounts. 1964, 1965, 1966.

KENYA

(All works prior to December 12, 1963, refer to the Colony and Protectorate of Kenya; all works after that date refer to the Republic of Kenya.)

Final Report of the Economic Commission of the East Africa Protectorate, 1919. Part I. Nairobi: Swift Press, 1919.

Native Land Tenure in Kikuyu Province: Report of Committee. Nairobi: East Africa Standard, 1929.

Settlement Committee Report. 1939.

Humphrey, N., ed. *The Kikuyu Lands.* Nairobi: Government Printer, 1945.

Land Utilization and Settlement: A Statement of Government Policy. Sessional Paper No. 8 of 1945.

Post-War Settlement Schemes: Proposed Schemes. Agricultural Production and Settlement Board. 1945.

Post-War Settlement in Kenya: Accepted Scheme for European Settlement. Settlement Board. 1945.

Proposals for the Reorganization of the Administration of Kenya. Sessional Paper No. 3 of 1945.

Mitchell, Sir Philip. *General Aspects of the Agrarian Situation in Kenya as It Affects the African Population.* Despatch No. 44, April 7, 1946.

Agricultural Policy in African Areas in Kenya. 1951.

Communiqué on Land Tenure Policy. White Paper No. 4 of 1951.

Correspondence of the Governor [Mitchell] and the Secretary of State [Lyttleton] on the East Africa Royal Commission, Land and Population in East Africa. November 16, 1951.

Troup, L. G. *Inquiry into the General Economy of Farming in the Highlands.* 1953.

Carothers, J. C. *The Psychology of Mau Mau.* 1954.

Report of the Commissioner [W. F. Coutts] Appointed to Enquire into Methods for the Selection of African Representatives to the Legislative Council. Sessional Paper No. 39 of 1955/56.

Swynnerton, R. J. M. *A Plan to Intensify the Development of African Agriculture in Kenya.* 1955.

Adjustments to the Boundaries of the Highlands under Section 67 of the Crown Lands Ordinance, Cap. 155. Sessional Paper No. 47 of 1956.

African Land Development in Kenya, 1946–1955. Ministry of Agriculture, Animal Husbandry and Water Resources. 1956.

Agricultural Census, 1955 (Highlands and Asian Settled Area). 1957.

Report on the Government's Eighteen-Point Statement of Policy: Achievements and Future Policy. 1957.

Adjustments to the Boundaries of the Highlands under Section 67 of the Crown Lands Ordinance, Cap. 155. Sessional Paper No. 1 of 1957/58.

Report of Working Party on African Land Tenure, 1957–1958. 1958.

Statement of Government Policy. Sessional Paper No. 1 of 1958/59.

Adjustments to the Boundaries of the Highlands. (Section 67 of the Crown Lands Ordinance, Cap. 155). Sessional Paper No. 7 of 1958/59.

Kolbe, L. H., and Fouché, S. F. *Land Consolidation and Farm Planning in the Central Province.* Department of Agriculture. 1959.

Land Control (Native Lands) Ordinance, 1959. Communiqué from Ministry of African Affairs. 1959.

Land Tenure and Control Outside the Native Lands. Sessional Paper No. 10 of 1958/59.

Report of the Working Party Set Up to Consider the Establishment of an Authority to Promote the Development of Cash Crops for Small Holders. [1959]

Dagleish, A. G. *Survey of Unemployment.* 1960.

The Development Programme, 1960/63. Sessional Paper No. 4 of 1959/60.

Land Tenure and Control Outside the Native Lands. Sessional Paper No. 6 of 1959/60.

Report of the Committee on the Organization of Agriculture. 1960.

Report of the Working Party Appointed to Consider Elections under the Lancaster House Agreement. Sessional Paper No. 7 of 1959/60. June 8, 1960.

Unalienated, Undeveloped, Underdeveloped Land. 1960.

Unemployment. Sessional Paper No. 10 of 1959/60.

African Land Development in Kenya, 1946–1962. Ministry of Agriculture, Animal Husbandry and Water Resources. 1962.

Observations on the Report of an Economic Survey Mission from the International Bank for Reconstruction and Development. Sessional Paper No. 1 of 1963.

Report of the Fiscal Commission. 1963.

Development Plan, 1964–1970. 1964.

Kenya Population Census, 1962. Advance report of Volumes I and II. 1964.

African Socialism and Its Application to Planning in Kenya. 1965.

High-level Manpower Requirements and Resources in Kenya 1964–1970. Ministry of Economic Planning and Development. May, 1965.

"Memo to Ministers for Lands and Settlement, Agriculture, and Economic Planning, re: 'Repayment Capabilities of Settlers.' " Director of Settlement (A. Storrar). April 22, 1965.

Development Plan, 1966–1970. 1966.

The Million Acre Settlement Scheme, 1962–1966. Department of Settlement. [1966]

"Some Preliminary Results of the Economic Survey of Settlement, 1964/65," Parts I and II. Survey conducted by the Farm Economics Survey Unit. Government Economist/Statistician. March 16, 1966.

PUBLICATIONS AND DOCUMENTS OF ORGANIZATIONS AND POLITICAL PARTIES

Kenya African National Union. *The KANU Manifesto for Independence, Social Democracy and Stability.* Nairobi [1960].

———. *What a KANU Government Offers You.* [1963].

Kenya Peoples Union. *KPU Manifesto for 1966 By-Elections.* Nairobi, May 19, 1966.

"Speeches and Articles by Michael Blundell, M.B.E., during his visit to the United Kingdom in May and June, 1959." Issued by the New Kenya Group. [1959].

INDEX